IDENTITY IN PERSIAN EGYPT

Identity in Persian Egypt

The Fate of the Yehudite Community of Elephantine

BOB BECKING

EISENBRAUNS | University Park, Pennsylvania

The writing of this book was made possible through the research project "Elephantine in Context" sponsored by the *Deutsche Forschungs Gemeinschaft* (2015–18).

Library of Congress Cataloging-in-Publication Data

Names: Becking, Bob, author.
Title: Identity in Persian Egypt : the fate of the Yehudite community of Elephantine / Bob Becking.
Description: University Park, Pennsylvania : The Pennsylvania State University Press, [2020] | Includes bibliographical references and index.
Summary: "Examines the Yehudite community in Elephantine in southern Egypt in its historical, social, and religious context"—Provided by publisher.
Identifiers: LCCN 2020016972 | ISBN 9781575067452 (hardback) | ISBN 9781646022441 (paper)
Subjects: LCSH: Jews—Egypt—Elephantine—History—To 1500. | Elephantine (Egypt)—Antiquities. | Elephantine (Egypt)—Ethnic relations. | Elephantine (Egypt)—Religion.
Classification: LCC DS121.5.B43 2020 | DDC 932/.3—dc23
LC record available at https://lccn.loc.gov/2020016972

Printed in the United States of America
Published by The Pennsylvania State University Press,
University Park, PA 16802–1003

Eisenbrauns is an imprint of The Pennsylvania State University Press.

The Pennsylvania State University Press is a member of the Association of University Presses.

It is the policy of The Pennsylvania State University Press to use acid-free paper. Publications on uncoated stock satisfy the minimum requirements of American National Standard for Information Sciences—Permanence of Paper for Printed Library Material, ANSI Z39.48–1992.

To the memory of Gary N. Knoppers
1956–2018
Colleague, Friend, Exemplary Human Being

TABLE OF CONTENTS

Introduction. ix
List of Abbreviations xiii

CHAPTER 1. How Persian Power Entered Egypt 1

1.1 Egypt Before the Persians 1
1.2 Persia's Rise to Power 3
1.3 Cambyses Came to Egypt 4
1.4 Darius's Consolidation 9
1.5 "The Silver and the Ebony Were Brought from Egypt" or: The Character of Persian Rule in Egypt 13
1.6 Elephantine 16
1.7 Who Was Cambyses, and What Exactly Is Meant by the Verb "To Conquer"? 17

CHAPTER 2. Yehudites at Elephantine: Provenance, Identity, and Religion 18

2.1 Jews, Judaeans, Judeo-Arameans, or Yehudites? 18
2.2 How Did They Come to Egypt? 20
2.3 Religious Identity 23
2.4 Yehudite Identity in Elephantine 52

CHAPTER 3. Multiethnic Elephantine: Some Remarks on Different Minor Ethnicities in a Persian Border Garrison 54

3.1 Eastern Satrapies 55
3.2 Anatolia 61
3.3 Phoenicians 63
3.4 Philistines 73
3.5 The Aegean Sea 73
3.6 Lybian Tribes 74

3.7 Arabs 75
3.8 Conclusion and Prospect 77

CHAPTER 4. Pax Persica: Cooperation, Cohabitation, and Acceptance 78
4.1 Intermarriage 78
4.2 Salutations in Letters 86
4.3 Trade Contacts 93
4.4 Oaths and Other Deities 94
4.5 An Interreligious Figurine 97
4.6 Conclusions and Questions 97

CHAPTER 5. Control Through Education, Law, and Military Power. . . 99
5.1 Two "Literary" Texts 99
5.2 Sayings of Aḥiqar as Scribal Propaganda 100
5.3 The Function of the Aramaic Version of the Bisitun Inscription 108
5.4 Law 115
5.5 Military 117
5.6 An Inadequate Analogy 117

CHAPTER 6. Disruptions of the Interethnic Solidarity 119
6.1 A Stone of Contention 119
6.2 A Conflict Between Egyptians and Yehudites 122
6.3 Burglary in Times of Turmoil 123
6.4 The Crisis Around the Demolition of the Temple of Yahô 128
6.5 A Thick Description 144
6.6 Concluding Question 146

CHAPTER 7. "Khnum Is Against Us Since Hananiah Has Been in Egypt": On Two Historical Movements in the Fifth Century BCE . . 147
7.1 From the Oasis in the Desert to the Land of the Pyramids 148
7.2 Egypt's Struggle for Independence 154
7.3. *Histoire Conjoncturelle* 162

CHAPTER 8. Beyond the Final Curtain: The Aftermath of Elephantine 163
8.1 Independent Under Nepherites 163
8.2 The Fate of the Yehudites and Other Minorities 164
8.3 Some Speculations 166
8.4 Conclusions 168

Bibliography 169
Index of Authors 195
Index of Ancient Sources 201

INTRODUCTION

The first time I heard about the presence of Yahwists on the island of Elephantine in Southern Egypt in the Persian period was while reading as an undergraduate Theo Vriezen's outline of the religion of ancient Israel.[1] I became aware of Aramaic documents excavated in the beginning of the twentieth century CE that revealed the presence of many Yehudites in the Persian border garrison during the fifth century BCE. Traditionally, they have been construed as Jews, albeit it with a slightly different form of Yahwism. This acquaintance started a lifelong engagement with a fascinating topic. Two questions have been puzzling me. How and why did the "Jews" migrate to Southern Egypt? Is their nonstandard form of Yahwism a relic of the religion in their homeland, Israel, or should it be construed as a syncretistic aberration as a result of being far away from Jerusalem and its temple?

In his 2014 monograph, the historian Simon Schama started his narrative on the story of the Jews in Egypt—not, however, with Moses and the Exodus, but with the community in Elephantine.[2] The reason for this unexpected starting point is twofold. On the one hand, Schama detected in the written documents an open-minded Jewish community with many references to daily life. On the other hand, he uses the antagonism between inclusive and exclusive Judaism—Ezra versus Elephantine—to describe the ongoing tensions within that religion. Reading Schama's book, my initial questions were only partially answered. I found his depiction of Elephantine slightly perfunctory, but I have to admit that twenty-four pages is a restricted space in which to tell the whole story.[3]

It was therefore a great pleasure for me to participate in the Elephantine in Context research project, sponsored by the Deutsche Forschungs Gemeinschaft

1. Vriezen, *De godsdienst van Israël* (translated into English as *The Religion of Ancient Israel*).
2. Schama, *Story of the Jews*.
3. Schama, *Story of the Jews*, 4–27.

(2015–18). I have learned much from the open discussions we had during our meetings at the Theologicum of the Humboldt Universität. I therefore thank the other protagonists in this project, Reinhard Gregor Kratz, Giulia Francesca Grassi, Bernd Ulrich Schipper, and Ann-Kristin Wigand, for the openminded atmosphere in which we could exchange ideas. I also thank the group of excellent scholars who contributed with papers and discussions that put our work on the Aramaic documents in context: Collin Cornell, Sebastian Hoedt, Tawny Holm,[4] Sylvie Honigman, James D. Moore, Joachim Friedrich Quack, Kim Ryholt, Karel van der Toorn, and Alexandra von Lieven. The presence of Verena Lepper, who is leading a team aiming at the publication of all documents from Elephantine—those published and those as yet unpublished—has been of great help. And finally, I thank three scholars who have earned their spurs in this area of research, "Mr. Elephantine" Bezalel Porten, Margaretha Folmer, and Ingo Kottsieper, for sharing with me their insights.

This book was born from my attempts to answer the questions formulated above. The process of carefully reading the texts and putting them in context has refined and redirected these questions. The aim of this book is to put the Yehudite—some say Jewish—community of Elephantine in its historical, social, and religious context. The majority of research on Elephantine in the Persian period overlooks the presence of other ethnic groups on the island and at the adjacent riverside city of Syene. In this book, I present my construction of the past. I am of the opinion that it is impossible to offer an exhaustive reconstruction of everything that happened. The reader will find my reenactment of the past subjective and open to challenge. I have tried, wherever possible, to present the primary source information to allow the reader to evaluate for him- or herself.

Chapter 1 constructs the way in which the Persians conquered Egypt and makes clear that Persian control over Elephantine and its environs had a hands-off character. As long as the yearly taxes were paid, the Persians generally did not interfere in local affairs. Of great importance to the Persians was the protection of their trade interests. For that reason, a garrison was stationed at Elephantine to protect the southern border and, more importantly, to control the trade with sub-Saharan Africa.

Chapter 2 discusses the Yehudite presence at Elephantine. Historically, it is unclear when they settled, and many possible options have been suggested, ranging from Judeans who escaped the fundamentalist policy of Josiah to recruitment by the Persians. I argue that the Yehudites came in waves. As for the identity of this group, they were Yahwists venerating Yahô in their own local sanctuary. They were familiar with the Sabbath and Passover, and they had a local *marzeaḥ* (a regular meeting of upper-class people meeting that included

4. I would like to thank Tawny Holm for her helpful remarks on chapters 5 and 7.

a banquet). Their form of Yahwism was probably aniconic, but certainly not monotheistic or monolatric. Other deities were accepted, as is clear from the salutation formulas in the letters from Elephantine. In addition to Yahô, some minor deities—Anat-Yahô, Eshem-Bethel, and Ḥerem-Bethel—were venerated.

Chapter 3 examines the variety of ethnic groups other than the Persians and the Egyptians. It appears that people from all corners of the Persian Empire were recruited to serve in the local garrison. In addition, there are clear references to Phoenicians and Ionians who visited the island for trade interests. Other groups—for instance, Carians, Libyans, and Philistines—served as laborers or slaves.

Chapter 4 sketches the relatively peaceful coexistence of all these ethnic groups. The groups were intertwined through endogamous marriages. They had common trade interests. Oath texts reveal that these Yehudites accepted the deities of others as witnesses to oaths. The documents evoke the image of a successful multiethnic society under the aegis of the *pax persica.*

How was this *pax persica* possible, and with which instruments was it maintained? Chapter 5 refers to a series of mechanisms the Persians used to control the local community. It is hypothesized that this friendly coexistence of several ethnic groups was only possible as an effect of Persian presence. Argument for this thesis are found in "literary" texts, such as as the Sayings of Aḥiqar (the narrative as well as the proverbs) and the Besitun inscription (an Aramaic version was found on Elephantine), both of which were used in school textbooks training local scribes. These texts functioned as propaganda, ingraining in the scribes an ideology of obedience and loyalty. In addition, the Persians controlled the balance between the groups through their military presence and judicial instruments.

Chapter 6 presents the breakdown of this multiethnic harmony. From 420 BCE onward, the situation changed. Several incidents bear witness to the decline of Persian power and the collapse of solidarity between the groups. A Yehudite was accused of stealing a precious stone, with consequence for the rest of the Yehudite community. Other Judeans were connected with a burglary as a consequence. Even more indicative of this breakdown is the destruction of the Yehudite temple by the priests of Khnum in collaboration with the garrison commander Vidranga. A closer analysis of the documents reveals that this act of destruction was not an isolated incident directed at the Yehudites. The destruction of the Temple of Yahô was part of a broader set of attacks against vital elements of the Persian administration aimed at destabilizing Persian power. Among these targets was the *ywdnʾ zy mlkʾ*, the granary of the king, where the taxes were collected in kind, and the well used to supply the garrison with water.

Chapter 7 tries to put this shift in interethnic relations into its historical and ideological context. First, I examine the difficult-to-understand Papyrus

Amherst 63, which dates from the late fourth century BCE but whose traditions go back earlier to a multiethnic community situated in the "fortress of palms" (or, as I alternately read it, "oasis in the desert") in the seventh century BCE. From this source, I argue that the Yehudite community of Elephantine was joined by additional Yehudite immigrants around 425 BCE, which led to a reformulation of their group identity and, in response to this, a backlash from the Egyptian community, especially the priests of Khnum. Second, I show that there was a recurrent Egyptian desire for independence, evidenced by a series of revolts dating back as far as the reign of Cambyses. I sketch the history of Egyptian resistance to Persian power and look at the political and economic background of these uprisings. I suggest that during the last quarter of the century, a sense of Egyptian self-esteem and anti-Persian feelings became more and more openly voiced. Together, these two factors contributed to the deterioration of multiethnicity harmony in Elephantine and its environs.

Chapter 8 looks at the aftermath. After the Egyptians achieved independence, the presence of the Yehudites as well as the other ethnic groups disappears from the documents. Aramaic, the official language of the Persian Empire, was replaced by the indigenous Demotic. The last Aramaic document is dated to 398 BCE. The fate of all the non-Egyptians from Elephantine and Syene can only be guessed at, but I explore and evaluate some of the possibilities that have been suggested.

I have written this book in a period in which the so-called Western democratic world has entered into a transition period. With the election of Donald Trump as the forty-fifth president of the United States of America, his political struggle to "make America great again," and the rise of alt-right on both sides of the Atlantic, the concept of an open society in which persons from different ethnic groups, diverging religious convictions, and a variety of views on same-sex marriages has begun to corrode. Studying the documents from Elephantine in their political, historical, and social context has strengthened my belief that such a society is possible. The possibly utopian dream, however, comes at a price and will always be vulnerable to the avarice and selfishness of those human beings who do not concede the "other" his or her freedom and way of life.[5]

5. See Lincoln, *Religion, Empire, and Torture*, who after discussing the "other side of paradise"—that is, the ideology of the Bisitun inscription—made some intriguing remarks on the American practice of torture in the Second Gulf War.

ABBREVIATIONS

ANEM	Ancient Near East Monographs/Monografías sobre el Antiquo Cercano Oriente
AOAT	Alter Orient und Altes Testament
BASOR	*Bulletin of the American Schools of Oriental Research*
BZAW	Beihefte zur Zeitschrift für die alttestamentliche Wissenschaft
CBET	Contributions to Biblical Exegesis and Theology
CdE	*Chronique d'Égypte*
CHANE	Culture and History of the Ancient Near East
Enchoria	*Enchoria: Zeitschrift für Demotistik und Koptologie*
FAT	Forschungen zum Alten Testament
HdO	Handbuch der Orientalistik
IrAnt	*Iranica Antiqua*
JAOS	*Journal of the American Oriental Society*
JBL	*Journal of Biblical Literature*
JEA	*Journal of Egyptian Archaeology*
JEgH	*Journal of Egyptian History*
JNES	*Journal of Near Eastern Studies*
JSJ	*Journal for the Study of Judaism in the Persian, Hellenistic, and Roman Periods*
JSJSup	Journal for the Study of Judaism Supplement Series
JSOTSup	Journal for the Study of the Old Testament Supplement Series
JSS	*Journal of Semitic Studies*
LSTS	The Library of Second Temple Studies
MHR	*Mediterranean Historical Review*
NASB	New American Standard Bible
OBO	Orbis Biblicus et Orientalis
OLA	Orientalia Lovaniensia Analecta
Or	*Orientalia* (NS)

OTS	Old Testament Studies
RB	*Revue biblique*
StD	Studia Demotica
TADAE	Bezalel Porten and Ada Yardeni. *Textbook of Aramaic Documents from Ancient Egypt*. Winona Lake, IN: Eisenbrauns, 1999.
Transeu	*Transeuphratène*
VT	*Vetus Testamentum*
VWGTh	Veröffentlichungen der Wissenschaftlichen Gesellschaft für Theologie
ZAW	*Zeitschrift für die alttestamentliche Wissenschaft*

CHAPTER I

How Persian Power Entered Egypt

IN 526 BCE, THE PERSIAN KING Cambyses conquered the land of Egypt.[1] This statement is in need of explanation: Who was Cambyses? And what exactly is meant by the verb "to conquer" in this connection? These questions will guide the following analysis of the advent of Persian power in Egypt.

1.1. Egypt Before the Persians

Although Egypt had a turbulent history, even from the time of the earliest pharaohs, the land had remained largely independent. Through the millennia, there had been many changes of dynasties. Periods in which one pharaoh ruled over Egypt in its entirety interchanged with periods of fragmentation of powers to local rulers. There were only a few periods of foreign rule. The first period was the reign of the Hyksos (Twenty-Fifthy Dynasty; ca. 1648–1550), mainly over northern Egypt. The Hyksos—named by the Egyptians as *ḥqꜣ(w)-ḫꜣswt*, "rulers from foreign lands"—ruled over Egypt from their capital city Avaris in the delta. Their land of origin, ethnic affiliation, and language still remain unknown, despite speculations on their Semitic or Indo-European background. Traditionally, the coming of the Hyksos to Egypt has been seen as the result of a military campaign; presently, however, the view that their migration into Egypt as well as their rise to power was a result of the Thirteenth Dynasty being weakened by famine and plague is gaining ground. The expansion of power of the Theban pharaohs of the Eighteenth Dynasty brought about the end of Hyksos rule, with the conquest of their administrative center, Avaris, by Pharaoh Ahmose I.[2]

1. On the date and its historiographic problems, see Kahn, "Note on the Time-Factor," 103–12; Quack, "Zum Datum der persischen Eroberung Ägyptens," 228–46 (with lit.); Müller, "Among the Priests of Elephantine Island," 234; Vittmann, "Arameans in Egypt," 229; Wigand, "Politische Loyalität und religiöse Legitimierung," 138.

2. See, e.g., Redford, "Hyksos Invasion," 1–52; Ryholt, *Political Situation in Egypt*, 118–50; Van Seters, *Hyksos*; Candelora, "Defining the Hyksos," 203–21.

In the seventh century BCE, the Neo-Assyrian Empire extended into Egypt. According to Amélie Kuhrt, "Egypt's repeated meddling in Palestine"—for instance, by supporting the Levantine rebels against Sennacherib in 701—triggered the Assyrian appetite to control the land of the Nile.[3] Stephen Ruzicka adopts a binary model of struggle between the eastern core of the ancient Near East (Mesopotamia) and the western core (Egypt) for domination over the central area (the Levant), a conflict spanning from the dawn of civilization.[4] By attacking Egypt directly, the Assyrians could tip the balance and become masters of the middle territory with its resources and trade routes. In the reign of Esarhaddon, the Assyrian army conquered Memphis (671):

> After the god Ashur and the great gods, my lords, had ordered me to march far along remote roads, (through) rugged mountains (and) great sand dunes, where (one is always) thirsty, I marched safely (and) in good spirits. As for Taharqa, the king of Egypt and Kush, the accursed of their great divinity, from the city Ishupri to Memphis, (his) royal city, a march of fifteen days overland, I inflicted serious defeats on him daily, without ceasing. Moreover, (with regard to) he himself, by means of arrows, I inflicted him five times with wounds from which there is no recovery; and (as for) the city of Memphis, his royal city, within half a day (and) by means of mines, breaches, (and) ladders, I besieged (it), conquered (it), demolished (it), destroyed (it), (and) burned (it) with fire. I carried off to Assyria his wife, his court ladies, Usanahuru, his crown prince, and the rest of his sons (and) his daughters.[5]

In order to consolidate his rule over Egypt, the Assyrian king campaigned a second time against Egypt, but he died en route. The Assyrian rule over Egypt was consolidated by his son Assurbanipal, who conquered Thebes in 663.[6] Assyrian rule, however, did not bring about complete Egyptian submission or Assyrianization of culture, religion, and daily life; Egyptians did not have to give up their religious and cultural identity, and the relations between the Assyrian king and the local rulers were relatively friendly.[7] Because the power of the Assyrian

3. Kuhrt, *Ancient Near East*, 499.

4. Ruzicka, *Trouble in the West*, 7–8.

5. Esarhaddon Victory Stele from Sinjirli: rev. 36–44; see, e.g., Spalinger, "Esarhaddon and Egypt," 295–326; Ruzicka, *Trouble in the West*, 7–8.

6. Streck, *Assurbanipal und die letzten assyrischen Könige*, 16 = Rm. Col II:37–39, and 164 = Ann. 1:74; Ruzicka, *Trouble in the West*, 8.

7. See Kuhrt, *Ancient Near East*, 499–500; Ruzicka, *Trouble in the West*, 6–9; Kahn, "Assyrian Invasions of Egypt," 251–67; for later reflections in demotic texts, see Ryholt, "Assyrian Invasion of Egypt"; Holm, "Sheikh Fadl Inscription," 193–224; Köhler, Driaux, Marchand, Holm, and Capirci, "Preliminary Report."

Empire waned in the last years of Assurbanipal and the weak kings that succeeded him, Egypt was able to regain its independence. The power vacuum that resulted from Assyria's decline was filled by local Levantine rulers, such as Josiah of Jerusalem, who regained independence. At the same time, Egypt tried to stretch its influence into the "central area." Dan'el Kahn has collected some evidence that hints at a growing Egyptian influence in the Levant in the decades preceding the rise of the Neo-Babylonian Empire.[8]

Nebuchadnezzar II of the Neo-Babylonian Empire succeeded in ending the Egyptian influence in Syria and Palestine, extending dominion into the southern Levant, right up to the border with Egypt. In 601/600 BCE Nebuchadnezzar invaded Egypt, albeit in vain. He was defeated by the pharaoh and had to withdraw: "In the month of Kislîmu he[9] took the lead of his army and marched to Egypt. The king of Egypt heard it and mustered his army. In open battle they smote each other's breasts and inflicted great havoc on each other. The king of Akkad turned back with his troops and returned to Babylon."[10] During the Saite period (Twenty-Sixth Dynasty; 644–526), Egypt was a prospering and united country.[11] This would drastically change, however, with the rise of the Achaemenid rulers from Persia to world dominion.

1.2. Persia's Rise to Power

In the sixth century BCE, a new power entered the stage of world history. The Persians had their power base in what is now the province of Fars in Iran. After securing Persian domination over the Medes, Cyrus the Great looked west and attacked the weakened Neo-Babylonian Empire: "In the month Nisanu, Cyrus, king of Parsu, mustered his army and crossed the Tigris below Arbela."[12] A full description of the surprising ascent of Cyrus from a local tribal ruler to a sovereign reigning from Afghanistan to the Aegean Sea and from the Caucasus to the border of Egypt, and the framework of the economic and political circumstances and shifts that made this rapid route to rule possible, is worthy of a monograph on its own.[13] But in view of the central inquiry of this book—the implications

8. Kahn, "Nebuchadnezzar and Egypt," 66–69.

9. Nebuchadnezzar II.

10. Grayson, *Assyrian and Babylonian Chronicles*: text 5 rev. 6'–7'; see Kahn, "Nebuchadnezzar and Egypt," 70–71.

11. See Kuhrt, *Ancient Near East*, 636–46; Kahn, "Nebuchadnezzar and Egypt."

12. Nabonidus Chronicle (Grayson, *Assyrian and Babylonian Chronicles*, text 7 II 15–16).

13. See, e.g., Dandamaev, *Persien unter den ersten Achämeniden* 91–107; Wiesehöfer, *Das antike Persien*, 25–52; Kuhrt, *Ancient Near East*, 647–61; Briant, *Histoire de l'Empire Perse*, 41–72; Ruzicka, *Trouble in the West*, 12–13; Zarghamee, *Discovering Cyrus*; Waters, *Ancient Persia*, 35–53; Siljanen, *Judeans of Egypt*, 20–25.

of waning Persian rule in Egypt for the multiethnic community in and around Elephantine—a full (re)construction of the processes is not necessary here. After the death of Cyrus in 530 BCE, his son Cambyses inherited a vast empire. Egypt, however, was not yet under Persian rule.

1.3. Cambyses Came to Egypt

"The great king of all foreign countries Cambyses came to Egypt, taking the foreigners of every foreign country with him. When he had taken possession of the entire country, they settled themselves down therein, and he was made great sovereign of Egypt and great king of all foreign countries."[14] With these words, the pro-Persian Egyptian official Udjaḥoresnet summarizes the conquest of Egypt by Cambyses. In his autobiography, he paints the Persian takeover of Egypt in relatively light colours. In Udjaḥoresnet's perception, Cambyses did not "conquer" the land, he just "came" almost as on a tourist outing. A comparable euphemism is used in describing the influx of officers, tax-contributors, merchants, and soldiers who came from all corners of the empire to put the Persian mark on Egypt. This is, as can be assumed, a flattering image of the process. Udjaḥoresnet obviously wanted to please the foreign ruler.[15]

The account in Herodotus's *Histories* is also biased, albeit in a different way. The Greek historian, however, offers a set of trustworthy details mingled with legendary stories.[16] After Cyrus's conquest of Lydia,[17] Pharaoh Ahmose II (570–526) made common cause with Polycrates of Samos, a Greek tyrant, probably aiming to weaken the Persian forces.[18] In the framework of this bond, Ahmose was able to conquer the island of Cyprus using the large fleet he had inherited

14. Autobiography of Udjaḥoresnet:11–12; text: Posener, *Première domination perse en Egypte*, no. 1; translation: Kuhrt, *Persian Empire*, 117–22; see, e.g., Rössler-Köhler, "Zur Textkomposition der naophoren Statue des Udjahorresnet/Vatikan Inv. Nr. 196," 43–54; Blenkinsopp, "Mission of Udjahorresnet," 409–21; Baines, "On the Composition and Inscriptions of the Vatican statue of Udjahorresnet," 83–92; Briant, *Histoire de l'Empire Perse*, 70–72; Grabbe, *History of Jews and Judaism*, 1:113; Lee, *Authority and Authorization of Torah*, 41–56; Lloyd, "Egyptian Attitude to the Persians," 185–98; Lopez, *Democede di Crotone e Udjahorresnet di Sais.*

15. Some scholars suspect him to have been a collaborator; see Lloyd, "Inscription of Udjaḥorresnet," 166–80; Fried, "Cyrus the Messiah?," 373–93; Fried, *Priest and the Great King*, 63–65; Rohrmoser, *Götter, Tempel und Kult*, 18–20; correctly nuanced by Fitzpatrick-McKinley, *Empire, Power, and Indigenous Elites*, 16; Smoláriková, "Udjahorresnet," 151–64.

16. See Kuhrt, *Ancient Near East*, 661–64; Brown, "Herodotus' Portrait of Cambyses," 387–403; Depuydt, "Murder in Memphis," 119–26; Serrano Delgado, "Cambyses in Sais," 31–52; Grabbe, *History of Jews and Judaism*, 1:12–22; Wesselmann, "Se non è vero," 130–54.

17. Herodotus, *Hist.* 1.79–81.84; translation: Kuhrt, *Persian Empire*, 62–63; see Evans, "What Happened to Croesus?," 34–40; Briant, *Histoire de l'Empire Perse*, 46.

18. On Polycrates, see Herodotus, *Hist.* 3.120–25; translation: Kuhrt, *Persian Empire*, 127–29; see Carty, *Polycrates, Tyrant of Samos.*

form his ancestor Neco II.[19] This event compelled Cambyses to build his own fleet, since he understood that he would need naval power to defeat Ahmose.[20] When the triremes were ready after a few years, the Persians first took control of Cyprus—probably in order to have control over the maritime routes in the eastern Mediterranean.[21] Herodotus narrates a legendary story about the relations between Cambyses and Ahmose that serves to explain the Cambyses's attack of Egypt. The Persian king had asked Ahmose for his daughter to become a concubine at the Persian court.

> After considering the matter, he (= Ahmose) did as follows. There was a daughter of the former king Apries, all that was left of that family, quite tall and pretty, and her name was Nitetis; this girl Ahmose adorned with clothes and gold and sent to Cambyses as his own daughter. But after a time, as he (= Cambyses) embraced her, addressing her as the daughter of Ahmose, the girl said to him, "O King, you do not understand how you have been made a fool of by Ahmose, who dressed me in finery and sent me to you as his own daughter, when I am in fact the daughter of Apries, the ruler Ahmose revolted from with the Egyptians and killed." This speech and this crime that occurred turned Cyrus's son Cambyses, furiously angry, against Egypt. So the Persians say.[22]

Herodotus makes this swindle the trigger for the war, casting the Persian king as a ruler led by emotions.

Cambyses's attack on Egypt coincided with a period of quarrels between the semi-independent kings in the delta region and the central power of Ahmose in Memphis, leading to a weakening of the natural defense line that is formed by the waters and the mud of the delta.[23] In the same period, Cambyses negotiated with Arab tribes on the Sinai Peninsula: "Cambyses, hearing what was said by the stranger from Halicarnassus, sent messengers to the Arabian and asked for and obtained safe conduct, giving to him and receiving from him pledges. . . . When, then, the Arabian had made the pledge to the messengers who had come from Cambyses, he devised the following expedient: he filled

19. Herodotus, *Hist.* 2.182; see Briant, *Histoire de l'Empire Perse*, 62.

20. Herodotus, *Hist.* 3.19, 44; translation: Kuhrt, *Persian Empire*, 110–12; see Briant, *Histoire de l'Empire Perse*, 61.

21. Herodotus, *Hist.* 3.19; see Schulz, "Zwischen Eroberungskrieg und Präventivschlag?," 651–52.

22. Herodotus, *Hist.* 3.1; translation: Kuhrt, *Persian Empire*, 107; see Wesselmann, "Se non è vero," 137–40; Yamauchi, "Cambyses in Egypt," 371–72; Briant, *Histoire de l'Empire Perse*, 61.914. The name Νίτητις, Nitetis, is certainly Egyptian. *Njtt-jj.tj*, daughter of Apries, unfortunately is not documented in Egyptian sources.

23. See Yamauchi, "Cambyses in Egypt"; Ruzicka, *Trouble in the West*, 14–17; Siljanen, *Judeans of Egypt*, 25–27.

camel skins with water and loaded all his camels with these; then he drove them into the waterless land and there awaited Cambyses's army."[24] The Persian king clearly aimed to attach Egypt on two fronts: through the desert and over sea, applying the age-old strategy of the pincer movement. While the Persian army marched through the desert in the direction of Memphis, the fleet attacked the Egyptians in the eastern part of the Nile delta. The Egyptians suffered many losses and withdrew to the capital city of Memphis. After a tragic incident with a Persian herald—while asking the Egyptians to surrender, he and all the men on his boat were massacred—the Persians besieged Memphis for ten days before the city fell into their hands. The new pharaoh, Psammetichus III, son of the deceased Ahmose, was put in prison. The Persians took over and tried to negotiate to extend their power to the southern border of Egypt.[25] From the available evidence, it is unclear whether or not Cambyses achieved this goal. It should be noted that the Yehudites of Elephantine—on the southern border of Egypt—claimed in their request to rebuild the demolished temple of Yahô, that "when Cambyses entered Egypt, he found the temple built. They [the Persians] overthrew all the temples of the Gods of Egypt, but one did not damage anything in that temple [=Yehudite temple]."[26] If that claim was correct, then Cambyses must have reached Egypt's southern border. There are indications that Cambyses campaigned to the south after his conquest of Memphis. The report in Herodotus, however, is rather vague on the outcome of the southern campaign: "Hearing this, Cambyses feared their becoming cannibals, and so gave up his expedition against the Ethiopians and marched back to Thebes, with the loss of many of his army; from Thebes he came down to Memphis, and sent the Greeks to sail away."[27] Here, the fact that the Persian soldiers had to eat grass is given as a reason to end the campaign against the south. Strabo, however, claims that Cambyses campaigned as far south as Meroe, hence beyond the fifth cataract, to present-day Bagrawiya in Sudan: "Further, when Cambyses took possession of Egypt, he advanced with the Egyptians even as far as Meroe; and indeed, this name was given by him to both the island and the city, it is said, because his sister Meroe—some say his wife—died there."[28] This was written by the end of

24. Herodotus, *Hist.* 3.7–9; translation (only partly): Kuhrt, *Persian Empire*, 110; see Briant, *Histoire de l'Empire Perse*, 64; Retso, *Arabs in Antiquity*, 236–37.

25. Herodotus, *Hist.* 3.10–11, 14–15, 17–21; translation: Kuhrt, *Persian Empire*, 112–17; Ruzicka, *Trouble in the West*, 18–19; Ctesias, *Persica* = Jacoby, *Die Fragmente der griechischen Historiker*, 3:688 Fr. F 13 (10), erroneously gives Amyrtaeus as the name of the imprisoned pharaoh; see Kahn, "Note on the Time-Factor," 106–7; see also Briant, *Histoire de l'Empire Perse*, 279–87; Sternberg-el Hotabi, "Die persische Herrschaft in Ägypten," 112.

26. *TADAE* A4.7:13–14 // *TADAE* A4.8:12–13; for a discussion of these events, see §6.3 below.

27. Herodotus, *Hist.* 3.26–27; translation: Kuhrt, *Persian Empire*, 115–16; see also Ruzicka, *Trouble in the West*, 21.

28. Strabo, *Geography* 17.1.5; translation: Kuhrt, *Persian Empire*, 116; Roller, *Historical and Topographical Guide*, 941–97; Schulz, "Zwischen Eroberungskrieg und Präventivschlag?," 651.

the first century BCE. The claim is not corroborated by other evidence, and the historicity of the campaign is far from certain. The reference is probably due to Strabo's inclination to describe the world by depicting its periphery.[29]

Despite the fact that he was enthroned as *mesutire*, "Re incarnate,"[30] and despite his examplary behavior as an Egyptian king, Cambyses was unable to consolidate Persian rule over Egypt. Already in 525/24 BCE, he was confronted with a rebellion, albeit an unsuccessful one, by Psammetichus III, the defeated son of Ahmose.[31] Excavations at Amheida in the Dakhla oasis have made clear that in 520 BCE Cambyses was confronted with a rival king: Petubastis IV, a descendant of the Saite pharaohs.[32] It was already known that Petubastis had conquered Memphis,[33] but these excavation have now shown that Petubastis also reigned over the western oases, shedding unexpected light on the western campaign that Cambyses conducted during his reign in Egypt. This campaign is narrated by Herodotus, who suggests that the army was defeated by a sandstorm and then buried in the past.[34]

> As for those who were sent to march against the Ammonians, they set out and journeyed from Thebes with guides; and it is known that they came to the city of Oasis,[35] inhabited by Samians[36] said to be of the Aeschrionian tribe, seven days' march from Thebes across sandy desert; this place is called, in the Greek language, Islands of the Blest. Thus far, it is said, the army came; after that, except for the Ammonians themselves and those who heard from them, no man can say anything of them; for they neither reached the Ammonians nor returned back. But this is what the Ammonians themselves say: when the Persians were crossing the sand from Oasis to attack them, and were about midway between their country and Oasis, while they were breakfasting a great and violent south wind arose,

29. See also Porten, *Archives from Elephantine*, 19–20; Kahn, "Note on the Time-Factor," 107–12; Roller, *Historical and Topographical Guide*, 975.

30. As narrated in Udjahoresnet's autobiography:14; translation: Kuhrt, *Persian Empire*, 118; see also Lloyd, "Egyptian Attitude to the Persians," 187–91; Lee, *Authority and Authorization*, 43; Ruzicka, *Trouble in the West*, 19–21; Granerød, *Dimensions of Yahwism*, 36.

31. See Herodotus, *Hist.* 3.14–15; translation: Kuhrt, *Persian Empire*, 113–14; see Briant, *Histoire de l'Empire Perse*, 128; Kaper, "Petubastis IV in the Dakhla Oasis," 125.

32. Kaper, "Petubastis IV in the Dakhla Oasis."

33. Possibly the *nšn ꜥꜣ*, "great rage," mentioned in the Autobiography of Udjaḥoresnet 33–34.40–41; see Kaper, "Petubastis IV in the Dakhla Oasis," 138.

34. Herodotus, *Hist.* 3.25; translation: Kuhrt, *Persian Empire*, 115; see also Ruzicka, *Trouble in the West*, 21; Kaper, "Petubastis IV in the Dakhla Oasis," 137–43. By way of a side remark, I first heard of the story of the lost army of Cambyses when reading as a youngster the Dutch translation of Johns, *Biggles Flies South*.

35. This word refers to the "Great Oasis" of Khargeh, about seven days' journey from Thebes.

36. A Lybian tribe, not the inhabitants of the Aegean island of Samos.

> which buried them in the masses of sand which it bore; and so, they disappeared from sight. Such is the Ammonian tale about this army.[37]

Olaf Kaper connects this story of the lost army of Cambyses with the rebellion of Petubastis. Defeating this counter-king was the aim of Cambyses's campaign, but Petubastis ambushed his army among sand dunes, and they never returned.[38]

The events that led to Cambyses's death and the accession of Darius are uncertain and only known in legendary and biased descriptions.[39] The transition of power and the propagandistic images depicting it deserves a careful historical survey, but I will here limit myself to a minimalistic picture. Cambyses had a brother named Bardiya—or Σμέρδις (Smerdis) in Herodotus[40]—who met a violent end. The circumstances of his death and its aftermath are, however, difficult to (re)construct. According to both Herodotus and the Bisitun inscription of Darius I, Cambyses killed his full brother.[41] The circumstances are further muddled by traditions about a somewhat enigmatic figure named Gaumāta. According to the Bisitun inscription of Darius:

> Afterwards, there was a certain man, a Magian, Gaumāta by name, who raised a rebellion in Paishiyauvada, on a mountain called Arakadrish. On the fourteenth day of the month Viyaxana he rebelled. He lied to the people, as follows:
>
> I am Bardiya, son of Cyrus, the brother of Cambyses.
>
> Then were all the people in revolt, and from Cambyses they went over unto him, both Persia and Media, and the other provinces. He seized the kingdom; on the ninth day of the month Garmapada. Afterwards, Cambyses died of natural causes.
>
> [...]
>
> There was no man, either Persian or Mede or of our own dynasty, who took the kingdom from Gaumāta, the Magian. The people feared him exceedingly, for he slew many who had known the real Bardiya. For this reason, did he slay them,

37. Herodotus, *Hist.* 3.26; translation: Kuhrt, *Persian Empire*, 115; see also Ruzicka, *Trouble in the West*, 21; Kaper, "Petubastis IV in the Dakhla Oasis," 137–43. By way of a side remark, I first heard of the story of the lost army of Cambyses when reading as a youngster the Dutch translation of Johns, *Biggles Flies South*.

38. Kaper, "Petubastis IV in the Dakhla Oasis," 137–43.

39. See Briant, *Histoire de l'Empire Perse*, 119–50; Schulz, "Zwischen Eroberungskrieg und Präventivschlag?," 652–53. On the folkloristic story of the omen through a bellowing horse—which in reality was a masked equerry—Herodotus, *Hist.* 3.84–89, see now Rollinger, "Altorientalisches bei Herodot," 13–42.

40. He is named Tanyoxarces by Ctesias and Sphendadates.

41. Darius I DB §10; translation: Kuhrt, *Persian Empire*, 143; Herodotus, *Hist.* 3.30; translation: Kuhrt, *Persian Empire*, 159–60.

> that they may not know that I am not Bardiya, son of Cyrus.
> There was no one who dared to act against Gaumāta, the Magian, until I came. Then I prayed to Ahura Mazda. Ahura Mazda brought me help. On the tenth day of the month Bagayadish, I, with a few men, slew that Gaumāta, the Magian, and the chief men who were his followers. At the stronghold called Sikayauvatish, in the district called Nisaia in Media, I slew him; I dispossessed him of the kingdom. By the grace of Ahura Mazda I became king; Ahura Mazda granted me the kingdom.[42]

According to this inscription, Gaumāta was an imposter who misled many people by presenting himself as Bardiya, and in doing so he was able to obtain power over Persia and Media. Darius, in turn, took advantage of the situation by killing Gaumāta and positing himself in power. In antiquity, Darius's proclamation that Gaumāta's claim to be Bardiya was incorrect was widely accepted.[43] In modern scholarship, there is a tendency to accept Gaumāta's claim that he was Bardiya, and Darius's Bisitun inscription is construed as a propagandistic account covering up the murder of Bardiya. By stating that Cambyses killed his own brother, Darius concealed the evil act he performed to take the throne.[44] Whatever exactly happened, Cambyses had to return from Egypt, but "he died on the road, before he had reached his native country."[45] Herodotus thinks Cambyses died in "Syrian Ecbatana."[46] As a result of all this trouble, the Persians were unable to consolidate their rule over Egypt under Cambyses.

1.4. Darius's Consolidation

Darius I was a usurper, although he tried to conceal this fact with an invented genealogy.[47] His claim to be, just like Cyrus, a descendant of *Hachaimenēs* (Ἀχαιμένης), the eponymous ancestor of the Achaemenid dynasty, cannot be substantiated. Amélie Kuhrt correctly argues that the fact that on the day of

42. Darius I DB § 10; translation: Kuhrt, *Persian Empire*, 143 (slightly changed). An enlarged version of this tale is present in Herodotus, *Hist.* 3.61–68; translation: Kuhrt, *Persian Empire*, 160–63.

43. See, e.g., Aeschylus, *Persians*, 765–79; Ctesias, *Persica* = Jacoby, *Fragmente der griechischen Historiker*, 3:688 Fr. F 13 (11–15); Justin, *Epitome* 1.9.4–13.

44. E.g., Dandamaev, *Persien unter den ersten*, 108–214; Wiesehöfer, *Der Aufstand Gaumātas*, 168–232; Shayegan, "Bardiya and Gaumāta," 65–76.

45. Demotic Chronicle Papyrus BN 215: 7–8; see Quack, "Zum Datum der persischen Eroberung Ägyptens"; Siljanen, *Judeans of Egypt*, 26.

46. Herodotus, *Hist.* 3.65–68; translation: Kuhrt, *Persian Empire*, 161–62.

47. Darius I DB §10; translation: Kuhrt, *Persian Empire*, 143.

Darius's ascension both his father and his grandfather were alive should be construed as a falsification of Darius's claim. If he really was an Achaemenid, his grandfather would have been inaugurated as king over Persia.[48]

Darius seized the throne after the murder of Gaumāta. According to the Bisitun inscription of Darius, Gaumāta, along with some of his brothers-in-arms, was killed by a group of seven Persian noblemen.[49] Herodotus offers a lively account of this story, embelished with many legendary details, such as the claim that Darius was assigned by an omen to be the killer of Gaumāta.[50] Darius's reign was contested; from all corners of the Persian Empire local leaders rebelled against his investiture. The king and his army undertook a series of campaigns to suppress these revolts, as is depicted in his Bisitun inscription.[51]

According to the Bisitun inscription one of the rebellious areas was Egypt: "While I was in Babylon, these provinces revolted from me: Persia, Elam, Media, Assyria, Egypt, Parthia, Margiana [Marguš], Sattagydia [Thataguš], and Scythia [Saka]."[52] In the second-century CE *Stratagems* of Polyaenus, there is a rather legendary note on Darius:

> The Egyptians revolted, on account of the cruelties inflicted on them by Aryandes, their satrap. In order to reduce them to obedience, Darius himself marched through the Arabian desert and arrived at Memphis, at the very time when the Egyptians were commemorating the death of Apis. Darius immediately made a proclamation that he would give a hundred talents of gold to the man who could produce Apis. The Egyptians were so impressed by the piety of the king that they took decisive action against the rebels and entirely devoted themselves to support of Darius.[53]

Polyaenus's remarks cannot be treated as historical evidence, although they are not completely without value. Darius's inscription does not mention a campaign against Egypt, but this does not mean that he did not campaign against Egypt. He obviously did, since later in his reign, he controlled Egypt. Herodotus refers to Darius's interference in Egyptian affairs: he removed Aryandes, who was appointed by Cambyses, and reinstalled Persian power in the framework

48. Kuhrt, *Ancient Near East*, 665.

49. Darius I DB §13; translation: Kuhrt, *Persian Empire*, 143.

50. Herodotus, *Hist.* 3.70–73; 76–79; translation: Kuhrt, *Persian Empire*, 167–70.

51. Darius I DB §16–75; translation: Kuhrt, *Persian Empire*, 144–51.

52. Darius I DB §21.

53. Polyaenus, *Strategemata* 7.11.7 (in Brodersen, *Polyainos: Strategika* [Sammlung Tusculum], Berlin: de Gruyter, 2017); see, e.g., Cameron, "Darius, Egypt, and the 'Lands Beyond the Sea,'" 307–13; Ruzicka, *Trouble in the West*, 23–24. On the historical value—or, better, lack of it—see the essays in Brodersen, *Polyaenus Neue Studien*.

of his 518 BCE campaign against Barca and Cyrene.[54] Whether or not Darius was helped by Arab tribes—just like Cambyses—is uncertain.[55] The trilingual Chalouf Stela remarks, "King Darius says: I am a Persian; setting out from Persia, I conquered Egypt. I ordered [them] to dig this canal from the river that is called Nile and flows in Egypt, to the sea that begins in Persia. Therefore, when this canal had been dug as I had ordered, ships went from Egypt through this canal to Persia, as I had intended." [56] This tradition of Darius digging a canal from Suez through the desert to the Nile to accommodate trade relations seems to be corroborated by a set of inscriptions in Akkadian, Egyptian, Elamite, and Persian along the route.[57]

In the next period of his reign—after having restored order in his realm—Darius took a series of measures aiming consolidating Persian rule. Of great importance in this regard is Darius's reorganization of the satrapies. Although the institution of the satrap (*xšaçapāvan*, literally "protector of the province") already existed in the period of Median rule, it was Cyrus who connected the function of satrap to a territory in the empire over which the satraps where installed as viceroys. Cyrus had the empire divided into twenty-six satrapies.[58] Darius improved the system and extended the duties of the satraps into the area of taxes. The satraps (by then numbered at twenty) had to collect a stipulated tribute both in money and in kind on a yearly basis.[59] As regards the satrapy of Egypt, Herodotus informs his readers about the following annual tribute: "The sixth province was Egypt and the neighboring parts of Libya, and Cyrene and Barca, all of which were included in the province of Egypt. From here came seven hundred talents, besides the income in silver from the fish of the lake Moeris; besides that silver and the assessment of grain that was given also, seven hundred talents were paid; for a hundred and twenty thousand bushels of grain were also assigned to the Persians quartered at the White Wall of Memphis and their allies." [60]

54. Herodotus, *Hist.* 4.165–67; 200; translation: Kuhrt, *Persian Empire*, 175–76; 189–93; Wijnsma, "Worst Revolt of the Bisitun Crisis," 157–73.

55. Pace Porten, *Archives from Elephantine*, 21.

56. Darius I DZc §3; translation: Kuhrt, *Persian Empire*, 485–86; see Redmount, "Wadi Tumilat," 127–35; Schulz, "Zwischen Eroberungskrieg und Präventivschlag?," 657.

57. See Posener, *Première domination perse en Egypte*, 48–87; Porten, *Archives from Elephantine*, 21–22; Sternberg-el Hotabi, "Die persische Herrschaft in Ägypten," 118–19; Kuhrt, *Ancient Near East*, 668–69; Fried, *Priest and the Great King*, 65–67; Wasmuth, "Political Memory," 205–11; Klotz, "Darius I and the Sabaeans," 267–80.

58. See the monograph by Klinkott, *Der Satrap*.

59. Herodotus, *Hist.* 3.89–97; translation: Kuhrt, *Persian Empire*, 674–77; see Monson, "Egyptian Fiscal History," 1–36.

60. Herodotus, *Hist.* 3.91; Moeris is a lake in the northeastern part of the Wadi Fayum; an important quarry was situated there, see Cruz-Uribe, "Lake of Moeris," 63–66; Briant, *Histoire de l'Empire Perse*, 412; Sternberg-el Hotabi, "Die persische Herrschaft in Ägypten," 115–16.

Some of Darius's policies attempted to win Egyptian favor. Darius, like his predecesors, presented himself as an Egyptian god-king.[61] He also improved the route from the Levant to Egypt through the northern Sinai, building a chain of way stations,[62] in the interest of facilitating trade, as well as tax collection. With these measures, Darius tried to structure and consolidate Persian control over Egypt.[63] However, there was another face to Persian rule over Egypt. In order to finance the Persian campaign against Greece, heavy taxes were laid upon Egypt.[64] These caused an anti-Persian attitude especially among the still semi-independent kings (or warlords) in the delta region, leading to a rebellion against Persia in the final years of Darius's reign.[65]

A set of three Demotic letters gives evidence of the interference of King Darius in the administration of the temple of Khnum in Elephantine.[66] When Pherendates was satrap over Egypt, the *wab*-priests of that temple corresponded with the satrap—as was apparentlytypical—on the appointment of a new *mr-šn*, "lesonis," for the temple.[67] For the Persians the choice of a trustworthy and loyal functionary in that position was of great importance. In one of the letters a job description is found: "Now, the *wab*-priest whom it is suitable to make *lesonis* is a great man, whom, it will happen, I will cause to carry out his functions, there being nothing that he has let fail, one who will be selected in accordance with that which Pharaoh Darius has ordered."[68] In doing so, Pherendates takes responsibility for ensuring that Darius's politics are spelled out even in this remote temple.

It was only under Darius's successor Xerxes that order was restored in Egypt. Xerxes also changed the basic politics of Persian rule over Egypt. He no longer construed himself as a pharaoh. In his view, the satrapy of Egypt was nothing more than an enslaved province: "After being persuaded to send an expedition against Hellas, Xerxes first marched against the rebels in the year after Darius death. He subdued them and laid Egypt under a much harder slavery than in the time of Darius, and he handed it over to Achaemenes, his own brother and

61. Ruzicka, *Trouble in the West*, 23–25.

62. Ruzicka, *Trouble in the West*, 24.

63. See also: Bresciani, "Satrapia d'Egitto," 132–88; Wasmuth, "Political Memory."

64. See Ruzicka, *Trouble in the West*, 26–28.

65. For details, see §7.2 below.

66. Edited by Spiegelberg, *Drei demotische Schreiben*, 82–91; translation in Porten, *Elephantine Papyri in English*, 288–94; see Hughes, "So-Called Pherendates Correspondence," 75–86; Briant, *Histoire de l'Empire Perse*, 490–91; Fried, *Priest and the Great King*, 75–76.80–84; Grabbe, *History of Jews and Judaism*, 1:113–14; Müller, "Among the Priests of Elephantine Island," 235–38.

67. A lesonis was responsible for the administrative and economic well-being of a temple.

68. P.Berl. 13540:4–5; see Spiegelberg, *Drei demotische Schreiben*, 82–91; Porten, *Elephantine Papyri in English*, 291–92.

Darius's son. While governing Egypt, this Achaemenes was at a later time slain by a Libyan, Inaros, son of Psammetichus."[69]

1.5. "The Silver and the Ebony Were Brought from Egypt" or: The Character of Persian Rule in Egypt

One of the aims of the Persians in conquering Egypt was to collect all sorts of taxes and tributes from this rich country. A few texts give evidence of this.

In a Demotic text called "the decree of Cambyses"—written on the verso of the Demotic Chronicle—a series of measures is ordered that would lead to lower income for Egyptian temples from the imperial coffers.[70] In doing so, Cambyses could claim that he continued the cult at several Egyptian temples and, at the same time, save money.[71]

After finishing the building of a new palace in Susa, Darius had a trilingual foundation inscription made in which he narrates the construction of the new palace—with the help of Ahura Mazda.[72] The inscriptions note that the new palace was built with materials from all corners of the empire. People from all satrapies had delivered resources and were instrumental in the building process. Stone columns came from Elam, cedarwood from the Lebanon. The inscription communicates a clear royal ideology: Darius is presented as king over an empire in which various people harmoniously served their suzerain.[73] The contribution from the satrapy of Egypt consisted of silver and ebony: "The silver and the ebony were brought from Egypt. The ornamentation with which the wall was adorned, that was brought from Yaunâ. The ivory that was wrought here was brought from Kush and from India and from Arachosia."[74]

At first sight, this seems strange. Egypt is not well known for its indigenous silver ore, and the ebony tree was not part of the native flora on the shores of the Nile. Noel H. Gale and Zofia A. Stos-Gale, however, have correctly argued that

69. Herodotus, *Hist.* 7.7; translation: Kuhrt, *Persian Empire*, 248; see Ruzicka, *Trouble in the West*, 28.

70. Demotic Chronicle Verso D:1–17; translation: Kuhrt, *Persian Empire*, 125–26; Grabbe, *History of Jews and Judaism*, 1:115.

71. See Fried, *Priest and the Great King*, 73–74; Sternberg-el Hotabi, "Die persische Herrschaft in Ägypten," 112–13; Granerød, *Dimensions of Yahwism*, 59–61.

72. Darius DSf; translation: Kuhrt, *Persian Empire*, 492–95; see Grabbe, *History of Jews and Judaism*, 1:115–16.

73. See Kuhrt, *Ancient Near East*, 669–70, who refers to the fact that the administrative texts from Persepolis confirm the multiethnic character of the enterprise. On the palace and its various aspects, see Perrot, *Palace of Darius at Susa*.

74. Darius DSf §11. Arachosia is a mountainous area in which is now the border territory between Afghanistan and Pakistan; see Vogelsang, "Early Historical Arachosia," 55–99.

although the local sources for silver were not abundant, a white shining alloy of gold and silver was mined in ancient Egypt.[75] Herodotus also claims that the yearly tribute from the satrapy of Egypt contained—among other things—large amounts of silver.[76] Ebony (*Diospyros ebenum*) is a kind of hardwood that is indigenous to India and Sri Lanka. Central Africa is the cradle of *Dalbergia melanoxylon* or African Blackwood, which in ancient Egypt as well in the ancient Near East was used for the production of luxury furniture, and which is still used for the production of musical instruments today. Since African Blackwood timber has much in common with the Asian ebony, the two species have often been confused. From prepharaonic times onward, "ebony," Egyptian *hbny* (probably African Blackwood), was part of the trade between Egypt and Central Africa.[77] The Persians took over this lucrative trade. The Susa inscription from Darius also refers to elements of ivory in the construction brought from "Kush and from India and from Arachosia." For many millennia, ivory from Kush, which is present-day Ethiopia, was traded through Egypt to Mesopotamia.[78] The importance of Elephantine as a transit market on this route will be discussed below.

Both the remark on the yearly tribute and the reference to the Egyptian contribution to the palace of Darius contain clues to the importance of Egypt for the Persians and the character of their rule.[79] In short: the Persians were not primarily interested in Persianizing ancient Egypt, its religion, or aspects of daily life; their interest was especially in trade, tribute, and taxes.

In her recent monograph, Anne Fitzpatrick-McKinley discusses the character of Persian power in the conquered territories. She rightly disputes the view that the Persians would have exercised an extremely liberal and tolerant form of government over the various peoples. This is what the Cyrus Cylinder wants us to believe. She also disputes the view that the Persians would have developed a system similar to medieval feudalism. In her opinion, the aim of Persian domination was to receive as much tribute as possible from the conquered countries. In order to achieve their goals, the Persians involved local elites in their strategies. These elites had to take care of the payment of tribute under the supervision of Persian officials.[80] Fitzpatrick shows in detail how these mechanisms were implemented in the various satrapies of the immense Persian Empire, taking into account the interests of the local elites and the nature of the population. Although

75. Gale and Stos-Gale, "Ancient Egyptian Silver," 103–15.

76. Herodotus, *Hist.* 3.91 (see above).

77. See Amin, "Ancient Trade and Trade Routes," 23–30; Roy, *Politics of Trade*, 253.

78. Roy, *Politics of Trade*, 255–57.

79. On the idea of clues as specific kinds of historical traces, see Ginzburg, *Clues, Myths and the Historical Method.*

80. On the Persian system of raising tributes, see Briant, *Histoire de l'Empire Perse*, 399–433.

the evidence is far from overwhelming, it shows that there were differences in regulations applied, for example, to Lycia and to the Arab Bedouins.[81]

As regards the satrapy of Egypt, there are clear indications of the Persians collecting the yearly tribute.[82] In his list of tributes to be paid to the Persian court, Herodotus mentions the taxation to be levied from Egypt.[83] The cooperation of the Persians with the local elites is depicted also in the Autobiography of Udjaḥoresnet, mentioned above. Muhammad A. Dandamayev and Vladimir G. Lukonin have made clear that after taking control over Egypt the Persians only replaced a small portion of the local Egyptian civil servants, leaving the majority of them in office.[84] Alejandro F. Botta has argued that the Egyptian calendar remained in use, albeit in various cases in parallel with the Persian, Babylonian-based calendar.[85] The Persian attitude toward Egyptian culture and religion can be illustrated with two examples. Decorations on the walls of the Temple of Hibis in the Egyptian Kharga Oasis depict Darius I as an Egyptian pharaoh as a way to thank him for rebuilding the sanctuary.[86] Here, Darius is cast as a friend of Egypt. Slightly different is the image in the inscription on a stela of Darius that was constructed to be set up in Heliopolis:

> A great god is Ahuramazda, who created this earth, who created yonder sky, who created man, who created happiness for man, and who made Darius king.
> This is the statue, made of stone, which Darius ordered to be made in Egypt. This is how everyone who will see this in the future will know that the Persian man ruled in Egypt.
> I am Darius, the great king, king of kings, king of all peoples, king in this great earth far and wide, the son of Hystaspes, an Achaemenid.
> King Darius says: May Ahuramazda protect me and what I did![87]

This inscription presents Darius in two capacities: he is a pious Egyptian warrior-monarch as well as a foreign conqueror.[88]

81. Fitzpatrick-McKinley, *Empire, Power, and Indigenous Elites*; for Egypt, see pp. 68–70.

82. See Bresciani, "Satrapia d'Egitto'; Ruzicka, *Trouble in the West*, 24–28; Monson, "Egyptian Fiscal History."

83. Herodotus, *Hist.* 3.91; see above.

84. Dandamaev and Lukonin, *Culture and Social Institutions*, 96–115; see Fitzpatrick-McKinley, *Empire, Power, and Indigenous Elites*, 11.

85. Botta, *Aramaic and Egyptian Legal Traditions*, 45–49, see also Neugebauer, "Origin of the Egyptian Calendar," 396–403; Claget, *Calendars, Clocks, and Astronomy*.

86. See Winlock, *Temple of Hibis in el Khargeh Oasis*; Cruz-Uribe, *Translations, Commentary, Discussions*, 227; see, however, the critical remarks by Lloyd, "Egyptian Attitude to the Persians," esp. 191; Wasmuth, "Political Memory," 212–15.

87. Darius I, DSab; Yoyotte, "Inscriptions hiéroglyphiques," 181–83, 213–14; translation: Kuhrt, *Persian Empire*, 477–79.

88. See Kuhrt, *Ancient Near East*, 688; Briant, *Histoire de l'Empire Perse*,491–92.

Alan Lloyd has correctly argued that these and other inscriptions and monuments present the Persian gaze.[89] The ideological character is clear: Darius wants to be seen as an Egyptian pharaoh. This ideology does not, however, make the inscriptions completely untrustworthy. In my view, this Persian gaze conceals the fact that the Persians, with their ambiguous politics of conquest and friendship, spread the seed for coming unrest. During the fifth century a growing Egyptian struggle for independence can be detected, leading eventually to the end of the Persian hegemony.[90]

1.6. Elephantine

Elephantine is the name of an island in the Nile in southern Egypt. The island was named *ꜣbw*, "ivory," in Old Egyptian. The name is probably connected with the role the island had in the millennia-old ivory trade. In Aramaic the island is called יב, and in Greek sources Ἰηβ. The island has been continuously inhabited from prehistoric times until this day. On the island temples for the deities Satet and Khnum were built.[91]

In view of the above, the island of Elephantine was important to the Persian Empire in the fifth century BCE for its location. The cascades of the first cataract were nearby, which made Elephantine a natural transit market. Commodities like ebony and ivory that came from Central Africa on small boats were transferred to the bigger ships that could sail the Nile but could not cross the cataract. The Persian presence on this island in the Nile and on the banks of that river in nearby Syene served several other Persian interests:

1. The border garrison—consisting of Persians and soldiers from all corners of the Empire—protected the trade routes going into Central Africa. Various commodities, including ebony and ivory, were transported on these routes to mainland Persia.[92]

89. Lloyd, "Egyptian Attitude to the Persians'; see also Fitzpatrick-McKinley, *Empire, Power, and Indigenous Elites*, 63–65.

90. See §7.2 below.

91. Müller, "Among the Priests of Elephantine Island," 213–43, offers a concise history of the island.

92. See Schulz, "Zwischen Eroberungskrieg und Präventivschlag?," 654–55. It should be noted that Elephantine was not the southernmost Persian stronghold. Upstream in Nubian territory a Persian fortress on the island of Dorginarti existed. The find of Phoenician amphorae at this site indicates the importance of the stronghold for the trade routes, although the amphora might have to be dated to an earlier period. See Heidorn, "Saite and Persian Period Forts at Dorginarti," 205–19; Briant, *Histoire de l'Empire Perse*, 397.

2. The border garrison defended the Persian presence in Egypt against Nubian and Cushite infiltration. Both peoples—living south of Elephantine—had a continuous inclination to meddle in Egyptian affairs.
3. Elephantine was a collection point for taxes, as becomes clear from the fact that both a granary and a "house of the king" are mentioned in the Aramaic inscriptions.
4. Some of the Aramaic documents give the impression that Elephantine has been a confluence point for the Persian "secret service." Xenophon refers to an intelligence network already in the era of Cyrus the Great: the king's eyes and ears informed the ruler about many movements in his empire and on the strive of disloyal officers.[93]

1.7. Who Was Cambyses, and What Exactly Is Meant by the Verb "To Conquer"?

Even from this rather brief analysis, it is clear that Cambyses was a Persian king who enlarged the realm he had inherited from his father. The conquest of Egypt in 525 BCE by him and the subsequent consolidation of Persian rule by Darius I—belated by the rebellion of Petubastis IV—did not devastate the local Egyptian culture and religion. Daily life was not very much interrupted. The main change was the fact that taxes and tributes were no longer paid to the Egyptian court but to the Persian overlord. This fact, however, was an ongoing source for Egyptian unrest and rebellion. In the next chapters, I will describe how the complex community in Elephantine and Syene played a role in the maintenance of Persian power in Egypt and how the presence of Persian power provoked once again the Egyptian desire for independence.

93. Xenophon, *Cyr.* 8.2.10–12; translation: Kuhrt, *Persian Empire*, 644; Bledsoe, "Conflicting Loyalties," 257.

CHAPTER 2

Yehudites at Elephantine: Provenance, Identity, and Religion

ELEPHANTINE IS THE NAME of an island in the Nile that was located at the southern border of the Persian Empire during the fifth century BCE.[1] Written documents give evidence of a "Jewish/Judean/Yehudite" section in the multicultural border garrison on the island at that time. In this chapter, I present this group, their provenance, and their religious identity.

2.1. Jews, Judeans, Judeo-Arameans, or Yehudites?

Time and again this group has been labeled as "Jewish." To give two recent examples, Stephen G. Rosenberg wrote an article claiming to be able to trace the remains of a Jewish temple at Elephantine,[2] and Simon Schama, although sometimes using the marker Yehudite, depicts the Yahwists of Elephantine as Jews.[3] I take these as representatives of a more general view that understands the identity of the Yehudites of Elephantine as Jewish. This classification, however, is problematic and requires discussion. A question of definition as well as identity is at stake.

In several of the texts on papyri and ostraca, this group is labeled—by themselves as well as by others—as *yhwdyʾ*. This Aramaic noun can be rendered as "Jewish" as well as "Yehudite." The Aramaic noun *yəhûdāy* occurs a few times in the Old Testament: Ezra 4:12, 13; 5:1, 5; 6:7–8, 14; Dan 3:8, 12. In these contexts, the noun signifies "a person coming from Yehud; a Judean." In various Aramaic texts from Qumran the noun clearly refers to a "Jew." It is possible to construe the Aramaic noun in the documents from Elephantine as "Jew(ish)."[4]

1. Porten, *Archives from Elephantine*, still is an instructive introduction.
2. Rosenberg, "Jewish Temple at Elephantine," 4–13; the classification "jew(ish)" is widespread among scholars.
3. Schama, *Story of the Jews*, 4–27.
4. Korpel, "Disillusion among Jews in the Postexilic Period," 135–57.

This classification, however, yields a problem as regards its specific meaning in the fifth century documents from Elephantine. "Jewish"—if understood as referring to formative, normative, or rabbinic Judaism—would clearly be an anachronism applied to fifth century BCE Yahwism.[5] On the other hand, the evidence from Elephantine—as will be made clear below—does not even show a religion, or religious identity, that equals Yahwism, as we know it from the Hebrew Bible. In accordance with Shaye Cohen, I use the classifier "Jewish" to refer to practitioners of "Judaism," the religion that was constructed in Hellenistic times. I construe the Persian era as a period of transition from Yahwism to Judaism.[6] Hence, I will refer to the *yhwdy'* of the Persian period distinctively as Yehudites.[7]

A problem that must be discussed in this connection is the fact that some Yehudites seem to have a double ethnic identity. Karel van der Toorn lists a number of Yehudites who are labeled as Yehudite in some documents, but as Aramaic in others.[8] The most striking example is a certain Mahseiah. He is known as "Mahseiah, son of Yedaniah, Aramean of Syene"[9] and as "Mahseiah, son of Yedaniah, a Yehudite who is in the fortress of Elephantine."[10] Several suggestions have been offered to explain this assumed double ethnic identity. They are, however, not convincing.[11] Some scholars assume that the double identity is caused by a process of acculturation between "Jews" and Arameans that also would have led to the syncretistic form of religion.[12] Others argue that the noun "Aramaic" should be construed as the indication of a language and that the "Jews" were seen as part of a larger Aramaic-speaking community.[13] Pierre Grelot and Alejandro F. Botta argue that these "Jews" were also called Arameans since they were administratively part of the Aramaic garrison.[14]

Recently, van der Toorn has offered a more elegant explanation. In his view the Yehudites could be called Arameans since they came from the Persian satrapy *ebir-nāri*, "beyond the river," a larger Aramaic area in the Persian Empire.[15] His analysis of Papyrus Amherst 63 led him to the assumption that the Arameans at Elephantine had migrated from the Palmyra oasis—the Jews

5. See, e.g., Grabbe, *Judaic Religion*, 29–36, 315–34; Collins, *Invention of Judaism*.
6. Cohen, *Beginnings of Jewishness*; Nodet, *Search for the Origin of Judaism*; Vittmann, "Arameans in Egypt," 230–31.
7. See also Bledsoe, "Conflicting Loyalties," 239.
8. Van der Toorn, "Ethnicity at Elephantine," 152–56.
9. *TADAE* B2.1:3–4.
10. *TADAE* B2.2:3–4.
11. See van der Toorn, "Ethnicity at Elephantine," 156–60.
12. Van Hoonacker, *Communauté Judéo-Araméenne à Éléphantine*.
13. Porten, *Archives*, 33; Joisten-Pruschke, *Das religiöse Leben*, 84.
14. Grelot, *Documents araméens d'Égypte*, 174; Botta, *Aramaic and Egyptian Legal Traditions*.
15. Van der Toorn, "Ethnicity at Elephantine."

mainly to the island and the Syrians and Babylonians to Syene. In his view the Yehudites had been Samarians who fled to Palmyra after the Neo-Assyrian attacks on Samaria and Jerusalem and adopted a Jewish identity in the second half of the fourth century BCE.[16] His proposal invites a discussion of both the provenance and the identity of the Yehudites in Elephantine.

2.2. How Did They Come to Egypt?

The inscriptions from Elephantine are silent about the provenance of the Yehudites on the island and in nearby Syene. The earliest texts referring to *yhwdy*ʾ date from the beginning of the fifth century BCE. This implies that they must have settled there not later than around 500 BCE. Some views, however, reckon the date of the arrival of the *yhwdy*ʾ in Elephantine even earlier. These views are based on the scarce scraps of evidence.[17]

Only for curiosity's sake, I will refer to the view of Evan MacLaurin who suggested that the "Yeb colony was descended from a body of Hebrews left behind at the time of the Exodus."[18] Although this view explains the nonstandard form of Yahwism among the Yehudites in Elephantine—this group had not received the Decalogue—it is not supported by any evidence.

In the famous request for the rebuilding of the devastated temple of Yahô on the island, the Yehudites claim that "when Cambyses came to Egypt, he found this temple built. They [the Persians] overthrew all the temples of the Gods of Egypt, but one did not damage anything in that temple [=Yehudite temple]."[19] Since there are no indications of a Yehudite presence in Elephantine before 500 BCE, this claim could be seen as an example of "invented tradition." If, however, there *were* already Yehudites in the area before the Persians took over Egypt, two interpretations are possible. The first construes the remark as a reference to an action in which Cambyses would have destroyed temples throughout Egypt. From an outsider perspective, the idea that Cambyses devastated all the sanctuaries in Egypt except the temple for Yahô in Elephantine should be construed as an example of hyperbolic appropriation of history. To insiders, the remark in the rebuilding request should be interpreted as an expression of group identity—they construed themselves as living in Elephantine "from the olden days."[20] The second interpretation construes the remark in

16. Van der Toorn, *Becoming Diaspora Jews*.
17. Siljanen, *Judeans of Egypt*, 45–54, gives a nice display of the various proposals.
18. MacLaurin, "Date of the Foundation of the Jewish Colony at Elephantine," 89–96.
19. *TADAE* A.4.7:14; 4.8:13.
20. Porten, *Archives*, 25–38; Porten, "Jews in Egypt," 378–79; Schäfer, *Judeophobia*, 121; Porten, "Settlement of the Jews at Elephantine," 457–60.

the letter from Elephantine as a reference to the destruction of temples in the era of Cambyses at the local scale of Elephantine.

In a side comment, the author of the Letter of Aristeas mentions that long before the Hellenistic times, "large numbers of Jews had come into Egypt with the Persian, and in an earlier period still others had been sent to Egypt to help Psammetichus in his campaign against the king of the Ethiopians. But these were nothing like so numerous as the captives whom Ptolemy, son of Lagus, transported."[21] Writing from a much later period, this author applies the anachronism "Jews" for the seventh-century Judeans. Building on this text, Gösta Ahlström assumes that many Judeans moved to Egypt in the end of the seventh century BCE to help Psammetichus I in his battles with the Ethiopians.[22] The inscription on the statuette of Asḥor—the commander of the fortress of Elephantine under Pharaoh Apries, son of Psammetichus I—might corroborate this claim. In the inscription, Asḥor brings thanks to the deity Khnum: "For you rescued me from an evil plight, from the mercenaries, the ⌜Libyans⌝, the Greeks, the Asiatics (*ʿꜣmw*), and foreigners who had it in their hearts . . . to go to Shassheret."[23] This text gives the impression that some mercenaries tried to escape their military duties. Among the Asiatics might have been Judeans.[24]

In the book of Jeremiah, in the aftermath of the assassination of Gedaliah the governor:

> Johanan, son of Kareah, and all the army officers led away all the remnant of Judah who had come back to live in the land of Judah from all the nations where they had been scattered. They also led away all those whom Nebuzaradan, commander of the imperial guard, had left with Gedaliah, son of Ahikam, son of Shaphan—the men, the women, the children and the king's daughters. And they took Jeremiah the prophet and Baruch, son of Neriah ,along with them. So, they entered Egypt in disobedience to YHWH and went as far as Tahpanhes.[25]

Jeremiah 44 narrates a debate among Judeans in Egypt on the question of whether idolatry—the veneration of the Queen of Heaven—had been the reason

21. Let. Aristotle 13; on this letter, see now Wright, *Letter of Aristeas*.

22. Ahlström, *History of Ancient Palestine*, 751, 760; see also Redford, "Origin and Termination of the Foreign Colony–Garrison at Elephantine," 149–57.

23. Breasted, *Ancient Records of Egypt*, 4:§994; see now Bassir, "Neshor at Elephantine in Late Saite Egypt," 66–95.

24. Thus, Porten, "Settlement of the Jews at Elephantine," 465–66; Rohrmoser, *Götter, Tempel und Kult*, 48.

25. Jer 43:5–7. I herewith abandon my previous view that Judeans fleeing to Egypt only settled in the delta area and did not reach southern Egypt: Becking, "Die Gottheiten der Juden in Elephantine," 203–26—thanks to Vittmann, "Arameans in Egypt," 232.

why YHWH had delivered Judah into the hands of the Babylonians.[26] On the basis of these remarks, in combination with the assumed presence of polytheistic elements in the religion of the Yehudites in Elephantine, many scholars take the view that these Yehudites were a mixed group of people who fled Judah after 587 BCE to Egypt together with former polytheistic inhabitants of the Northern Kingdom of Israel.[27]

The Aramaic documents from fifth-century Elephantine give the impression that the Yehudites were recruited—voluntarily or forced—by the Persian military system. This would hint at the possibility that they were mercenaries and descendants of the Israelite soldiers who fought in the Assyrian army and had kept their Ephraimite form of Yahwism.[28] These mercenaries could also have been brought to Egypt from the Persian province of Yehud after the exile. The recently published texts from the area of *al Yahudu*, "the city of Judah/Yehud," and *al ša* ᴾ*na-šar*, "the City-of-Nashar" ("Eagleton"), in Babylonia indicate that Yehudites were still living in the Babylonian countryside after the Persian takeover.[29] This opens the possibility that some of the Yehudites from Elephantine were brought there from that area of Mesopotamia. It might well be that these Yehudites, coming from an Aramaic satrapy, were one of the reasons why some Yehudites in and around Elephantine could also be labeled as *ʾrmyʾ*. Anne Fitzpatrick-McKinley recently argued that some Yehudites serving in Elephantine might have been recruited from the Borsippa area, where Judean mercenaries are attested side by side with Carians in the fifth century BCE.[30]

Elaborating on a remark by Richard Steiner, van der Toorn recently suggested that a group of persons from various ethnic backgrounds migrated from Palmyra to Elephantine and Syene in the early years of Persian rule over the land of the Nile. These people had been living in an "oasis in the desert" as exiles from Syria, Babylonia, and Israel.[31] With their migration they brought a

26. See on this chapter: Becking, "Jeremiah 44," 255–64.

27. Niehr, *Der höchste Gott*, 43–45; Redford, *Egypt, Canaan and Israel*, 441–45; van der Toorn, "Anat-Yahu, Some Other Deities, and the Jews of Elephantine" (he later specified this position; van der Toorn, "Eshem-Bethel and Herem-Bethel"); Niehr, *Religionen in Israels Umwelt*, 162; Grabbe, "Israel's Reality after the Exile,"25–32; Schama, *Story of the Jews*, 12–13; Siljanen, *Judeans of Egypt*, 45–54.

28. As surmised by Weippert, "Synkretismus and Monotheismus," 170–71.

29. See the edition by Pearce and Wunsch, *Documents of Judean Exiles*; Alstola, *Judeans in Babylonia*, 102–63.

30. Fitzpatrick-McKinley, "Preserving the Cult of Yhwh," 419–20; she refers to the text VS 6 128 that deals with the assignment of Judeanas in Borsippa and was drafted in 510 BCE, see Waerzeggers, "Carians of Borsippa," 8.

31. On the term "oasis in the desert," see below §7.1.

syncretistic form of religion—as expressed in Papyrus Amherst 63—with them to Egypt.[32]

All these proposals have their merits and their weaknesses, and at the same time they are not mutually exclusive.[33] In light of this, I take the position that the Yehudites did not come to Elephantine in one wave but should be seen as the merger of various groups who—for different reasons and in various periods—ended up in Elephantine.[34]

2.3. Religious Identity

Much can be said and has been written about the religious identity of the Yehudites in Elephantine. Simon Schama observed that they did not hold to the letter of the law in observance.[35] The question is: What can positively be said about their religious identity? Recent studies by Angela Rohrmoser, Gard Granerød, and Esko Siljanen have explored many elements of their religious identity.[36] In the next sections, I summarize their findings through the lens of such aspects of life as time, space, and the "other."

2.3.1. Identity and the Organization of Time

In their request to rebuild the demolished temple of Yahô, the Yehudites of Elephantine claimed that "when Cambyses entered Egypt, he found the temple built. They [the Persians] overthrew all the temples of the Gods of Egypt, but one did not damage anything in that temple [=Yehudite temple]."[37] This remark refers to an internal tradition of the Yehudites that they had been living in Egypt from the days before Cambyses came to Egypt. Whether or not this claim is correct, it is a feature on their linear conception of time. In addition to this linear dimension of time is the calendrical experience of time, which serves as an even greater identity marker. Time as such has no inherent divisions other than the rhythms of day and night and the four seasons. The calendrical organization of

32. See Steiner, "Aramaic Text in Demotic Script," 362–63; van der Toorn, *Papyrus Amherst 63*; van der Toorn, *Becoming Diaspora Jews*; with my remarks in §7.1 below.

33. See also Kratz, *Historical and Biblical Israel*, 137–38.

34. See already Anneler, *Zur Geschichte der Juden von Elephantine*, 101–17.

35. Schama, *Story of the Jews*, 14.

36. Rohrmoser, *Götter, Tempel und Kult*; Granerød, *Dimensions of Yahwism*; Siljanen, *Judeans of Egypt*, 218–95.

37. *TADAE* A4.7:13–14 // *TADAE* A4.8:12–13; for a discussion of these events, see §6.3 below.

time marks the worldview of a community.[38] As far as I can see, the Yehudites in Elephantine largely adopted the local Egyptian calendar system but kept some aspects of their own calendar.[39] The cultic calendar of Yahwism—originally based in the cycles of the agricultural year but slightly extracted from these roots in the priestly calendar developed during and after the exile[40]—can be discerned from the inscriptions from Elephantine only in two elements: the assumed festival of Passover/Matzot and the celebration of Sabbath.

2.3.1.1. Passover[41]

Among the documents from Elephantine is an interesting letter that is generally known as the "Passover Letter" (P.Berl. 13464; *TADAE* A4.1). Below, I will evaluate whether or not this label is correct. First, I present a transliteration and translation of this badly damaged document based on a recent photograph made at the Staatliches Museum zu Berlin:[42]

Transliteration

Recto

1. ⸢. . . *y*⸣*dnyh wknwth ḥ*⸢*ylʾ*⸣,[43] *yhwdyʾ ʾḥwkm ḥnn*⸢*y*⸣*h ʾlhyʾ* [. . .]
2. [. . .] *wkʿt šntʾ 5 drywhwš mlkʾ mn mlkʾ šlyḥ ʿl ʾrš*⸢*m*⸣
3. [. . .] *yʾ kʿt ʾntm kn mnw ʾrb*⸢*ʿt . . .*⸣
4. ⸢. . . *ʿb*⸣*dw wmn ywm 15 ʿd ywm 21 l* [. . .]
5. [. . .] *dkyn hww wʾzdhrw ʿbydh ʾ*⸢*l . . .*⸣
6. [. . .] *ʾl tštw wkl mndʿm zy ḥmyr ʾl* [. . .]

Verso

7. ⸢. . . *b*⸣*mʿrb šmšʾ ʿd ywm21 lnys*[. . .]
8. ⸢. . . *h*⸣*nʿlw btwnykm wḥtmw byn ywmyʾ* [. . .]
9. [. . .]
10. [. . .] *kḥy*[44] *ydnyh wknwth ḥylʾ yhwdyʾ ʾḥwkm ḥnnyh b*⸢*r . . .*⸣

38. Zerubavel, "Easter and Passover," 284–89.

39. Neugebauer, "Origin of the Egyptian Calendar," 396–403; Claget, *Calendars, Clocks, and Astronomy*; Botta, *Aramaic and Egyptian Legal Traditions*, 45–49.

40. Wagenaar, *Origin and Transformation*; Albani, "Israels Feste im Herbst und das Problem des Kalenderwechsels in de Exilszeit," 111–56.

41. This section is based on Becking, "Centre, Periphery, and Interference," 65–78.

42. See http://elephantine.smb.museum/record/ID100463.

43. The reading *ḥ*[*ylʾ*], "force," as is generally accepted, is supported by the repetition of the phrase "his colleagues of the Yehudite force" in line 10.

44. The first sign in this line has generally been read as an *ʾāleph*. Hence the first word was read *ʾḥy*, "my brothers," as an indication for "Yedaniah and his colleagues'; see the edition by Porten and Yardeni. Except from the fact that it is uncertain whether *ʾḥy* is a noun in the plural with a first person singular suffix, see, e.g., Folmer, *Aramaic Language*, 211; Muraoka and Porten, *Grammar of Egyptian Aramaic*, §12. The sign on the photograph differs too much from the other *ʾāleph*s in the

Translation

Recto

1. ⸢... J⸣edaniah and his colleagues of the Yehudite f[orce], [from] your brother Hanania[h]. May God [...].[45]
2. [...] And now, this[46] year, year 5 of Darius the king, from the king has been sent to Arsh[ames ...]
3. [...] you will count fou⸢r ...⸣
4. ⸢... of⸣fer. You will count from day 15 up to day 21 of [...]
5. [...] be undefiled and take heed. Work [...]
6. [...] you will not drink,[47] and anything that is leavened you shall not [...]

Verso

7. [...] setting of the sun until day 21 of Nisa⸢n ...⸣
8. ⸢... b⸣ring to your chambers and seal (it) between the days [...]
9. [...]
10. [...] my power; Yedaniah and his colleagues of the Yehudite force, your brother Hananiah, so⸢n of ...⸣

Ever since the discovery of this document, the gaps in the texts have been filled based on passages from the Hebrew Bible and Jewish tradition. Already in 1912 William Arnold produced a full and flowing text.[48] This tradition has been continued even in the critical edition of Bezalel Porten and Ada Yardeni.[49] As a result, a text emerges in which clear instructions can be read concerning the

text. In my view, the sign should be read as a *kaph* leading to a word *kḥy*, "my power," indicating the role of Hananiah in the Persian rule. As far as I can see, the noun *kḥ*, well known in Biblical Hebrew, is not attested elsewhere in Ancient or Persian period Aramaic inscriptions. In the Aramaic of the targumim the noun occurs a few times; see Tg. Psalm 16:3; 22:31; 71:18; 80:3; Job 36:19; Ruth 3:15.

45. Porten and Yardeni translate the end of line 1: "May God/the gods [seek after] the welfare of my brothers," probably based on the salutation-formulae in other letters. There is, however, not much space for such an addition.

46. The demonstrative pronoun *zʾ* clearly has a deictic function referring to the then actual year; see Muraoka and Porten, *Grammar of Egyptian Aramaic*, §41a.

47. Grelot suggests that the object of (non)drinking would have been *škr*, "beer." He refers to some passages in Mishnaic law that indicate that the drinking on Passover of *zythos*, an Egyptian beer, was forbidden, Mishnah Pesachim 3.1: "These items are a transgression on Pesach: Babylonian *kutach*, Median beer, Edomite vinegar, Egyptian ale (זותום), bran water from dyers, working dough from cooks, and glue from scribes"; see Grelot, "Études sur le 'Papyrus Pascal' d'Éléphantine," 361–62; see also Porten, *Archives*, 82.129; Rohrmoser, *Götter, Tempel und Kult*, 384–85. This argument is, however, not convincing.

48. Arnold, "Passover Papyrus from Elephantine," 1–33.

49. See, e.g., Grelot, "Papyrus pascal d'Éléphantine nouvel examen," 114–17; Porten, *Archives from Elephantine*, 128–30; Whitters, "Some New Observations," 282–85; Kratz, "Temple and Torah," 84–86; Lee, *Authority and Authorization of Torah*, 72–82; Wagenaar, *Origin and Transformation*, 142–43; Schama, *Story of the Jews*, 16–17; Kratz, *Historical and Biblical Israel*, 141.

character of the Passover festival. Erasmus Gass—correctly—warned of the pitfall of such overinterpretation and circular reasoning.[50]

Already Edouard Sachau classified this text as “Sendschreiben betreffend das Passafest.”[51] The letter is commonly known as the “Passover Letter.” Already in 1912, however, Hedwig Anneler construed the letter as referring to the feast of unleavened bread and avoids the term Passover in this connection.[52] I will return to this classification later. Suffice it for now to make the observation that the text as we now have it contains a few references in the direction of a spring festival:

- the fragmentary clause “You will count from day 15 up to day 21 of” could refer to the days of the Matzot festival; the fifteenth day is mentioned in Lev 23:6–8 and Num 28:17 as the starting day of this festival
- the Aramaic noun *ḥmyr*, “leavened” (line 6), is quite well known from the targumim as the Aramaic cognate of Hebrew *ḥameṣ*
- the clause in line 6 is reminiscent of the prohibition in Exod 12:10, “You shall eat nothing leavened”
- most probably the month Nisan is mentioned in line 7: “Nisa⸢n . . .⸣”[53]

Due to the absence of words like *psḥ*, “Passover,” or *mṣwt*, “unleavened bread,” in the parts of the letter that survived the ages, an exact reference to a specific festival cannot be established. We are left with relative uncertainty. Nevertheless, the letter makes clear that on behalf of the Persian administration instructions were given for a Yehudite festival.

The addressee of the letter is clear: it was to be received by the leaders of the Yehudite community. Yedaniah—referred to in a couple of other documents from the same period—is apparently seen as the spokesman and contact person. The sender is less clear. Of course, the document refers to a certain Hananiah as the author of the letter. He functioned as some sort of a civil servant for Yehudite affairs under the satrap Arshames.[54] He must have had a double loyalty being a

50. E. Gass, “Der Passa-Papyrus (Cowl 21I),” 55–68; his view was adapted by Schwiderski, *Die alt-und reichsaramäischen Inschriften*, 2:6; Grabbe, *History of Jews and Judaism*, 1:211–12; Joisten-Pruschke, *Das religiöse Leben*, 151–57; Rohrmoser, *Götter, Tempel und Kult*, 342–44; Granerød, *Dimensions of Yahwism*, 172–75.

51. Sachau, *Aramäische Papyrus und Ostraka*, 36.

52. Anneler, *Zur Geschichte der Juden von Elephantine*, 85.

53. See also Wagenaar, *Origin and Transformation*, 142–43; Rohrmoser, *Götter, Tempel und Kult*, 341–42.

54. On Hananiah, see Porten, *Archives from Elephantine*, 130; Kratz, “Judäische Gesandte im Achämenidenreich,” 377–98; Kratz, “Second Temple of Jeb and of Jerusalem,” 247–64; Joisten-Pruschke, *Das religiöse Leben*, 75; Kratz, “Zwischen Elephantine und Qumran,” 138–41; Kratz, “Judean Ambassadors,” 421–44; Schama, *Story of the Jews*, 17 (who incorrectly believes Hananiah is

Yehudite in the Persian administration since he was both peripheral and central at the same time.[55]

A few things about the origin of the letter, however, remain unclear. It is uncertain from where the letter has been sent. Three options are open: (1) from the administrative seat of Hananiah, probably in Memphis,[56] (2) from the Yehudite temple in Jerusalem, or (3) from the imperial palace in Susa or Ecbatana. The second possibility is only a vague possibility. Other than in the request for the rebuilding of the temple, the so-called Passover Letter does not contain a reference to Jerusalem or Samaria.[57]

The uncertainty about the sender is connected to two other questions. First, line 2 seems to reference a memorandum sent by King Darius to Ars⌜hames . . .⌝. Darius here is Darius II. Ars⌜hames . . .⌝ refers to Arshames the satrap, who was in charge of Egypt in the latter years of the fifth century. It seems unlikely that the present letter would have been the memorandum sent to Arshames. It is more likely that Hananiah excerpted the section relevant for the Yehudites from a text that would have contained a variety of topics.

Second, who was the "real" sender? Or phrased differently: Whose power was behind the instructions? It seems unlikely that King Darius himself would have been involved in religious matters in the periphery of his empire. Most likely, he only gave his approval to a suggestion made to him by an advisor. Who, however, was this advisor or group of advisors? What had triggered this advice? Was it a reaction to a request from the Yehudite community at Elephantine? Did the priesthood in Jerusalem broach the subject? Was the letter written under the impact of the canonization of the Torah, as Porten suggests?[58] Unfortunately, all suggestions to this topic remain speculative, in view of the lack of evidence. A few years later a letter was written from Elephantine to Samaria and Jerusalem requesting the rebuilding of the temple of Yahô after the priests of Khnum destroyed it with the approval of the wicked Vidranga.[59] This letter could be seen as comparative evidence, but it is far from decisive for the view that the Yehudite community in Elephantine itself had requested regulations on the festival. It only opens up the possibility but does not rule out other options.

---

identical with חנני, "Hanani," the brother of Nehemiah in Neh 1:2; 7:2); Kratz, *Historical and Biblical Israel*, 146; Granerød, *Dimensions of Yahwism*, 34–37; van der Toorn, "Ezra in Egypt?," 602–10.

55. See Porten, *Archives*, 130; Kottsieper, "Die Religionspolitik der Achämeniden," esp. 150–58.

56. Thus, Kratz, "Zwischen Elephantine und Qumran," 140–41.

57. This observation makes the assumption of Nihan, *From Priestly Torah to Pentateuch*, 573–74; Jonker, "Achaemenid Understanding of Law and Justice in Darius I's Tomb Inscriptions," 33–35; that by 419 BCE the Yehudites of Elephantine acknowledged the authority of the temple in Jerusalem is very improbable. In my opinion, the "Passover Letter" cannot be used as an argument for the dating of the Holiness Code/Tradition in the Hebrew Bible.

58. Porten, *Archives*, 133; nuanced by Collins, *Invention of Judaism*, 49–50.

59. *TADAE* A.4.7=8; *TUAT* I, 254–58; see §6.3 below.

Despite all these uncertainties it seems safe to assume that the letter is part of the communication between center and periphery. The reference to the Persian king Darius, as well as the noun *kḥ*, underscores this assumption. The application of this spatial metaphor to the power structure of the Persian Empire is not just an invention of a latter-day historian. As Bruce Lincoln suggests, the metaphor is already present in the presentation of Darius I in the rock relief in Bisitun.[60]

Does this letter give any hint of celebration of Passover, as has often been assumed?[61] Ingo Kottsieper argued for the connection between this letter and the festival of Matzot.[62] The text is too broken to make a decision. The only conclusion to be drawn here is that at the end of the fifth century the Yehudites felt the need for a calendrical organization of time, especially in connection to their sanctuary. Matzot is not referred to in any texts. The theme of Passover is present in two ostraca. One text refers to Passover but is not informative as regards the character of the festival;[63] the other text was written seventy to eighty years before the so-called Passover Letter and contains a question: "Please inform me whether you celebrate Passover (תעבדון פסחא)."[64] One can speculate whether this seasonal festival had been an older tradition of the Yehudites that needed some revision, or whether the troublesome times at the end of the fifth century BCE invited them to start this festival. Whether a renewal of tradition or an invented tradition, this festival functioned as an identity marker of the Yehudites.

2.3.1.2. Sabbath

In Judaism the observance of the Sabbath is an important identity marker to this day. The origin of this weekly day of observance is still unclear. In the postexilic community, whose festivals and holy days were no longer so closely connected to the agricultural cycle, the weekly Sabbath became a fundamental part of calendrical worldview based on order and calculated time.[65] The inscriptions from Elephantine evidence the existence of the Sabbath institution among the

60. Lincoln, *Religion, Empire, and Torture*, 17–23.

61. Since Arnold, "Passover Papyrus from Elephantine"; via Porten, *Archives*, 82.129; up to Siljanen, *Judeans in Egypt*, 250–53.

62. Kottsieper, "Die Religionspolitik der Achämeniden"; also Granerød, *Dimensions of Yahwism*, 170–71; van der Toorn, "Ezra in Egypt."

63. *TADAE* D7.24; see Porten, *Archives*, 131; Siljanen, *Judeans in Egypt*, 249; G. Granerød, "Canon and Archive," 356.

64. *TADAE* D7.6:9; see Porten, *Archives*, 72, 131; Siljanen, *Judeans in Egypt*, 248–50.

65. See Grabbe, *History of Jews and Judaism*, 1:220–23; Hartenstein, "Der Sabbath als Zeichen und heilige Zeit,"103–31; Wagenaar, *Origin and Transformation*, 121–55; Grund, *Die Entstehung des Sabbats*, 189–298; Rohrmoser, *Götter, Tempel und Kult*, 328–34; Smith-Christopher, *Religion of the Landless*, 139–51.

Yehudites, discussed below. One relevant document is a private letter to Yedaniah requesting provisions, which reads as follows: "Greeting, Yedanyah! Now, were I to put [in] the provisions, then it would be commanded: "[Let] them [*not*] withhold from him bread and water." ⸢*Now* . . . let⸣ Ahutab [take] out for me. But, ⸢. . . d⸣ay of the Sabbath. Now, if they did not capture Nathan there, let him go out to me, and I will go grind [. . .]. Moreover, dispatch to me [. . .] and I shall write [. . .] and do not [. . .]."[66] This letter is not easily understood. The anonymous writer seems to be worried about the deliverance of food and provisions to him. The connection with the Sabbath is unclear. On the basis of this broken text no conclusions can be drawn as to the character of the Sabbath at Elephantine.

Another pertinent document is an ostracon written by a certain Islah, most probably a woman:

> Behold, I will send vegetables tomorrow.
> Meet the boat tomorrow on the Sabbath, so that they will not get lost.
> By the life of Yahô, if not, (then) I will take your life.
> Do not rely on Meshullemeth or Shemaiah.
> Now, send me barley in return.
> Now, by the life of Yahô, if not, (then) you will be responsible for the account.[67]

This ostracon indicates that on the day of the Sabbath, there obviously existed some trade in vegetables. It might, however, be that this was a case of emergency. The letter by Islah might have been a cry from the bottom of a crisis. One problem with this interpretation—although it seems to defend a basically strict Sabbath observance—is that the inscription does not hint at a case of emergency. The language of apology for trespassing the Sabbath is absent. On the other hand, to conclude that this ostracon reflects standard procedures in Elephantine is premature. What can be adduced is the fact that at least a few Yehudites had no moral or religious problems with trade on a Sabbath.[68]

For a more traditional view, see Friedman, "Sabbath in Israel," 93–98; Robinson, *Origin and Development*; MacKay, *Sabbath and Synagogue*,11–42; Veijola, *Moses Erben*, 61–75; Granerød, *Dimensions of Yahwism*, 182–96.

66. *TADAE* D7.10; see Porten, *Archives*, 126.277; B. Porten, "Religion of the Jews of Elephantine in Light of the Hermopolis Papyri," 116–21; Grabbe, *History of Jews and Judaism*, 1:221; Rohrmoser, *Götter, Tempel und Kult*, 331–33; Granerød, *Dimensions of Yahwism*, 192–93.

67. *TADAE* D7.16:1–9; see Porten, *Archives*, 126; Porten, "Religion of the Jews of Elephantine"; Grabbe, *History of Jews and Judaism*, 1:221; Rohrmoser, *Götter, Tempel und Kult*, 331–33; Granerød, *Dimensions of Yahwism*, 192–93.

68. See Rohrmoser, *Götter, Tempel und Kult*, 333–34.

The other ostraca are not very informative. One inscription mentions that Sabbath came, but the context is very unclear.[69] In three texts there seems to be a rather loose connection between salt and Sabbath.[70] A fragmentary letter that mentions bread also reads: "And now, bring to me on the Sabbath."[71] This inscription, too, seems to imply that (economic) activities could take place on a Sabbath.

We can also draw some conclusions about Sabbath practice from the fact that many of the Yehudites functioned as soldiers in the Persian army. This implies that they were supposed to be on military duty all days of the week. If, however, the scheme of a seven-day week with the Sabbath as a day of complete rest was already operational in Elephantine, then full-time military duty would have caused moral or religious problems, since one cannot expect the Persians to have taken into account the various religious wishesof its multiethnic garrison. The inscriptions from Elephantine do not bear witness to such a conflict. This, however, is no proof of the absence of the Sabbath, but only an indication that the Yehudites had a liberal stance toward the demand of the powers that were.[72]

In sum, the tiny pieces of evidence only allow a few glimpses into the reality of ancient Elephantine. There are no indications that the Sabbath was the weekly day of rest yet, as it was in early Judaism.[73] Indications for a seven-day scheme are absent from the inscriptions of Elephantine. This absence of evidence is not, however, evidence of absence. It should be noted that there is also no mention of other days of observance as mentioned in the Hebrew Bible like the "New Moon."[74] The suspension of almost all activities—as is so important in later Jewish tradition—is not attested, neither are there clues about worship practices in the form of celebrations or ritual. In other words, the Sabbath was known, but no strict observation is attested.[75]

It should be noted, however, that a simple comparison between these reports from daily life and the formative codes as known from the Hebrew Bible and later Jewish tradition cannot be made. The codes should be construed as part of the official (or book) religion, while the texts from Elephantine reveal religion at the level of the household and the local community. These two classifications should not be confused, but at the same time the existence of a more

69. *TADAE* D7.12:9; Grabbe, *History of Jews and Judaism*, 1:221.

70. *TADAE* D7.28; 7.35; Grabbe, *History of Jews and Judaism*, 1:221; Lozachmeur, *Collection Clermont-Ganneau*, #205; Rohrmoser, *Götter, Tempel und Kult*, 331–33.

71. *TADAE* D7.48:4–5; Grabbe, *History of Jews and Judaism*, 1:221.

72. 1 Macc 2:41, later, allows warfare on the Sabbath, but as I see it only as an act of defence; see Nodet, *Search for the Origin of Judaism*, 63–92.

73. See also Kratz, "Temple and Torah," 86; Kratz, "Zwischen Elephantine und Qumran," 142; Schama, *Story of the Jews*, 16; Kratz, *Historical and Biblical Israel*, 141.

74. See, e.g., Ps 81:3; 2 Kgs 4:23; Amos 8:5.

75. Grabbe, *History of Jews and Judaism*, 1:221.

open-minded or liberal practice reveals that the normativity of the religious and moral codes was not always mirrored in daily life and that the reality often was more refractory than the official documents would like us to believe.

2.3.2. *Identity and the Life Cycle*

Important information about a group's identity—and how it construed itself—can be discerned from its views on and rituals for the various phases in the cycle of life.[76] A few aspects of the life cycle will be discussed here.

2.3.2.1. *Circumcision*

In many cultures, past and present, circumcision of young adults is part of a rite of passage to adulthood. By giving away a part of the *membrum virile* they became member of the tribe.[77] It is possible that in ancient Israel before the Babylonian exile, circumcision was such a rite of passage to adulthood. The struggle to reformulate the religious identity after the exile might have been an important factor in the change to a ritual performed seven days after the birth of boys.

As far as I can see, no mention is made in the documents from Elephantine of the practice of circumcision either with male babies or with young adults. Schama assumes that all Yehudite boys in Elephantine were circumcised, given the context that circumcision at the threshold of adulthood was common in ancient Egypt.[78] There is no evidence for this claim. The absence of evidence, however, cannot be taken as evidence of absence for this ritual, especially since circumcision has always been part of the religious habits at the family level and hence has often escaped the written record.[79]

76. Capps, "Beatitudes and Erikson's Life Cycle Theory," 226–44.

77. In Africa, for example, circumcision is widespread. While this custom is known among the Yoruba and Igbo of Nigeria, boys of the Zulu, Lemba, and AmaXhosa tribes in southern Africa are also circumcised. See Junod, *Social Life*, 72–73, 94; Le Roux, *Lemba*, 209–24. In traditional Masai culture, boys of about twelve are circumcised in a *rite de passage* to adulthood. See Eilberg-Schwartz, *Savage in Judaism*, esp. 149–53. Aboriginals of Australia traditionally take part in a comparable ritual. As part of a ritual associated with attaining full tribal membership, initiates must sacrifice body parts such as teeth, hair, and foreskin, as a test of bravery; Doyle, "Ritual Male Circumcision," 279–85. With the Native Americans the habit was known among the Incas, Mayas, and Aztecs; Doyle, "Ritual Male Circumcision," 279. In the Philippines, ritual circumcision (*tuli*) is still practiced. During this rite, which is understood as both a marker of male identity and an improvement to the penis, boys are circumcised as a sign of their transition into adulthood; see Glick, "Real Men," 155–74.

78. Schama, *Story of the Jews*, 15.

79. Porten, *Archives*, 251–52.

2.3.2.2. *Marriage, Divorce, and Intermarriage*

Among the documents from Elephantine, three marriage contracts mentioning Yehudites were found.[80] These documents have been discussed by various scholars.[81] These contracts contain a set of stipulations especially regarding the extent of the dowry, the eventual distribution of the inheritance, and the unfortunate case of the ending of the marriage in a divorce. The agreement is made before witnesses whose names are listed. These contracts form the legal side of marriages for well-to-do Yehudites in Elephantine. They do not hint at the form of the marriage ceremony, except for the fact that the phrase "She is my wife and I am her husband from now on to eternity"[82] might refer to the actual formulation of the promise in the wedding.

Some documents make clear that divorces took place, although it is unknown at what scale. The marriage contracts mentioned above stipulate that both man and woman had the right to start the process leading to the dissolution of the marriage. In either case formulaic language is needed. A declaration must be made *śn'ty*, literally "I hate." "Hatred" must be construed as a legal term that goes beyond the sphere of mere emotion. The verb refers to the fact that the person uttering these words is of the opinion that the marriage had lost its formal and emotional ground. He or she is willing to pay the *ksp śn'*, "hatred money," which means that financial questions must be settled, probably by returning the dowry.[83] The woman had to leave the matrimonial home.[84]

It is interesting to note that in Elephantine exogamous intermarriage was accepted. Various texts refer to such marriages.[85] Illuminating, but probably also exceptional, is the biography of Mibtaiah, daughter of Mahseiah.[86] She was first married to her fellow Yehudite Jezaniah, son of Uriah. Bride and groom were part of the upper social stratum. After the death of her first husband, Mibtaiah entered into a contract with Pia, son of Paḥi, a builder of the fortress of Syene, that cannot, however, be seen as a marriage contract.[87] Later on, she married

80. *TADAE* B.2.6; B.3.3. and B.3.8.

81. E.g., Yaron, "Aramaic Marriage Contracts from Elephantine," 1–39; Porten, *Archives*, 187–263; Fitzmeyer, "Re-study of an Elephantine Aramaic Marriage Contract," 137–68; Nutkowicz, "Concerning the Verb *śn'*," 211–25; Botta, "Aspects of the Daily Life," 63–84; Botta, "Hated by the Gods," 105–29; Azzoni, *Private Lives of Women*; Nutkowicz, *Destins de femmes à Eléphantine*; Granerød, *Dimensions of Yahwism*, 49–51; Ilan, "Women's Archives," 171–78.

82. E.g.. in *TADAE* B.2.6:4; the same phrase also occurs in marriage contracts in which Yehudites were not involved, e.g., *TADAE* B.6.1:3–4; the phrase might refer to royal legal customs.

83. See Botta, "Hated by the Gods."

84. Nutkowicz, "Concerning the Verb *śn'*."

85. See §4.3.

86. Porten, *Archives*, 240–55.

87. *TADAE* B.2.8; see below §4.1.

her second husband, Ashor, the builder of the king, also an Egyptian.[88] Marriages with persons from the Aramean ethnos probably were not unknown, but limited.[89]

2.3.2.3. *The Final Threshold*

Death is the final and inevitable phase in the cycle of life. As far as I can see, the documents from Elephantine do not contain any references to ideas about a beatific afterlife. Here too the absence of evidence, however, cannot be taken as evidence for the absence of ideas about life after death. In view of the longstanding Egyptian traditions on this topic,[90] it would be suprising if the inhabitants of Elephantine—of whatever ethnic background—would not have speculated about their בית עלם, "eternal home; grave." Unfortunately, we are not informed about the character of their speculations. One exception, however, should be noted. As will be discussed below, one text from Elephantine hints at the existence at Elephantine of the *marzēaḥ*—a regular meeting of upper-class people that included a banquet.[91] The ancient Near Eastern institution of the *marzēaḥ* was often, but not always, connected with the cult of the dead and the veneration of the ancestors.[92] In other words the presence of the *marzēaḥ* at Elephantine might indicate the existence of the veneration of deified ancestors and hence some perception of an afterlife.

It is interesting to note that at least the well-to-do Yehudites made arrangements regarding their inheritance. Several contracts deal in minute detail with the distribution of property after the death of its owner. These texts have been thoroughly discussed with regard to legal aspects.[93] In this connection it is important to note that these measures were based on the concept of continuity. The settling of the inheritance not only organizes the continuation of control over property and means within one's own extended family but also hints at the responsibility for the continuation of the community in its entirety.

88. *TADAE* B.2.6.

89. Porten, *Archives*, 174.

90. See Taylor, *Death and the Afterlife*.

91. *TADAE* D.7.29; see, e.g., Porten, *Archives*, 179–86; McLaughlin, *Marzēah in the Prophetic Literature*, 36–37; Becking, "Temple, *marzēaḥ*, and Power at Elephantine," 37–47; Dvorjetski, "From Ugarit to Madaba," 17–39; Na'aman, "Four Notes," 215–22; Amadasi Guzzo and Zamora, "Phoenician *Marzēaḥ*," 187–214.

92. McLaughlin, *Marzēah in the Prophetic Literature*; Dvorjetski, "From Ugarit to Madaba"; Amadasi Guzzo and Zamora, "Phoenician *Marzēaḥ*."

93. E.g., Gottlieb, "Succession in Elephantine and Jewish Law" 193–203; Szubin and Porten, "Testamentary Succession at Elephantine," 35–46; Botta, *Aramaic and Egyptian Legal Traditions*, 56–58.

2.3.3. Identity and the Topography of Space

A temple functions as a sacred space, as a delimited area qualified by the presence of a specific divine presence. In Elephantine there was a temple dedicated to the veneration of Yahô. This temple is first referred to in the prescript of an early fifth-century letter written by Oshea to his brother Shelonam: "[. . . . . to the (?) t]emple of Yahô in Jeb."[94] Correspondence between Yedoniah and Bagohi provides details on the destruction of the temple by a coalition of the priests of Khnum and the wicked Vidranga and on its subsequent rebuilding.[95] Archaeological traces of this temple are still uncertain.[96]

In Yedoniah's letter to Bagohi, the Persian satrap of Yehud, requesting support for the rebuilding of the demolished temple, he remarks that "Yahô dwells in the temple of Yeb." This phrase, which resembles a formulation used elsewhere in the ancient Near Eastern, expresses the spatial identity of the temple.[97] The divine dwelling qualifies this secluded space. It is likely that cultic gatherings functioned also as a boundary marker for the group. The cult of Yahô was not, however, completely monotheistic. The deities Eshem-Bethel and Anat-Bethel are referred to in the so-called collection account for the Temple of Yahô.[98] Comparable divine names are Anat-Yahô and Ḥerem-Bethel, whose identity will be discussed below. The inscriptions from Elephantine also refer to many other deities, such as Khnum and Nabû, El and Shamash, Bêl and Nergal, that were not part of the cult of Yahô itself.

2.3.4. Identity and Social Stratification

I assume the existence of social stratification within the Yehudite group in Elephantine, which is also suggested by the fact that some Yehudites were in high enough a socioeconomic position that it was necessary to make contractual arrangements for marriage and inheritance. In this connection, it is worth discussing the presence of a *marzēaḥ* in Elephantine.

94. P. Padua 1 = *TADAE* A3.3:1. For other references to this temple apart from the Yedoniah correspondence, see *TADAE* D7.18; *TADAE* B2.7:13–14. See Ayad, "From the Archive of Ananiah Son of Azariah," 37–50.

95. *TADAE* A 4.7 and 4.8; Reinhard Kratz has published and discussed these texts in "Second Temple of Jeb and of Jerusalem," 247–64.

96. Pace Von Pilgrim, "Textzeugnis und archäologischen Befund," 485–97; Rosenberg, "Jewish Temple at Elephantine"; Rohrmoser, *Götter, Tempel und Kult*, 161–85; see also the discussion in Granerød, *Dimensions of Yahwism*, 81–127.

97. See various texts in the Hebrew Bible and the bilingual inscription for Tell Fekherye; Abou-Assaf, Bordreuil, and Millard, *Statue de Tell Fekherye*, 65. On the concept, see Mettinger, *Dethronement of Sabaoth*, 38–79.

98. *TADAE* C3.15 VII:126–28; see Anneler, *Zur Geschichte der Juden von Elephantine*, 83–84; Porten, *Archives*, 160–64 (who connects the collection account with the Festival of Weeks); Becking, "Temple, *marzēaḥ*, and Power at Elephantine"; Granerød, *Dimensions of Yahwism*, 69–73.

To Haggai
I spoke to Ashian about the silver for the *marzēaḥ*
Thus, he said to me:
There isn't any.
Now I shall give it to Haggai or Igdal
Get to him that he may give it to you![99]

This institution implies the existence of an elite group within the Yehudite community that apparently was in need of a distinctive and separate identity. Elsewhere, I have argued that the so-called Collection Account from Elephantine—which records the donation of two sheqels each for the temple of Yahô by 128 Yehudites—should be construed as the administrative upper layer of the Yehudites of Elephantine.[100] I assume that this elite group is roughly the same as the group who attended the *marzēaḥ*.

2.3.5. *Identity in Crises*

Rituals that are performed in times of crisis are indicative of the religious identity of a community. One such ritual, known from the Old Testament, is the practice of wearing sackcloth as a sign of mourning. Saul Olyan has correctly noted that mourning rites are not limited to the process of coping after a death but were also executed in situations of vehement disturbance of the balance in existence.[101] In addition, fasting was sometimes used in ancient Israel as a ritual of mourning with the aim of satisfying God. Both are mentioned together in the book Jonah.[102]

In the letter in which Yedoniah seeks support for the rebuilding of the demolished temple of Yahô, he described their ritual of mourning for the temple destroyed by the Khnum priests:

We wore sackloth with our women and children,
fasted and prayed to Yahô, the Lord of Heaven[103]

This shows that the Judeo-Israelite—or perhaps generally ancient Near Eastern—practices of mourning were also known in Elephantine. By fasting they might persuade Yahô to reinstall the balance in their existence.

99. *TADAE* D.7.29; see, e.g., Porten, *Archives*, 179–86; McLaughlin, *Marzēah in the Prophetic Literature*, 36–37.
100. Becking, "Temple, *marzēaḥ*, and Power at Elephantine."
101. Olyan, *Biblical Mourning*.
102. Jonah 3:5.
103. *TADAE* A.4.7:20 // A.4.8:19.

2.3.6. Identity and the Divine

The veneration of the divine is formative for the identity of a group or a religion. In this section, I will present the various deities that formed the pantheon of the Yehudites in and around Elephantine.

In Elephantine Yahô was worshiped. The fact that other deities were worshiped, or that the divine was also known by other names, should not distract from the fact that YHWH is the most frequently mentioned deity in the Aramaic papyri and ostraca. The name appears in a variety of forms:

- The tetragrammaton יהוה is not attested in the inscriptions from Elephantine.
- As a rule, the name of the Yehudite God is represented in the papyri as יהו.
- In ostraca the spelling is mostly יהה.
- The formula from the Hebrew Bible יהוה צבאות, "the Lord of Hosts,"[104] is written as יוה צבאת.[105]
- As a theophoric element in personal names, the short form יה is always applied, both at the beginning of a name and at the end of a name.

On the basis of this evidence, it can be concluded that the name was probably pronounced as *yahô*.

Knowing the pronunciation of the divine name, however, does not inform us about the nature of the divinity or the nature of its worship. The inscriptions from Elephantine contain no evidence for a full-fledged theology, or coherent symbol system.[106] However, there are some aspects that can be discerned about Yahô's nature from the extant evidence.

2.3.6.1. Epithets

The archive of Elephantine contains the remains of a correspondence about the restoration of the temple of Yahô.[107] The most important letter is written in an emergency by Yedoniah to Bagohi, the Persian administrator of Yehud.[108] In 411 BCE Arshames, the Persian satrap of Egypt, was not in Egypt but present at the court of Darius II. During his absence, the priests of the Khnum temple in

104. See Mettinger, *In Search of God*, 123–57.

105. E.g., in Ostrakon Clermont Ganneau J8 (175+185), ed. Lozachmeur, *Collection Clermont-Ganneau*, I:324–24 (175); 334–35 (185) and 447–48 (J8): 2; see Rohrmoser, *Götter, Tempel und Kult*, 122–26; Grassi, "Bemerkungen zu Ostrakon Clermont-Ganneau J8 (175+ 185) aus Elephantine," 84–97.

106. On this concept, see Geertz, *Interpretation of Cultures*, 91–93; for a different approach, see Granerød, *Dimensions of Yahwism*.

107. *TADAE* A.4.7–9.

108. *TADAE* A.4.7//8; see §6.3 below.

Elephantine conspired with a person named Vidranga, then the regional governor (Persian *fratrarakas*). Priests and governor thus abused the power vacuum for a set of evil acts.[109] One of their violent acts was the destruction of the temple of Yahô and the burning of the goods of the sanctuary. A few years later, Yedoniah wrote his request for support for the rebuilding of the temple. In his letter, Yahô is referred to in multiple ways:

- in the opening sentence of the letter, "the God of Heaven" (אלה שמיא; line 1) is invoked for Bagohi's health and well-being
- in line 6, יהו, "Yahô," is presented as the god who is in Yeb, that is in Syene/Elephantine
- the Yehudites pray to "Yahô, the god of the sky" (יהו אלה שמיא; line 15);
- יהו, "Yahô," is the god worshiped in Yeb (lines 24–25)
- if Bagohi responds positively to the request, he will be favored by "Yahô, the God of Heaven" (יהו אלה שמיא; lines 27–28)

It is noteworthy that in this communication directed to a non-Yehudite—Bagohi, the Persian administrator of Samaria—Yedoniah uses the epithet "God of Heaven," which was presumably used by the Persians for their god Ahura Mazda.[110] The epithet is also used in a memorandum that allegedly summarizes the decision by Arshames—that is, in official communication.[111] However, the epithet is also evidenced in inner-Jewish communication—for example, greetings at the beginning of letters.[112]

Thomas M. Bolin has interpreted the epithet "God of Heaven" in a political, diplomatic sense. In his opinion, the epithet does not reveal to us the nature of the idea of God in Elephantine, but the use of the epithet is part of diplomatic courtesy.[113] Others argue that the use of this epithet reflects a turn from henothe-

109. See §6.4 below.

110. On the Persian deity, see Skjaervo, "Ahura Mazdā and Ārmaiti," 399–410; Hintze, "Monotheism the Zoroastrian Way," 225–49. The assumption seems to be based on Herodotus, *Hist.* 1.131. In a passage describing the Persian religious system, the Greek historian, however, does not use the term "god of heaven." He only states that the Persians identify the "whole circuit of heaven" with Zeus. Koch, "Weltordnung und Reichsidee im alten Iran," 310, has indicated that in Persian inscriptions a direct parallel is absent. The idea of Ahura Mazda as creator of heaven is often mentioned in Old Persian texts. The epithet "the great god, the lord of heaven" for Horus-Behdety in the Horus Myth C from Edfu (VI, 111,4; see Kurth, *Edfou VI.*, 192) is of a too late—Ptolemaic—date to be of influence in this discussion.

111. *TADAE* A.3.8:3–4.

112. See *TADAE* A3.6:1; A4.3:1–2, with Schwiderski, *Handbuch des nordwestsemitischen Briefformulars*, 115–20.

113. Bolin, "Temple of יהו at Elephantine," 127–42; see also Frey, "Temple and Rival Temple," 175n32.

ism to universalism within the Israelite religion.[114] However, it must be borne in mind that the epithet is attested already before the Persian period. Emil Kraeling and Herbert Niehr interpret the epithet "God of Heaven" (אלה שמיא) as an equivalent to the Phoenician בעלשמין. They postulate thus a concord of features between the Aramaic-Phoenician deity Baal-Shamayin in the concept of Yahô in Elephantine.[115] The epithet is already attested in the Hebrew Bible.[116]

2.3.6.2. Theophoric Personal Names

In the texts from Elephantine several personal names containing the theophoric element *yahô* are attested.[117] First, it is noticeable that almost all theophoric names of the Yehudites contain *yhw* or *yh* as the theophoric element. The element *ʾdn*, "Lord; master," is not attested. At least one Yehudite name from Elephantine containing *bʿl*, "Baal," is known.[118] It is, however, unclear whether or not this name belonged to a Yehudite. The element *ʾl*, "God," in appellative sense, is not attested in Elephantine as a theophoric element. In Ezra and Nehemiah, on the other hand, it is often used. The number of names from Elephantine as a whole is too small—around 250—to yield far-reaching conclusions. Second, it can be assumed that personal names containing the elements *yhw* or *yh*, if they are not all traditional, are expressions of personal piety.[119] They should be interpreted, with caution, as an expression of the parents' faith. The names reflect a belief in Yahô as a god giving hope. A few examples are:

- מוזיה Mauziah, "Yahô is my refuge"
- תקותיה Tiqwatiah, "Yahô is my hope"
- עמנויה Immanuiah, "Yahô is with us"

2.3.7. The Other Deities

So far, my remarks might give the impression that Yahô was the sole god worshiped by the Yehudites in Elephantine. This would mean that the Aramaic papyri and ostraca reflected a form of the emerging Jewish religion that would

114. Porten, "Jews in Egypt," 385–86; Thompson, "Intellectual Matrix of Early Biblical Narrative,"107–24.

115. Kraeling, *Brooklyn Museum Aramaic Papyri*, 84; Niehr, *Der höchste Gott*, 43–68; Niehr, "JHWH in der Rolle des Baalšamem," 307–26; Rohrmoser, *Götter, Tempel und Kult*, 118–22.

116. See, e.g., Gen 24:7; 2 Chr 36:23 // Ezra 1:2; Ezra 5:12; 6:9–10; Neh 1:4–5; 2:4.20; Ps 136:16.

117. See Silverman, *Religious Values*.

118. בעלעזר, "Baal-Ezer/Azar," *TADAE* D11.10:1.

119. Albertz and Schmitt, *Family and Household Religion*, 245–386; Rohrmoser, *Götter, Tempel und Kult*, 296–304; Granerød, *Dimensions of Yahwism*, 162–64; Siljanen, *Judeans of Egypt*, 139–44.

be characterized as monotheistic. However, these texts also mention אלהיא אחריא, "other deities." I will discuss below some of the deities other than Yahô venerated by the Yehudites of Elephantine.

2.3.7.1. Blessings Within Letters

In the letter of a certain Giddel to his master Michaiah, Yahô and Khnum are mentioned in parallel:

> I send you peace and well-being.
> I bless you by Yahô and Khnum.[120]

This formula gives the impression that both deities were of equal importance. There is also a letter from Yarḥu to his brother Haggai with a blessing in the name of "Bêl and Nabû, Shamash and Nergal."[121] In addition, several letters have been found that are written by people with theophoric names containing Yahô and still use a blessing formula with plural gods: "May all deities seek your well-being at all times."[122] The collective talk of "deities" in these formulas is probably not a meaningful indicator of the complexity of the Yehudite pantheon in Elephantine, though. The references in these documents are of too general and too formal a character to support this view.[123]

2.3.7.2. The Collection Account

In Elephantine a very interesting document was found dating to the year 400 BCE.[124] This document lists donations for the temple. After the date, the text starts as follows: "These are the names of the Yehud garrison, who gave silver for the god Yahô."[125] The document lists around a hundred individuals. Most have specific Hebrew names, such as Hoshea, Nathan, or theophoric personal names containing Yahô, such as Zephaniah and Zebadiah. The end of the list, however, contains a surprise. A list of this sort would typically conclude with the formula "so and so many sheqels / much silver for Yahô." This list ends quite unexpectedly:

120. *TADAE* D7.21.

121. *TADAE* D7.30:2–3; see below.

122. E.g., *TADAEA* A3.7; A4.2; A6.1; see Porten, *Archives*, 158–60; Schwiderski, *Handbuch des nordwestsemitischen Briefformulars*, 130–37; Rohrmoser, *Götter, Tempel und Kult*, 293–96.

123. See also Niehr, *Höchste Gott*, 48.

124. *TADAE* C3.15; see Frey, "Temple and Rival Temple," 174–75.

125. *TADAE* C3.15:1.

126	In it: for Yahô:	126 sheqel
127	For Eshem-Bethel:	70 sheqel
128	For Anat-Bethel:	120 sheqel silver.[126]

This text implies that two deities, Eshem-Bethel and Anat-Bethel, were connected to the temple of Yahô in Elephantine. Porten has tried to explain this fact by assuming that Eshem-Bethel and Anat-Bethel were worshiped by "non-Jews."[127] But this would not explain why the deities then appear in a list for the temple of Yahô. Rainer Albertz, in a remark before he comes to the discussion of the passages, argues that the "other gods"—Anat-Bethel, Eshem-Bethel, etc.—were limited to the field of personal piety.[128] But the level of temple piety is further reaching than the level of the personal piety, and the gods mentioned obviously play a role in the local cult.

Porten has proposed a connection between collection account and the "Jewish" festival calendar.[129] The text is dated on the "third of Phamenoth, year 5." Palaeographic and orthographic considerations hint at a date in the reign of Amyrtheus, which implies that the text was written in the last quarter of the fifth century BCE. But more important than the year is the calendrical date in the text. The month of Phamenoth roughly coincides with the Israelite month of Sivan. Porten makes a strong case that this Phamenoth 5 in 400 BCE is a date "on or around the day on which the Festival of Weeks" was celebrated. The date for this festival is seven weeks after Passover or fifty days from the "day after the Sabbath" (Lev 23:15–21). In the Hebrew Bible it is stated that on the occasion of the Festival of Weeks "an offering of new grain" had to be brought for YHWH. Porten then suggests that the Collection Account from Elephantine should be related to the this festival and should be construed as the administration of gifts for a communal festival.[130] This is an interesting proposal that—if correct—would shed light on the religious community in Elephantine. But is it correct?

Two things are notable. First, no goods are offered, but money is given. According to Lev 23:16, "You shall bring from your settlements two loaves of bread as an elevation offering, each made of two-tenths of an ephah; they shall be of choice flour, baked with leaven, as first fruits to the LORD." Second, except for Leviticus 23—considering it part of the Priestly redaction—there are no clear references from the Persian period to the celebration of the Festival of Weeks. In the calendar of Ezek 45:18–25 the festival is not mentioned. It is only in later traditions, in Qumran, in the book of Jubilees, and in the New Testament that this festival becomes pivotal.

126. *TADAE* C3.15 VII:126–28; see, e.g., Winter, *Frau und Göttin*, 496–97.
127. Porten, *Archives*, 163n41.
128. Albertz, *Religionsgeschichte Israels*, 380–81.
129. Porten, *Archives*, 160–64.
130. Porten, *Archives*, 163.

What was the societal context of the collection account? Next to the arguments from the realm of religion, attention should be paid to arguments of a more sociological character. Therefore, I would like to answer the question whether Porten's suggestion is correct by making a detour of a sociological character. As far as I can see, 300–325 "Israelite" personal names are known from the archives of Elephantine, 60–65 percent of which occur in the Collection Account. Some of the names/persons do not occur for the obvious reason that they are attested in early fifth-century BCE documents and therefore predate the Collection Account, dated to 400 BCE. The Collection Account contains a very high percentage of Yehudite individuals known to us from around 400 BCE. It is interesting that women are listed too. Porten and others correctly assume these women represented their household while their husbands were apparently not present or were on duty elsewhere.[131] Women apparently could act on behalf of their husbands even in religious matters, as is also evidenced by a few other documents.

Based on the above considerations, one could hypothesize that the Collection Account lists *all* the Yehudite population of Elephantine in and around 400 BCE. The fact that all economic units are donating the same amount of money (two sheqels) can be interpreted as an indication that the old dream of an egalitarian society had not yet died out. Far away from Jerusalem, they felt united and construed themselves as members of one body. The "other"—here represented by the Persian administration, as well as by the Egyptian Khnum-priests, drove them together into an egalitarian identity, for which the temple of Yahô in Elephantine was a visible symbol. The aim of the donation of two sheqels per household still remains unclear, but it might have been related to the communal function of the temple.

This is an interesting hypothesis, but there are good reasons to doubt that the Collection Account lists *all* Yehudites from Elephantine. Not all people in a society are mentioned in the textual evidence reflecting their social lives, especially in societies and communities that did not register all their members. This is the case across the ancient Near East, including the Yehudite community in Elephantine. Based on the 128 economic units referred to in the Collection Account, the number of this community, including children and slaves, could be estimated at 450 to 650 persons.[132]

Another approach to calculating population is to start from the garrison size. According to the Elephantine texts, the Yehudite garrison consisted initially of four, but later three, *dglyn*. The Aramaic noun *dgl* is a Persian military term denoting a cohort of foreign soldiers that were under one banner. A *dgl* was built up from at least two companies. According to E. A. Knauf, in the relatively

131. Porten, *Archives*, 160–64.

132. For these calculations, see also Knauf, "Elephantine und das vor-biblische Judentum," 181–82.

peaceful circumstances of Elephantine, these companies might have consisted of sixty to eighty persons, which means that a *dgl* consisted of at least 120 to 160 persons.[133] With this taken into consideration, the whole Yehudite garrison would contain some five hundred soldiers. This number leads to an estimated Yehudite population of about 2,500.[134] Knauf's calculation, however, is a minimalistic one, since he assumes that in the relatively peaceful conditions at Elephantine, the extent of the military units was limited. If we instead assume that the groups in the *dgl* really consisted of one hundred soldiers, the calculation would yield an even larger number of 3,600 Yehudites. The calculations based on the garrison size yield an population estimate about five to ten times the calculation based on the Collection Account.

These calculations shed another light on the number of 128 economic units mentioned in the Collection Account. The magnitude of difference highlights the fact that not all individuals in a community were so important that their names were documented in writing. The names in the Collection Account should not be construed as *the* Yehudite community but as the social upper class of this community. In this regard, I would like to adopt Christianne Karrer's characterization of the Elephantine Yehudite community as a *Bürger-Tempel Gemeinde* (citizen-temple community), a community that was not in all aspects egalitarian but had an elite core, which can be discerned in the Collection Account as well as in the *marzēaḥ*.[135]

At the end of the Collection Account Eshem-Bethel and Anat-Bethel are mentioned as deities for whom money is collected. The identity and the provenance of these divine beings is debated among scholars.[136] The god Eshem-Bethel is not mentioned elsewhere in documents from Elephantine.[137] Anat-Bethel might be identical with Anat-Yahô, mentioned in an oath text from Elephantine.[138]

In the letter to Bagohi requesting restoration of the temple of Yahô, Yedoniah mentions the demolition of the *ʿmwdyʾ zy ʾbnʾ*, "stone pillars that were there."[139] This detail has given rise to the assumption that the Israelite deity was represented by one or more standing stones in the temple at Elephantine. It should be noted that the Aramaic noun *ʿmwdyʾ* is in the plural, and therefore the pillage of several standing stones is implied.

133. See Porten, *Archives*, 28–35; Hoftijzer and Jongeling, *Dictionary of the North-West Semitic Inscriptions*, 240–41 [with lit.]; Knauf, "Elephantine und das vor-biblische Judentum," 181–82.

134. As has been estimated by Knauf, "Elephantine und das vor-biblische Judentum," 181–82.

135. Karrer, *Ringen um die Verfassung Judas*.

136. See below.

137. The name assumedly occurs three times in the Palmyra-section of Papyrus Amherst 63 (ed. van der Toorn, *Papyrus Amherst 63*) XVI 1.14.15: ʾšbtylG.

138. *TADAE* B7.3. See Porten, *Archives*, 109.154–56; Winter, *Frau und Göttin*, 497–98; van der Toorn, "Herem-Bethel."

139. *TADAE* A.4.7:9 // A.4.8:8.

I would like to combine these two features, the reverence of Anat-Bethel and Eshem-Bethel and the presence of "standing stones" in the temple of Yahô, into the following proposal. The institution of the *marzēaḥ* was often, but not always, connected with the cult of the dead and the veneration of the ancestors.[140] Quite often, protective deities were part of the inventory of a *marzēaḥ*. This leads me to the assumption that Anat-Bethel and Eshem-Bethel might have been the protective deities of the *marzēaḥ* of Elephantine and were represented by the *ʿmwdyʾ zy ʾbnʾ*, "stone pillars."

2.3.7.3. Oaths

Several texts from Elephantine refer to the practice of swearing an oath. It should be noted that swearing by the deity of another group within Elephantine was not uncommon. One deity, or more, acts as a kind of heavenly guarantor of the oath. The oath conveys that the person who swears in the name of this speaks the truth. Apparently, it was believed that the gods have power over the swearer, functioning as a kind of "metaphysical controller" of the human conscience.[141] On a legal document on the withdrawal of goods, the Yehudite woman Mibtaiah, daughter of Mahseiah, satisfied the heart of her opponent, the Egyptian Pia, by swearing an oath by the goddess Sati. Sati is an alternative spelling of Satet, who was the deification of the flooding of the Nile and was also venerated as the protective deity of southern Egypt.[142]

In an oath text intended to settle a quarrel between two Yehudites, Menachem, son of Shallum, son of Ho[shiah(?) . . .] and Meshullam, son of Nathan, over the ownership of a she-ass that is the possession of Pa[mose, son of Pa]meṭ, Menachem swears by "Ḥ[. . .] the [god] in the place of veneration and by Anat-Yahô."[143] The first deity is often thought to be Ḥerem, perhaps as a short form of Ḥerem-Bethel.[144]

In another oath text, Ḥerem-Bethel is more clearly documented.[145] Malchiah, son of Yashobiah, states under oath that he did not break into the house of a person namedArtafrada, that he did not beat Artafrada's wife, and that he was

140. See McLaughlin, *Marzēah in the Prophetic Literature*.

141. See Conklin, *Oath Formulas in Biblical Hebrew*.

142. *TADAE* B2.8; on this formula, see Westbrook, "Phrase 'His Heart Is Satisfied,'" 219–24; Nutkowicz, *Destins de femmes à Eléphantine*, 297–98.

143. *TADAE* B7.3. See Porten, *Archives*, 109.154–56; Winter, *Frau und Göttin*, 497–98; Porten, "Jews in Egypt," 391.393–94; Porten, "Aramaic Oath Contract," 563–75; van der Toorn, "Anat-Yahu"; Mondriaan, "Anat-Yahu," 537–52; Rohrmoser, *Götter, Tempel und Kult*, 139–41, with recent translation at 425–26; Siljanen, *Judeans of Egypt*, 222–25. On the possibility that "the place of veneration" would refer to a deified altar, see §2.3.7.5 below.

144. See, however, Rohrmoser, *Götter, Tempel und Kult*, 144–49, 426: W[eihegabe des Gotte]s.

145. *TADAE* B7.2. See also Winter, *Frau und Göttin*, 498.

not a thief. Artafrada accused him of doing these things. Malchiah is a typical Israelite name, as is the name of his father. He is, however, marked in the text as Aramaic. He declares his innocence to Ḥerem-Bethel and in the presence of four law enforcement officers.[146]

Do we have a testimony for a deity named Ḥerem-Bethel here? A few factors warrant an alternate interpretation. The noun *ḥerem* appears as a theophoric element in personal names from Elephantine—for example, Ḥeremnathan.[147] But this does not mean that the word *ḥerem* by implication would refer to a deity on all occasions.[148] The element *ḥerem* does not refer to a deity named Ḥerem, but is better interpreted as an adjectival element that modifies a divine name.[149] The word *ḥerem* means something like "consecrated object; invulnerable object," an object that is inviolable because of a taboo. It is a perceptible, sacred representation of the divine.[150] Van der Toorn is of the opinion that the vow was made on a taboo object in the temple.[151] The practice of swearing by objects in the temple is attested in from a later period in the rebuke in Matt 23:16: "Woe to you, blind guides! You say, "If anyone swears by the temple, it means nothing." But anyone who swears by the gold of the temple is bound by that oath." What do these points mean for the question of the identity of Ḥerem-Bethel? The divine name Ḥerem-Bethel indeed refers to a deity, but in the form of an epithet: "the Inviolable of Bethel."[152].

I turn now to explore the connections between Anat-Yahô, Bethel, and Yahô. The first oath text mentioned above contains the name Anat-Yahô. This goddess may be the same as Anat-Bethel from the list of temple offerings. Already Sachau has noticed that Anat is here a goddess and argued that the compound name should be read as "the Anat of Yahô." The name hence refers, according to Sachau, to a goddess, who was the πάρεδρα (consort) of Yahô.[153] This interpretation has been widely accepted.[154] It implies that in Elephantine a goddess was revered by the Jews as the wife of Yahô, such as Yahweh and his Asherah in Kuntillet ʿAjrud and Khirbet el-Qom.

146. *TADAE* B7.2:2; see Granerød, *Dimensions of Yahwism*, 47.

147. *TADAE* B3.912; B6.4:9.

148. See van der Toorn, "Herem-Bethel," 285.

149. Silverman, *Religious Values*, 227.

150. This meaning is attested in Nabatean—Hoftijzer and Jongeling, *Dictionary of Northwest Semitic Inscriptions*, 405 s.v. hrm—in the Hebrew Bible and in Qumran (11QT 55.11; 3QTr 9.6; 11.7). A verb *ḥrm*, "to consecrate," is attested in various Northwest Semitic Languages (Moab. Mesha Inschrift KAI 181.17; Imperial Aramaic; Nabatean; Hatraean; Biblical Hebrew). See Winter, *Frau und Göttin*, 501; Silverman, *Religious Values*, 227; van der Toorn, "Herem-Bethel," 283.

151. Van der Toorn, "Herem-Bethel," 282–85; see also Niehr, *Höchste Gott*, 47.

152. See Silverman, *Religious Values*, 227; van der Toorn, "Eshem-Bethel and Herem-Bethel," 675–78.

153. Sachau, *Aramäische Papyri und Ostraka*, xxv.

154. Recently by Albertz, *Religionsgeschichte Israels*, 394–95; Niehr, *Religionen in Israels Umwelt*, 162; Frey, "Temple and Rival Temple," 174.

This interpretation, however, is not without its problems. Anat was a Northwest Semitic goddess who was worshiped at Ugarit in the second millennium BCE.[155] She was a goddess of war and hunting. Her connection to Baal is controversial. Sometimes she is interpreted as a goddess of fertility and Baal's most important wife. Peggy Day has challenged this view.[156] She argues that Anat's religious function is similar to that of Ishtar in Mesopotamia. Some Phoenician and Punic inscriptions document veneration of her continuing into the first millennium BCE. There are traces of worship of her as an independent goddess in Egypt through the Hellenistic and Roman periods. In the Hebrew Bible the goddess Anat is not attested, apart from theophoric elements in some difficult-to-interpret personal and place names. The identification of Anat with the "queen of heaven" (Jer 7 and 44) is based on an argument from silence.[157] The facts make it difficult to believe that former Israelites in Elephantine worshiped a goddess Anat as the wife of Yahô.

Van der Toorn has made a connection between Anat-Yahô and the Phoenician goddess ^{d}*anati-batil*, which is mentioned in two texts by Esarhaddon.[158] Both in the treaty with King Baal of Tyre and also in the *adê* swearing Esarhaddon in to the throne, she is, along with the god Bethel, the subject of a curse. If King Baal of Tyre or one of the vassals of Esarhaddon breaks the oath: "May Bethel and Anat-Bethel [deliver] you to the paws of a man-eating lion."[159] The origin of the deities Bethel and Anat-Bethel is still unclear.[160] Perhaps they are to be regarded as the most important divine couple of the kingdom of Bit Agusi. The question is, what connection can be construed between Phoenicians in the seventh century and Yehudites in southern Egypt in the fifth century BCE? Van der Toorn initially hypothesized that the Yehudites of Elephantine—among others—are the offspring of the inhabitants of the former Northern Kingdom of Israel. After the downfall of Samaria, people from Babylon, and also from Syria, were deported to the Assyrian province of Samarina, according to van der Toorn. Members of this group later moved to Egypt and immigrated to Elephantine, "carrying with them" their deities assimilated to Yahwism.[161] The reedition of Papyrus Amherst 63, however, later made van der Toorn change his mind: the divine element Bethel is a contribution of the Syrian and Samaritan groups in the "oasis in the desert," from which the deities migrated to Elephantine.[162]

155. See P. L. Day, "Anat," in: *DDD*², 36–43.
156. Day, "Anat," 36–38 (with lit.).
157. See Day, "Anat," 41–43.
158. Van der Toorn, "Anat-Yahu," 80–101.
159. *SAA* II 5 iv:6–7; 6:467.
160. See W. Röllig, "Bethel," in *DDD*², 173–75; Rohrmoser, *Götter, Tempel und Kult*, 127–34.
161. Van der Toorn, "Anat-Yahu," 80–101; Niehr, *Religionen in Israels Umwelt*, 162; van der Toorn, *Papyrus Amherst 63*, 26–37.
162. See van der Toorn, *Papyrus Amherst 63*; van der Toorn, *Becoming Diaspora Jews*, 89–114.

Bethel, then, was a Phoenician god and Anat-Bethel his πάρεδρα. The divine name Bethel is to be interpreted as the deified cult stele. In Jer 48:13 it is said in the context of an oracle of doom against Moab: "And Moab will be ashamed of Kemosh, as the house of Israel has become ashamed of Bethel, his confidence."[163] The identity of Bethel here is much discussed. Is it a real divine name in Jeremiah, or is it a sobriquet? I believe that Jeremiah wanted to make a distinction between Yahweh as he was worshiped aniconically and monolatrously in the temple of Jerusalem and the god of the same name as he was worshiped in the former Northern Kingdom of Israel. The mention of Bethel would then be an indication that around 600 BCE this Phoenician god was also worshiped in (northern) Israel and that there was a process of assimilation that led to the identification of the deities Yahô and Bethel.[164] This assimilation or identification is already attested in Gen 31:13: "I am El (with the names) Bethel.

This theory is supported by the fact that in the vicinity of Elephantine the deity Bethel was also worshiped and that at Elephantine Anat-Yahô was identified with Anat-Bethel. Hermopolis Papyrus 1, a letter sent to Syene, starts with a temple salutation: "Hail the Temple of Bethel and the Temple of the Queen of Heaven."[165] Papyrus Amherst 63 contains five important passages in connection to the Bethel question. The Aramaic version of Psalm 20 contains a prayer to "our Lord" with the following request:

> May Lord, our God is Yahô!
> May our bull be with us.
> May Bethel answer us tomorrow.[166]

In this section Yahô and Bethel seem to be mutually identical. Papyrus Amherst 63, although found in Egypt and dating from the last part of the fourth century BCE, reflects a syncretistic form of religion from an earlier age.[167] The texts show the continuation of the worship of the god Bethel.[168]

163. See Holladay, *Chapters 26–52*, 358.

164. See Mettinger, *No Graven Image?*, 131.

165. Bresciani and Kamil, *Lettere aramaiche di Hermopoli*, No. 4 = *TADAE* A.2.1.

166. P. Amherst 63 (ed. van der Toorn, *Papyrus Amherst 63*) XI 17–18. See Vleeming and Wesselius, "Aramaic Hymn," 501–9; Nims and Steiner, "Paganized Version of Psalm 20:2–6," 261–74; Kottsieper, "Anmerkungen zu P. Amherst 63," 217–44; van der Toorn, "Celebrating the New Year," 634–37.645–49 (with extensive literature); Steiner and Nims, "Aramaic Text in Demotic Script," 45–46; van der Toorn, "Psalm 20 and Amherst Papyrus 63," 244–61; van der Toorn, *Becoming Diaspora Jews*, 69–73.

167. See van der Toorn, *Papyrus Amherst 63*; van der Toorn, *Becoming Diaspora Jews*.

168. See the other occurrences of the name: P. Amherst 63 (ed. van der Toorn, *Papyrus Amherst 63*) VI 22; VIII 13; IX 9.13; X 9; XVII 15; van der Toorn, *Becoming Diaspora Jews*, 65–77.

All these observations make it clear that Anat-Yahô and Anat-Bethel are identical deities. The meaning of the theophoric element Anat remains uncertain, as even in the Iron Age Phoenicia a goddess Anat occurs only on the edge of the pantheon. The πάρεδρα of the chief god is mostly Astarte in Phoenicia. Perhaps then the element Anat in Anat-Yahô/Bethel does not refer to an independent goddess but to a feminine noun functioning as representation of a divinity. Here I would follow William Albright's suggestion.[169] On the basis of Akkadian, he interprets it to mean "sign." Anat in Anat-Yahô and Anat-Bethel, in my opinion, refers to a female cult symbol.

Above, I have already indicated that the name Ḥerem-Bethel should be interpreted as "the inviolable of Bethel." The presupposed identitification of Yahô with Bethel leads to an interesting conclusion. Both Anat-Yahô/Bethel and Ḥerem-Bethel would thus be interpreted as a female or male cult object, each regarded as a representation of Yahô/Bethel, a visible sign and a taboo object. The Yahô/Bethel cult in Elephantine was therefore not strictly aniconic. The form and nature of these images are unclear.[170]

Finally, I turn to the deity Eshem-Bethel. Within the Elephantine inscription his name is only attested in the Collection Account mentioned above. Richard Steiner, Sven Vleeming, and Jan-Wim Wesselius have argued that Eshem-Bethel is also referred to in a prayer in Papyrus Amherst 63.[171] In the context of that prayer, Eshem-Bethel would be a strong martial deity.[172] Kottsieper, however, is quite skeptical of this suggestion. He reads the photo of the by-then-unpublished text just like Steiner: *ʾšʾbytl* (line 14) and *ʾšbytl* (line 15). But he does not take the liberty of interpreting the name as *ʾš*(*m*)*bytl*,[173] which would require an (otherwise unusual) assimilation of */šm/* to */šš/*. In his recent edition of Papyrus Amherst 63, van der Toorn notes that the text reads ʾšbytlG, אשביתל, but argues that the name should be construed as Eshem-Bethel. His argument is built on the observation that before a */b/* there is quite often the elision of the */m/*.[174] This does, however, not account for the variant spelling ʾšʾbytlG, "Esh(e)bethel," in line 14.

169. See Niehr, *Religionen in Israels Umwelt*, 118–26.

170. Mettinger, *No Graven Image?*, 131, assumes that Yahô was represented by a *maṣṣēbāh* in the temple of Elephantine.

171. P. Amherst 63 (ed. van der Toorn, *Papyrus Amherst 63*) XVI 1.14.15; Steiner, "Papyrus Amherst 63," 205 ; Vleeming and Wesselius, *Studies in Papyrus Amherst 63*, 2:11–12; Steiner and Nims, "Aramaic Text in Demotic Script," 57.

172. Especially in P. Amherst 63 XVI 13–17; see Steiner and Nims, "Aramaic Text in Demotic Script," 61–62.

173. I. Kottsieper in a private communication (2002).

174. Van der Toorn, "Eshem-Bethel and Herem-Bethel," 670–75; van der Toorn, *Papyrus Amherst 63*, 189–90.

For the interpretation of the name Eshem-Bethel there are three alternatives. First, Eshem-Bethel could be a compound name in which the god Bethel is combined with the god Ashima. In 2 Kgs 17:29–31 we are informed about the deities of the Assyrian settlers in the province of Samarina:

> But every nation still made gods of its own and put them in the shrines of the high places that the Samaritans had made, every nation in the cities in which they lived. The men of Babylon made Succoth-benoth, the men of Kutha made Nergal, the men of Hamath made Ashima, and the Avvites made Nibhaz and Tartak; and the Sepharvites burned their children in the fire to Adrammelech and Anammelech, the gods of Sepharvaim."

Parallel to this is the interpretation of the name element *'šm* as a noun *šm* with a prosthetic aleph. This then leads to an interpretation of Eshem-Bethel as the deified "name of Bethel."[175]

Second, the element *'eshem* could also be interpreted not as referring to a deity as such, but instead, just like Anat and Ḥerem, specifying noun. For example, Michael H. Silverman suggests translating the name as "sacrifice; guilt offering of God" ("Schuldopfer des/für Bethel").[176]

A third possibility has recently been offered by van der Toorn.[177] He observed that in Papyrus Amherst 63, Eshem-Bethel is often connected with the element of "fire," for instance in his epithet "the burning one."[178] He therefore revives the old idea that Eshem might be related to the Mesopotamian warrior-god Ishum, whose name is etymologically connected with the Semitic noun *'š*, "fire."[179] This interpretation of the name Eshem-Bethel as "fiery one of Bethel" might also explain the orthographic variant 'Š'bytlG, "Eshbethel," in Papyrus Amherst 63 xvi:14.

2.3.7.4. Function in the Framework

What role did these three minor deities play in the religious life of the Yehudites of Elephantine? In order to answer that question, I draw on Lowel Handy's model of the ancient Near Eastern pantheon, whichh divides the heavenly

175. So Winter, *Frau und Göttin*, 501–2 (with lit.).

176. Silverman, *Religious Values*, 221–31; Frey, "Temple and Rival Temple," 175.

177. Van der Toorn, "Eshem-Bethel and Herem-Bethel," 670–75.

178. P. Amherst 63 (ed. van der Toorn, *Papyrus Amherst 63*) XVI 1; note that Steiner and Nims, "Aramaic Text in Demotic Script," 57, have a different reading here.

179. Van der Toorn, "Eshem-Bethel and Herem-Bethel," 674–75 (with lit.); on the minor deity Išum known from Mesopotamian texts, see now George, "Gods Išum and Ḫendursanga," 1–8; Krul, *Revival of the Anu Cult*, 68, argues that Išum and Ḫendursanga might be identical.

royal household into four tiers, paralleling the hierarchy of the earthly royal household.[180]

In the upper register we find the *authoritative deities*,[181] typically a divine couple: the King and Queen of Heaven. In Ugarit this couple is Ilu and Athiratu.[182] The authoritative deities are construed as the owners of the palace in heaven, and to them have been given all power in heaven as well as on earth. Their rule is powerful, but based on eternal wisdom. They have the right to appoint the other deities to their positions. In the Ugaritic pantheon, Ilu is a wise, aged god, famous for his wisdom and his grey hair. Athiratu is not so much a fertility goddess or a mother goddess but is the ruling Queen of Heaven.[183]

The second register is housed by the most important *active deities*.[184] These are gods who from time to time leave the heavenly abode to enter the world of living humans. In this category we find deities like Baal determining the seasons, Shapshu the judge,[185] and Anat the goddess of battle. Not unlike high officers in a royal household, they are given the authority, by mandate of Ilu and Athiratu, to actually govern the universe and steer its history.

In the third register we find the so-called *artisan deities*.[186] These gods were the craftsmen of the heavenly household. A perfect example can be found in Ugarit, where Kothar-wa-Hasis is the smith of the gods, who, for instance, supplies the deities with bows and arrows.

In the lowest register are the "servants" of the gods, especially the *messenger deities*.[187] The Hebrew Bible quite often refers to the "the messenger of YHWH/God," in later times seen as an angel.

A connection can be made between the complexity of a society and the magnitude of its pantheon. A complex society with many different public functions and officers quite often has a divine household with many specialized deities. The panethones of Mesopotamia and Egypt are goodexamples. Both countries had complex bureaucracies that were needed for the organization of labor, the supply of water, and the distribution of goods and food. Their heaven was more crowded than the heaven of Ugarit. In the pantheons of countries like Israel, Judah, Ammon, Moab, and Edom, which developed a bureaucracy only at a late stage, no more than half a dozen deities were venerated. I classify the three minor deities of the Yehudites in Elephantine in the category of active deities.

180. Handy, *Among the Host of Heaven*; see also Niehr, *Religionen in Israels Umwelt*, 25–39.
181. Handy, *Among the Host of Heaven*, 65–96.
182. The counterparts of El and Asherah.
183. See, e.g., Niehr, *Religionen*, 25–29.
184. Handy, *Among the Host of Heaven*, 97–130.
185. The Ugaritic counterpart of the Mesopotamian *Šamaš*, see also Hebrew *šāmaš*, "sun."
186. Handy, *Among the Host of Heaven*, 131–48.
187. Handy, *Among the Host of Heaven*, 149–68.

TABLE 1. Function of Deities in Various Pantheons

	Ugarit	Hebrew Bible	Egyptian Elephantine	Yehudites of Elephantine
Authoritative Deities	Ilu Athiratu	יהוה	Re	Yahô
Active Deities	Shapshu Anath Balu Motu and others		Khnum Satis/Satet Anuket	Anat-Yahô/ Bethel Eshem-Bethel Herem-Bethel
Artisan Deities	e.g., Kothar-wa-Hasis			
Messenger Deities	various deities	"the messenger of YHWH/God"		

They are not to be seen as authoritative deities (this position was occupied by Yahô), yet they are more important than artisan deities. Artisan and messenger deities are not mentioned in the documents from Elephantine concerning the Yehudites, though this does not necessarily imply that they were absent in the lived religion of daily life.

There is one thing that puzzles me. Of the documents from Elephantine in which these three deities are mentioned, all are written in the last two decades before the Egyptian independence:

1.	Collection Account	400 BCE
2.	B7.2 oath	401 BCE
3.	B7.3 oath	late fifth century BCE.

Next to that, it is remarkable that Bethel, Eshem, and Ḥerem occur as theophoric elements in personal names from Elephantine only in texts later than 420 BCE. There is, however, one exception. In a document regulating the obligation to deliver grain from 483 BCE, the commander—ביתאלתקם, *bethel-taqum*—is twice mentioned, although not in an active role.[188] It is of course difficult to argue from silence. It is uncertain whether or not these deities were part of the pantheon of the Yehudites from the time they arrived at Elephantine. No traces are found, however. This raises a question: Why do these deities

188. *TADAE* B4.4:6–10; see Szubin and Porten, "Aramaic Joint Venture Agreement," 67–84; Porten, "Comprehensive Table of Bethel Names," 223–44.

appear in the last two decades of the existence of the Persian garrison in Elephantine? I do not yet have an answer, but will come back to the question in chapter 7.

2.3.7.5. A Deified Altar?

Before coming to a conclusion on Yehudite identity in Elephantine and its vicinity, I would like to make a side comment on one of the oath texts mentioned above. In this text, Menaḥem swears by "H[. . .] the [*god*] in the place of veneration and by Anat-Yahô."[189] The Aramaic noun,generally translated as "place of veneration" here is מסגד. The noun occurs here in a complex syntactic construction:

Main clause:	Oa⌜th . . .⌝
Subordinate clause:	that Menaḥem, son of Shallum, son of Hoshaiah,] swore to Meshullam, son of Nathan, by H[. . .]d, by the place of veneration, and by Anat-Yahô.
Next main clause:	He swore [. . .]

Within the subordinate clause three adverbial adjuncts qualify the verb ימא, "to swear": (1) by H[. . .]d, (2) by the place of veneration, and (3) by Anat-Yahô. The first two are asyndetically connected, the third one is syndetically connected. This construction raises the question of whether or not מסגד should be construed as a third divine entity. Javier Teixidor is quite clear in his interpretation: "Among the Jews of Elephantine oaths were taken by the god *mesgida*."[190] As an argument in favor of his view, he refers to the veneration of deified altars in later Hellenistic times such as the deities Madbachos and Bomos.[191] There are, however, two observations that plead against his interpretation.

The first is the meaning of the noun מסגד. The Aramaic noun can refer to an "object serving as a permanent sign of adoration of the god to whom it is dedicated."[192] This meaning, however, is only attested in late Nabatean inscriptions from the Greco-Roman period. In Imperial Aramaic the noun certainly refers to a building or a temple in which a god was worshiped.[193] Granerød, correctly, argues that the noun, like Arabic *misgad*, "mosque," refers to a building and not to a deified object.[194]

189. *TADAE* B7.3.
190. Teixidor, *Pagan God*, 86; see also Rohrmoser, *Götter, Tempel und Kult*, 14.426.
191. Teixidor, *Pagan God*, 86
192. Hoftijzer and Jongeling, *Dictionary of the North-West Semitic Inscriptions*, 663.
193. Hoftijzer and Jongeling, *Dictionary of the North-West Semitic Inscriptions*, 663.
194. Granerød, *Dimensions of Yahwism*, 108.

The second is the syntactical construction of the adverbial adjuncts. The Aramaic preposition ב can have various functions, including locative, instrumental, and the ב-*essentiae*.[195] The fact that there is no connecting ו between the first two adverbial adjuncts indicates that the expression "by the place of veneration" is more aptly construed as subordinate to the preceding qualifier indicating the place, where the oath should be sworn. This is not decisive, however, since in the Aramaic texts from Elephantine enumerations can also be constructed asyndetically.[196] The preposition ב has, in my opinion, a local function in the clause "at the temple," while it has instrumental force in the other two occasions. On the basis of the syntax, the rendition "by the temple," however, cannot be excluded.

All in all, the assumption that the Yehudites at Elephantine venerated a deified altar does not seem to be based on solid evidence. The clause should be rendered as "(1) by H[. . .]d, (1a) at the temple, and (2) by Anat-Yahô."

2.4. Yehudite Identity in Elephantine

I have argued that the label "Jewish" seems to be an anachronism for fifth-century BCE Yahwism. The Yehudites were not (yet) Jews. What distinguishes them from "common Judaism," for instance, is the nonstrictness in their observation of the Sabbath. On the other hand, the inscriptions from Elephantine do not show a religion, or religious identity, that equals Yahwism as we know it from the Hebrew Bible. Although the Yehudites of Elephantine venerated Yahô, they were not Yahwists in the "Deuteronomistic" sense of the word. This can be illustrated by the presence of a *marzēaḥ*.

The Yehudites can be differentiated from the "Ezra group" in and around Jerusalem. In Elephantine "mixed marriages" were accepted. There existed an openness to the "other" and no strict fence around the community was constructed.[197]

My final question is an almost unanswerable one. How should we interpret the identity of the Elephantine Yehudites within the historical development of Yahwism? It is difficult to resolve this issue because emergence and provenance of the Yehudites remain uncertain and the evidence on the development of Yahwism is still very scanty.The Elephantine evidence hints at the following supposition. The Yehudites were the descendants from a branch, or various

195. See Muraoka and Porten, *Grammar of Egyptian Aramaic*, 330.

196. See for instance: *TADAE* A4.3:1; 6.11:1; 6.12:1; 6.13:1, with thanks to Margaretha Folmer who hinted me at this construction.

197. See also Collins, *Invention of Judaism*, 44–61.

branches, of the poly-Yahwism that can be construed as in existence in Judah before the "Yahweh alone" movement. Whether they fled in the age of Josiah, were recruited form the Persian province of Yehud or even from the area around Al-Nashar and New Jerusalem in Mesopotamia, or migrated from the "oasis in the desert," they seem to have been able to retain their prebiblical form of Yahwism. Identity, however, is always on the move. Their fundamental attitude of openness made them able to adapt the local situation and to negotiate their identity in the multicultural setting of Persian-period Elephantine.

CHAPTER 3

Multiethnic Elephantine: Some Remarks on Different Minor Ethnicities in a Persian Border Garrison

ALTHOUGH SCHOLARS ARE AWARE of the presence of many other ethnic groups besides Babylonians, Judeo-Arameans, and Egyptians at Elephantine, not much attention is paid to these groups.[1] In this chapter, I will collect the information known on the other groups who lived at Elephantine and Syene. A first reading of the Aramaic and Demotic inscriptions evokes the impression that they can be divided into four groups: people from the eastern satrapies, people from western Asian satrapies, Phoenicians, and a few people from neighboring areas. The focal question in analyzing the material will be: What role(s) did persons from these groups play in the community in and around Elephantine? Were they merchants, mercenaries, general laborers, or part of the administration?[2]

A few dozen times in the Aramaic documents from Elephantine, individuals are classified as ארמי, "Aramean," in all cases with the addition of "from Elephantine" or "from Syene."[3] This raises the question of whether the Arameans of Syene and Elephantine should be treated as a separate ethnic group. A few observations are necessary:

1. The great majority of these Arameans have West Semitic and mostly Hebrew names. Many of their names contain the theophoric element *-yhw*.
2. Many of the Arameans are in other documents classified as Yehudites.[4]

Author's note: This chapter is based on Becking, "Other Groups That Were . . . ," 820–48.

1. Some remarks are made in Porten, Zadok, and Pearce, "Akkadian Names in Aramaic Documents," 1–2.

2. On the way the Persians made use of mercenaries throughout their empire, see Tuplin, "Mercenaries and Warlords," 17–35.

3. See, e.g., *TADAE* B4.6:2—⌜Shal⌝lum, an Aremean of Elephantine—and B4.7:1—Nanaishurim an Aramean of Syene.

4. To give an example: "Maḥseyah the son of Yedanyah" is referred to as an "Aramean of Syene" in *TADAE* B2.1:2–3; and as a "Yehudite who is in the fortress of Elephantine" in *TADAE* B2.2:3–4.

3. "Aram" was unlike the areas discussed below since it was not known as an administrative territory in the Persian Empire. Neither a satrapy nor a province of Aram is referred to in the sources. The territory of the former Aramaic kingdoms was known as the satrapy "beyond the river" in Persian texts as well as in the Hebrew Bible.

I therefore propose that these Arameans should be construed not as a separate ethnic group but as Yehudites who were seen as coming from Aramaic-speaking areas.[5]

3.1. Eastern Satrapies

3.1.1. Medes and Magians

The Medes were an Iranian group who were formerly an independent and powerful nation. After the conquest by Cyrus the Great of their territories in 550 BCE, the Median area in the Zagros Mountains became a satrapy in the Achaemenid Empire.[6] The Persians apparently moved people from Media to its military outpost in Egypt. Only once in the documents from Elephantine is someone indicated as "a Mede": the witness Atṛafarna, son of Naisaya, a Mede, who is one of the three witnesses to the testamentary manumission by which the Yehudite Meshullam, son of Zakkur, releases his handmaiden Tapamet.[7]

The Magians were a subtribe of the Medians.[8] Greek prejudice and misunderstanding has led to the incorrect idea that the Magians were magicians of some sort.[9] The Persepolis Fortification Texts, which date from the reign of Darius I, offer a more historically trustworthy picture.[10] Here, the Magians are depicted in their two functions: they were involved in the Persian administration,

5. See also Rohrmoser, *Götter, Tempel und Kult*, 6; Vittmann, "Arameans in Egypt," 229–31. Van der Toorn, "Ethnicity at Elephantine: Jews, Arameans, Caspians," 161–68; van der Toorn, *Becomin Diaspora Jews*, has developed the theory that all—or almost all—"Arameans" from Elephantine and Syene are the descendents of a group that migrated from an oasis in the Arab desert to Egypt; see my remarks in §7.1 below.

6. Briant, *Histoire de l'Empire Perse*, 23–40; Wiesehöfer, *Das antike Persien*, 391–96.

7. *TADAE* B3.6:16–17; on the name Atṛfarna, see P. Skjærvø, "Farnah-," 241–59; Tavernier, *Iranica in the Achaemenid Period*, 62. On this document, see §4.1.2 below.

8. Already noted by Herodotus, *Hist.* 1.101.

9. Attested in a quote of Heraclitus of Ephesus apud Clement of Alexandria, *Protrepticus* 2.13: "And in *truth* against these Heraclitus the Ephesian prophesies, as the night-walkers, the *magi*, the bacchanals, the Lenæn revellers, the initiated. These he threatens with what will follow death, and predicts for them fire." See Papatheophanes, "Heraclitus of Ephesus," 101–61; De Jong, *Traditions of the Magi*, 487–90.

10. See Briant, Henkelman and Stolper, *Archive des fortifications de Persépolis*.

especially as what we now would call financial experts, and they were among those responsible for the *lan* sacrifice, an important part of the cult of Ahura Mazda.[11]

In a legal document registering the gift of the Yehudite Ananiah of "half of the large room and its chamber" to "Tamet, his wife, in affection,"[12] the following witnesses are mentioned: Gemeriah, son of Mahseiah; Hoshiah, son of Yatom; Mithrasara the Magian; and Tata the Magian.[13] Next to two Yehudites are two Magians, called *mgšy*, "Magians; Magoi," in Aramaic.[14] The noun is a cognate of Aramaic *mgwš*, which is used in the Aramaic version of the Bisitun inscription to indicate the ethnic background of the rebellious Gaumāta as Magian.[15] The name Mithrasara is clearly Median: "Living in a bond with Mithra."[16] In a document concerning the donation by Mahseiah, son of Yedaniah, of his house to his daughter Mibtaiah, a "Mithrasara, son of Mithrasara" is listed as one of the witnesses. Although an ethnic indicator is absent in this text, it might refer to the same person.[17] The personal name Tata has an Indo-European background, since it can be connected to Old Indian/Sanskrit *tātā*-, "father."[18] The name is attested in Neo-Babylonian inscriptions but does not occur elsewhere in the documents from Elephantine.

The documents are not informative as to the role the Medians and the Magians played within the community of Elephantine. In view of their cultic function and administrative role in Persepolis, the Magians may have held comparable positions in Elephantine. The lack of further evidence, however, makes this suggestion neither falsifiable nor verifiable.

3.1.2. Khwarezmians

In ancient times the Khwarezmians were the inhabitants of Khwarezm or Chorasmia, a province in the eastern part of the Persian Empire. The area became part of the Persian Empire before 522 since it is listed in the Bisitun inscription as one of the areas over which Darius reigned.[19] Ctesias remarks that Cyrus the Great would have installed on his deathbed his youngest son Tanyoxarkes as

11. See, e.g., *PFT* 758. The *lan*-sacrifice and the not-exclusive role of the Magi in it, is discussed by Henkelman, *Other Gods Who Are*, 181–304.

12. *TADAE* B3.5 (Anani-archive, see §4.1.2 below).

13. *TADAE* B3.5:23–24.

14. See *DNWSI*, 595.

15. DB Aramaic *TADAE* C2.1:74–75. The versions in Persian, Elamite and Babylonian corroborate this interpretation; see Kuhrt, *Persian Empire*, 141–57.

16. See Tavernier, *Iranica in the Achaemenid Period*, 251.

17. *TADAE* B2.7:18 (Mibtaiah-archive).

18. See Tavernier, *Iranica in the Achaemenid Period*, 322.

19. DB:6; Kuhrt, *Persian Empire*, 141.

lord over a group of satrapies, among them Khwarezmia.[20] The area was famous for its lapis lazuli.[21] The trilingual Susa foundation charter of Darius I mentions that the turquoise stones in his palace were brought there from Chorasmia.[22] This might be related to a remark in Herodotus that the Khwarezmians had to pay a (yearly) tribute to Darius I of three hundred talents.[23] In a Persian inscription from the reign of Xerxes, Khwarezmia is mentioned in a list of people who were under the Persian law.[24] The Persian or Greek sources do not reveal any reason why Khwarezmians would have been brought to serve in the garrison in Elephantine. Herodotus mentions the existence of a Khwarezmian cohort in the army of Xerxes that was led by a certain Artabazus,[25] and it is not impossible that mercenaries from this cohort were recruited to serve in Elephantine. Arrian only gives the name of an Achaemenid satrap over the Khwarezmians from the time of Alexander the Great: Φαρασμάνης.[26]

Two interesting documents from the Mibtaiah archive from Elephantine refer to "Dargamana, son of Xvarshaina, a Khwarezmian."[27] His name, as well as the name of his father, is Old Persian.[28] The two legal documents refer to a quarrel about a piece of land between Dargamana and the Yehudite Mahseiah, son of Yedaniah. The first document is dated to the year Artaxerxes I ascended to the throne (= 464 BCE). Dargamana complained that Mahseiah had illegaly taken his property into possession. The judge—the Persian Damidata—ordered Mahseiah to swear an oath—"You swore to me by Yahô and satisfied my heart about that land"[29]—after which Dargamana relinquished his claim.[30] Some five years later, Mahseiah bequeaths this plot of land and the building upon it to his daughter Mibtaiah. In the cadastral boundaries in the document on that bequest it is stated that "above it [= the land of Mahseiah/Mibtaiah] the house of Dargamana, son of Xvarshaina, adjoins."[31] Most probably Dargamana had become or

20. Ctesias, *Persica* = *FrGH* 688 F 9; see Kuhrt, *Persian Empire*, 101. Tanyoxarkes is more well-known under the name Bardiya or Smerdis.

21. See Ferrier, "Persepolis," 23–27; Von Rosen, *Lapis Lazuli in Geological Contexts*.

22. DSf:10; Kuhrt, *Persian Empire*, 492.

23. Herodotus, *Hist.* 3.93; see Kuhrt, *Persian Empire*, 674.

24. XPh §3; see Lecoq, *Inscriptions de la Perse achéménide*, 256–58; Kuhrt, *Persian Empire*, 304–06.

25. Herodotus, *Hist.* 7.66; see Barkworth, "Organization of Xerxes' Army," 149–67; Kuhrt, *Persian Empire*, 519.

26. Arrian, *Anab. Alex.* 4.15.4; see also Livshits "Some Khwarezmian Names," 319.

27. *TADAE* B2.2; B2.3; Botta, *Aramaic and Egyptian Legal Traditions*, 123–26; van der Toorn, "Ethnicity at Elephantine," 160–61; Becking, "'Exchange, Replacement, or Acceptance?,'" 39–43.

28. See Tavernier, *Iranica in the Achaemenid Period*, 168; Livshits, "Some Khwarezmian Names," 318–19: "Long-minded."

29. *TADAE* B2.2:11–12.

30. *TADAE* B2.2.

31. *TADAE* B2.3:5–6.

remained the owner of another adjacent plot. From the two documents, it can be deduced that the Khwarezmian served in the garrison and that his position was important enough to make him the owner of a property. He is labeled as someone "whose place is made in Elephantine," indicating that he had a fixed position in the garrison.[32] In chapter 4, I will return to these two documents to show that they contain evidence for the peaceful coexistence of various groups in Elephantine.

Only one other text refers to a Khwarezmian. This accounts fragment, however, is badly damaged, making it impossible to reconstruct the name of this person or his role in the community.[33]

3.1.3. Caspians

In ancient times, Caspia was the area on the southwestern shore of the Caspian Sea. Caspians are not mentioned in the Persian lists of nations, which could be construed as a sign that they were of minor importance to the Persians.[34] It was part of the eleventh satrapy.[35] Its inhabitants had to pay tribute to the central Persian government. The Caspians have traditionally been seen as a pre-Indo-European nation related to or identical with the Kassites and, like them, speaking a non-Indo-European language.[36] In the documents from Elephantine a few Caspians are mentioned by name.[37] The fact that their names are etymologically related to ancient Persian, however, indicates that these Caspians might have spoken an Iranian language.[38] This argument—strong as it is—is not completely convincing, since the Caspians might have taken over some personal names from their Persian overlords.

In a document recording the sale of an abandoned property to Ananiah, a Yehudite, the sellers are Caspians.[39] Their names are clearly Iranian: Bagazushta, son of Buza, and Ubil, daughter of Shatibara. Bagazushta and his father-in-law Shatibara are presented as Caspians from the *dgl* of Namasava. Hence, they were mercenaries. Bagazushta is an Old Iranian personal name: **Baga-zušta-*, "beloved of the god(s)."[40] The fact that he and his wife were able to sell

32. *TADAE* B2.2:2–3. That he was a general, as argued by Gropp, "Development of Near Eastern Culture," 20, is slightly hyperbolic.

33. *TADAE* D3.39b:3; see below.

34. DNe; A²Pa.

35. See Herodotus, *Hist.* 3.92, 93.

36. Herzfeld, *Persian Empire*, 195–99.

37. See also van der Toorn, "Ethnicity at Elephantine," 160–63.

38. See Grelot, "Notes d'onomastique," 101–7.

39. *TADAE* B3.4; see Porten and Szubin, "Abandoned Property"; Botta, *Aramaic and Egyptian Legal Traditions*, 108–11; Porten, Zadok, and Pearce, "Akkadian Names in Aramaic Documents," 5.

40. See Grelot, "Notes d'onomastique," 108; Hinz, *Altiranisches Sprachgut der Nebenüberlieferungen*, 55. The name is attested about ten times mainly in documents from the fifth century BCE from various parts of the Persian Empire.

a property in the center of Elephantine might be an indication that they belonged to the upper class.[41] Among the witnesses to this contract are "*ḥwḥ/ḥyrw*, son of *'trly*, a Caspian; house of *vyzbl*, a Caspian."[42] The role of these witnesses in the community is not mentioned. The same property is referred to in a document registering the gift by the same Ananiah of "half of the large room and its chamber" to "Tamet, his wife, in affection."[43] The house as such is referred to as the one that Ananiah bought from "Ubil, daughter of Shatibara, and from Bagazushta."

Another Bagazushta is mentioned in a document concerning the sale by Ananiah, son of Azariah, and his wife Tapamet of their house to Ananiah, son of Haggai.[44] It is twice stated in the document that the house once belonged to "Bagazushta, son of Pallin, a Caspian" and that earlier the property was in the hands of "Yanbuly, son of Misday(a), a Caspian," who was a hereditary property holder in Elephantine, which implies that the property was given to him as a reward for military duties.[45] Among the witnesses no Caspians are listed.

Other Caspians are given as witnesses in a document concerning the donation by Mahseiah, son of Yedaniah, of his house to his daughter Mibtaiah.[46] Their names are "*vyzb[l(w)]* son of *'trly*, a Caspian; Barbari, son of Dargi(ya), Caspian."[47] The remark might indicate that *vyzbl* was a brother of *ḥwḥ/ḥyrw*, son of *'trly*, mentioned above.

The texts do not indicate why these Caspians were brought to Elephantine. No signs of problematic relations with other groups are available. Van der Toorn has argued that Caspians and Khwarezmians lived peaceful and in close proximity to each other in Elephantine/Syene.[48]

3.1.4. Bactrians

Bactrians were the inhabitants of the satrapy of Bactria, an area in the eastern Persian Empire in present-day Afghanistan.[49] The area was incorporated by Cyrus the Great into his empire. Ctesias notes that after Cyrus had incorporated the last independent Median king Astyages—who had caused trouble in

41. *TADAE* B3.4:7–10 describe the boundaries of the property as between the Temple of Khnum and the Temple of Yahô.

42. *TADAE* B3.4:23–24; the identity of the second person is uncertain.

43. *TADAE* B3.5.

44. *TADAE* B3.12.

45. *TADAE* B3.12:4–5.12. On the Persian army, see http://www.cais-soas.com/CAIS/History/hakhamaneshian/achaemenid_army.htm.

46. *TADAE* B2.7.

47. *TADAE* B2.7:18–19.

48. Van der Toorn, "Ethnicity at Elephantine," 160–63.

49. See Shaked, *Satrape de Bactriane et son gouverneur*, 2003.

the region—into his royal household, the once inimical Bactrians submitted themselves to Cyrus.[50] Ctesias remarks that Cyrus the Great, on his deathbed, intended to install his youngest son Tanyoxarkes as lord over a group of satrapies, among them Bactria.[51] Bactria is mentioned in the Bisitun inscription in the list of territories over which Darius became ruler.[52] In a Persian inscription from the reign of Xerxes, Bactria is mentioned in a list of people who were under the Persian law.[53] The Persian or Greek sources remain silent on the reason why Bactrians would have been recruited to serve in the border garrison in Elephantine. Herodotus remarks that Bactrians were incorporated into the army of Xerxes.[54] According to Quintus Curtius Rufus, Bactria supplied the Persian army with no less than 30,000 horsemen: "Therefore, the cavalry of the Bactrians had amounted to 30,000."[55] The large number might be due to an exaggeration in a late source, but the text makes clear that there was a memory up through Roman times of an important Bactrian contribution to the Persian army. It is not impossible that some of them were recruited for service in Egypt. Ctesias remarks that in the early days of the reign of Artaxerxes I a rebellion against the central Persian power took place, though the historicity of this has been challenged.[56] The recently published Aramaic documents from Bactria only deal with internal affairs in homeland Bactria in the middle of the fourth century BCE.[57]

As far as I can see, only one Bactrian is mentioned in the texts from Elephantine. A contract dated to 403 BCE reads: "[Ba]rznavara, son of Artabazana, that is Patu, a Bactrian, whose [p]lace is fixed in Elephantine, the fortress, of the detachment of Marya, to Yedaniah, [son of Na]than, a Y[ehudi]te, wh[o] is hereditary property holder in Elephantine, the fortress, in the detachment of [. . .]."[58] The personal names of the Bactrian and his father are clearly Persian.[59] From the inscription, it can be deduced that [Ba]rznavara held an important military position, comparable to that of Dargamana, the Khwarezmian.

50. Ctesias, *Persica* = *FrGH* 688 F 9:2; see Kuhrt, *Persian Empire*, 58.

51. Ctesias, *Persica* = *FrGH* 688 F 9; see Kuhrt, *Persian Empire*, 101. Tanyoxarkes is more well-known under the name Bardiya or Smerdis.

52. DB:6; see *Kuhrt, Persian Empire*, 141.

53. XPh § 3; see Lecoq, *Inscriptions de la Perse achéménide*, 256–58; Kuhrt, *Persian Empire*, 304–06.

54. Herodotus, *Hist.* 8.113; see Kuhrt, *Persian Empire*, 272–73.

55. Quintus Curtius Rufus, *History of Alexander* VII 4:30; see Wu, "'Land of the Unrule-ables," 264.

56. Ctesias, *Persica* = *FrGH* 688 F 14 (35); see Neuffer, "Accession of Artaxerxes I," 60–87; Kuhrt, *Persian Empire*, 315.

57. Edited by Naveh and Shaked, *Aramaic Documents from Ancient Bactria*; see also Shaked, *Satrape de Bactriane*.

58. *TADAE* D2.12:2–4; see Hoftijzer, "Unpublished Aramaic Fragment," 45–48.

59. See Porten, "Persian Names in Aramaic Documents," 165–86.

3.2. Anatolia

3.2.1. Carians

I will now move to Western Asia or Anatolia. One of the Persian satrapies was Caria, to be found in southwestern Anatolia. The Carians were an indigenous Hittite-Luwian people probably already referred to in Hittite and Mesopotamian inscriptions as Karkissa. They might be identical with a tribe of the Sea People, Qarqisha, mentioned in texts from the period of Ramses II.[60] Homer's *Iliad* presents a mythic memory of the Carians as soldiers siding with the Trojans.[61] I will not discuss here the question whether or not the Hebrew noun *kərētî* could refer to Carians as mercenaries in the Hebrew Bible.[62] Herodotus (*Hist.* 2.152, 154) remarks that Carians were settled in Daphne, Migdol, and later Memphis during the Saite dynasty.[63] Some very short Greek inscriptions from Abu Simbel and the reports in the Egyptian Annals give rise to the conclusion that Carians—as well as Greeks and Phoenicians—participated in the campaign of Psammetichus II against Nubia in 593 BCE.[64] This seems to be corroborated by Herodotus who in the context of Cambyses's campaign notes: "When the Persians had crossed the waterless country and encamped near the Egyptians intending to engage them, the Egyptian mercenaries, Greeks and Carians, devised a plan to punish Phanes, angered at him for leading a foreign army into Egypt."[65] Throughout Egypt Carian graffiti, funerary and votive inscriptions have been found dating from before the Persian period.[66] These inscriptions might hint at the role of the Carians in Persian-period Egypt as stonemasons.[67] With the Persian conquest of Egypt, the Carians seem to have lost their mercenary status. At Elephantine or Syene, no Carian inscriptions have been found. Sheldon Gosline has, incorrectly, argued that some mason marks discovered at Elephantine would have

60. See Franklin, "Masons' Marks," 113–11.

61. Homer, *Iliad* 2.867.

62. 2 Sam 8:18, 15:18, 20:23; 2 Kgs 11:4, 11:19; as has been suggested by Masson, "Nom des cariens," 406–14; Franklin, "Masons' Marks," 113–14; Avishur and Heltzer, "Carians as Skilled Masons," 87–90.

63. On Carians in Egypt, see Vittmann, *Ägypten und die Fremden*, 155–79; Fitzpatrick-McKinley, "Preserving the Cult of Yhwh," 408–18.

64. Phoenician graffiti: *CIS* I, 112; Greek inscriptions: Bernand and Masson, "Inscriptions grecques d'Abou-Simbel," 1–46; stela of Psammetichus II: Lichtheim, *Late Period*, 85; see now Ray, "Soldiers to Pharaoh," 1185–94; Schmitz, "Phoenician Contingent," 321–37; Schmitz, *Phoenician Diaspora*; Rohrmoser, *Götter, Tempel und Kult*, 78–79; Fischer-Bovet, *Army and Society*, 35; Vittmann, "Arameans in Egypt," 232.

65. Herodotus, *Hist.* 3.11; translation: Kuhrt, *Persian Empire*, 112–17. Phanes of Halicarnassus was a military advisor of Ahmose.

66. Ray, "Carian Inscriptions from Egypt," 181–98; Peden, *Graffiti of Pharaonic Egypt*; see now Adiego, *Carian Language*, 22–127.

67. Franklin, "Masons' Marks," 112–13.

a Carian origin.[68] Ignacio Adiego has shown that the letters on these marks are clearly not from the Carian alphabet.[69] The remarks in Herodotus and in the Egyptian annals could hint at the fact that the Carians at Elephantine were settled there as mercenaries.[70] This assumption, however, is not confirmed by the documents at our disposal.[71]

As for Elephantine, Carians are mentioned in a document concerning the authorization of the repair of a boat dated to 411 BCE.[72] From this text, it becomes clear that a group of Carians—whose names are not mentioned—were the users of a boat owned by Psamsineith that they hold in hereditary lease. The maintenance of this boat is overdue, and the Carians not only receive the right of repair but are also supplied with the necessary commodities for restoration, including copper.[73] The *prmnkry'*, "responsible foreman,"[74] Shamou, son of Kanufi, an Egyptian, functioned as a middleman between the satrap Arshames and the Carians. Since the character of the ship is not mentioned, it remains uncertain whether the Carians functioned as merchants or mercenaries.

3.2.2. Cilicians

Cilicia had been a Persian satrapy in southeastern Anatolia. The area was brought under Persian rule under Cyrus the Great. The area was ruled by tributary native kings. The Persian or Greek sources remain silent on the reason why Cilicians would have been recruited to serve in Egypt. According to Herodotus, the Cilicians paid a yearly tribute of 360 white horses and 500 talents in the days of Darius, a part of which was spent on the cavalry guarding the Cilician region.[75] This, however, is no direct evidence for Cilician mercenary activities in Egypt.

In the documents from Elephantine, some Cilicians are mentioned. In the late fifth century, the satrap Arshames sent a letter to Artavant, who held an important legal office.[76] In this letter, Arshames requests the release of a group of thirteen Cilician slaves who during the Egyptian uprising had run away from

68. Gosline, "Carian Quarry Markings," 43–50; see also Avishur and Heltzer, "Carians as Skilled Masons"; Franklin, "Masons' Marks."

69. Adiego, *Carian Language*, 26.

70. As suggested by Porten, *Archives*, 8–9; Kaplan, "Cross-Cultural Contacts," 1–31.

71. As noted by Fischer-Bovet, *Army and Society*, 34.

72. *TADAE* A6.2; this papyrus was discovered at Elephantine; see Cowley, *Aramaic Papyri*, 89–102.

73. Stieglitz, "Hebrew Seafaring in the Biblical Period," 5–15; Granerød, *Dimensions of Yahwism*, 66.

74. A Persian loanword, see Hinz, *Altiranisches Sprachgut*, 121.

75. Herodotus, *Hist.* 3.90; see *Kuhrt, Persian Empire*, 673–77.

76. *TADAE* A6.7.

their duties.[77] The Cilicians had been working at various domains of Arshames in Upper and Lower Egypt. The names of these thirteen persons are given; they are mainly of an Anatolian character.

In another letter, Arshames sends a request to *Mrdk* for the delivery of rations to—among others—"two Cilicians persons (and) one artisan" who are his servants. Their names are not given, and it is also unclear at which domain they worked. Arshames hopes that they will receive each day one handful of flour per caput.[78] *Mrdk* is to be construed not as the god Marduk but as the personal name of a Persian official.[79] In a third letter, Varfish orders Nakhtor to return five Cilician slaves to Arshames.[80] Finally, *TADAE* D6.7, a very broken and fragmented text, mentions Cilicians, but nothing can be deduced.

The extant evidence suggests that the Cilicians belonged to the lower societal stratum at Elephantine and Syene.

3.3. Phoenicians

The term "Phoenicians" does not really refer to a single ethnic group by is an ethnic label for a variety of seafarers from different city states on the Levantine coast and is an anachronism in the fifth century BCE. As Josephine Quinn has extensively argued, the label "Phoenician" for people from locations such as Byblos, Tyre, Sidon, and Ashkelon was only imposed on them by later Greek and Roman authors.[81] Although I agree with her that in the fifth century BCE there was not yet a common Phoenician identity or culture, I still use the label for convenience sake.

As for the these so-called Phoenicians, Kaplan argues that their presence in Achaemenid Egypt had a military function.[82] Others stress their function as traders.[83] Generally the Phoenicians lived harmoniously with the other groups, probably due to the power of the Persian control. It is only in the final quarter of the fifth century that, parallel to Egypt's strife for independence, quarrels between the different groups occur, such as the devastation of the Yehudite

77. They are characterised as *'bšwkn*, an Old Iranian loan word meaning "those who run away," cf. Hinz, *Altiranisches Sprachgut*, 18.

78. *TADAE* A6.9; on this text, see Colburn, "Connectivity and Communication," 29–52.

79. Like *Mordekay* in the Book of Eshter; Marduka in the Murashu archive; and Mardu/aku in the Persepolis fortification texts, e.g., PFT 81; 412; 489; 1858, see Yamauchi, "Mordecai," 272–75; Henkelman, *Other Gods Who Are*, 244.

80. *TADAE* A6.15; on these letters, see Whitehead, *Early Aramaic Epistolography*.

81. Quinn, *In Search of the Phoenicians*; as she herself admits, she was not the first to make this observation.

82. Kaplan, "Cross-Cultural Contacts."

83. E.g., Porten, *Archives*, 9, 85; Briant, *Histoire de l'Empire Perse*, 395–98.

temple of Yahô by the priests of Khnum in conspiracy with the Persian officer Vidranga.[84]

The documents show the presence of some Phoenicians on and around the island. In the following, I consider three questions about te Phoenicieans at Elephantine: (1) How vast was their contingent? (2) What role did the play in the local society? (3) Did they contribute to the harmony between groups?

3.3.1. Phoenicians in Egypt Through the Centuries

Already in prepharaonic times there had been trade contacts between Egypt and the Phoenician harbor cities. Although on a small scale, Phoenician sailors transported merchandise from the Levant and sometimes from Mesopotamia to the Egyptian delta in that era.[85] Phoenician trade with Egypt continued over time.[86] There is no room here for a full history on the mercantile relations of Phoenicia and Egypt; I will only hint at a few pieces of evidence for the ongoing trade and the presence of Phoenician merchants in Egypt. The "serpent spells" in the Egyptian Pyramid Texts from the third millennium contain incantations against *kbnw*, "Byblite snakes," that would have come as stowaways on Phoenicians ships to Egypt.[87] The report on the travel of Wenamun to Byblos makes clear that at the end of the second millennium the Egyptians obtained the timber for the great ark of Amun-Re from Phoenicia and that Phoenician ships regularly sailed to the delta.[88] Herodotus refers to a Phoenician presence in Memphis, in the area of the palace where trade took place: "Round about this enclosure dwell Phoenicians of Tyre, and this whole region is called the Camp of the Tyrians."[89] A few Phoenician inscriptions from the Neo-Babylonian and Achaemenid periods have been found in Egypt. Phoenician graffiti was inscribed on a stele of a seated Ramesses II from Abu-Simbel, which demonstrates that Phoenicians participated in the campaign of Psammetichus II against Nubia in 593 BCE.[90] In North Saqqara two dozen

84. On this incident and its aftermath, see *TADAE* A4.7 // A4.8; and §6.4 below.

85. See, e.g., Prag, "Byblos and Egypt in the fourth millennium BC," 59–74; Joffe, "Egypt and Syro-Mesopotamia," 113–23; Elayi, *Histoire de la Phénicie*, 39–95.

86. See Pons Mellado, "'Trade of Metals," 7–16.

87. See Steiner, *Early Northwest Semitic Serpent Spells*.

88. Schipper, *Die Erzählung des Wenamun*, 111–38.

89. Herodotus, *Hist.* 2.112; on the relialibility of Herodotus's remarks on Egypt—or the lack of it, see already Josephus, *Contra Apionem* 1.73; Africa, "'Herodotus and Diodorus on Egypt," 254–58.

90. Phoenician graffiti: *CIS* I, 112; Greek inscriptions: Bernand and Masson, "Inscriptions grecques d'Abou-Simbel," 1–46; stela of Psammetichus II: Lichtheim, *Late Period*, 85; see now Ray, "Soldiers to Pharaoh"; Schmitz, "Phoenician Contingent"; Schmitz, *Phoenician Diaspora*, 32–42; Rohrmoser, *Götter, Tempel und Kult*, 78–79; Fischer-Bovet, *Army and Society*, 35; Vittmann, "Arameans in Egypt," 232.

Phoenician ostraca have been unearthed.[91] In Abusir near Memphis, three short inscriptions in Phoenician were discovered in a funerary context.[92] Unfortunately, these inscriptions are not very informative as to the role of the Phoenicians in Egypt; they mainly contain some personal names. Nevertheless, they inform us about the widespread presence of Phoenicians in Egypt. Phoenician amphorae have been found throughout Egypt even as south as the fortress of Dorginarti situated near the second cataract in present-day Sudan. The numerous Phoenician amphorae from the Persian period indicate that the Levantine trade had spread deep into Africa.[93] Although the majority of the evidence hints at a mercantile background for the Phoenician presence in Achaemenid Egypt, the participation in the campaign against Nubia makes a military background possible too.[94]

3.3.2. Evidence from Elephantine

There are some indications of the presence of Phoenicians in Elephantine and Syene specifically. Although the evidence is not very abundant—especially when compared with the documents referring to the Yehudite community on the island—a few inferences can be made.

3.3.2.1. Inscriptions on Jar Fragments

Already in 1911, Sachau published a set of inscribed jar fragments found at Elephantine, the majority of which had a Phoenician inscription—the others were written in Aramaic.[95] One year later Mark Lidzbarski offered an improved reading of the material.[96] The collection consists of about fifty inscriptions, almost all of which contain personal names in the formula "(to) X (son of Y)." Some examples:

1. "to Ger-Baal, son of Yotan-Apis."[97]
2. "Abd-Baal, son of Chalpas."[98]
3. "Shamel."[99]

91. Edition: Segal, *Aramaic Texts from North Saqqâra*.
92. See Dušek and Mynářová, "Phoenician and Aramaic Inscriptions," 53–69.
93. See Heidorn, "Saite and Persian Period Forts"; Briant, *Histoire de l'Empire Perse*, 397.
94. See also Vittmann, *Ägypten und die Fremden*, 44–83, on Phoenicians in Egypt during the Persian period.
95. Sachau, *Aramäische Papyrus und Ostraka*.
96. Lidzbarski, *Phönizische und aramäische Krugaufschriften*.
97. Text 2.
98. Text 10.
99. Text 23.

I construe the second and third forms to be abbreviations of the fuller first form. It stands to reason, in view of the material on which the small inscriptions were written, that these texts were parts of the administration of commodity deliveries. Lidzbarski assumes that the jars might have contained wine,[100] based on jar forms that he considers to be Phoenician as well as a passage from Herodotus: "Into Egypt from all parts of Hellas and also from Phoenicia are brought twice every year earthenware jars full of wine."[101] The (reconstructed) jars were about 50 to 65 centimetres high.[102] They were coated on the inside in order to be impermeable. The type of jar on which the inscriptions were written were similar to the Phoenician amphorae well known in many examples from the Persian period.[103] Although they resemble jars found in Egypt that were used for the transport of wine, they also might have contained grain to supply the garrison at Elephantine.[104] In sum, it can be inferred that the Phoenicians acted as merchants.

Of great importance are the personal names in the inscriptions, since they show a broad ethnic background among the recipients of the commodities.[105] Table 2 makes clear that the Phoenician merchants were supplying an international clientele. Next to that, the inscriptions testify to harmonious relations between the various groups. The jar fragments were found on the island of Elephantine.[106] It is not clear whether the Phoenician merchants and their clientele lived on the island or in Syene on the banks of the Nile. The find spot could have been either the dwelling of a Phoenician merchant or a storehouse.

3.3.2.2. Erased Customs Account

It has long been assumed that on the scroll on which the Aramaic Sayings of Aḥiqar found at Elephantine was written an earlier text had been erased.[107] It was not until 1993, however, that the erased text was recovered and reconstructed by Ada Yardeni.[108] The text contained notes on the administration of duties and taxes that had to be paid on cargo brought to Egypt by boat. They were part of

100. Lidzbarski, *Phönizische und aramäische Krugaufschriften*, 20.

101. Herodotus, *Hist.*, 3.6; see Porten, *Archives*, 85.

102. See the excavation report by Honroth, Rubensohn, and Zucker, "Bericht über die Ausgrabungen auf Elephantine," 162–209.

103. See also Bettles, *Phoenician Amphora Production*.

104. See Porten, *Archives*, 85.

105. On the ethno-linguistic background of these names, see Gardiner, *Ancient Egyptian Onomastica*; Benz, *Personal Names*; Kornfeld, *Onomastica aramaica aus Ägypten*; Tairan, *Die Personennamen*; and the forthcoming monograph by Gulia Grassi on the onomasticon of Elephantine.

106. See Honroth, Rubensohn, and Zucker, "Bericht über die Ausgrabungen auf Elephantine."

107. Already by Sachau, *Aramäische Papyrus und Ostraka*, 148.

108. *TADAE* C3.7; Yardeni, "Maritime Trade and Royal Accountancy," 67–78; see also: Kuhrt, *Persian Empire*, 681–703.

the *mindāh*-duty. The Aramaic noun *mindāh* or *middāh*—compare Akkadian *mandattu*, "gift"—was a tax that had to be payed to the Persian king in silver or in kind. The taxation was mainly based on the number of acres of land a person owned, but it could also be levied on the import of merchandise.[109] The destination of the revenues was always the *byt mlk*ʾ, "(store)house of the king."[110] The text is dated to "year eleven," most probably of the reign of Xerxes I, which is 475 BCE.[111] In the account, two groups of ships are referred to. The first is comprised of two types of ships, clearly large Ionian sea vessels: the *spynh rbh* and the *ʾswt kḥmwš spynh rbh*.[112] In the account, these vessels are sometimes said to be steered by an Ionian captain. Some names of the captains are mentioned in the text—for instance, "Timokedēs, son of Mikkos."[113] The second group is comprised of two types of ships—*dwgy qnd/rt*ʿʾ and *dwgy qnd/rtšyry*—that are not connected with a land or region of origin.

Before discussing the area of origin of this second group of vessels, a few remarks must be made about the commodities that are charged with taxes in this document. Goods that are levied with the *mindāh* duty are, among others, *mšḥ*, "oil"; *ḥmr*, "wine"; *spn ryqnn*, "empty jars"; *ʿq*, "wood(en implements)"; *ʿq ʾrz*, "cedar wood"; *ntr*ʾ, "natron";[114] and *lq*, "oar." Interestingly, two types of wine are mentioned: (1) *ḥmr ywn*, "wine of Ionia," referring to Greek wine,[115] and (2) *ḥmr ṣydnyn*, "wine of the Sidonians."[116] This distinction has led to the assumption that the other group of ships would have been Phoenician in origin.[117]

Twice, the "Phoenicians ships" are referred to as *spnt kzd/ry*, "ships from X."[118] Pierre Briant—who reads *spnt kzry*—toys with the idea that all Levantine ships in this account came from Gezer, but he ultimately rejects this proposal since Gezer was not a harbor city. He then opts for an identification of *kzr* with "Gadaron, a city of Sidon" mentioned by Pseudo-Skylax (*Periplus* 3.35).[119] Oren Tal

109. On this tax, which is also referred to in Ezra 4:13 and Neh 5:4, see e.g., Wiesehöfer, *Das antike Persien* 94–98.

110. On the transfer of taxes from Egypt to Babylonia, see *TADAE* A6.13 with Kuhrt, *Persian Empire*, 720.

111. Thus Yardeni, "Maritime Trade," 67; Briant, *Histoire de l'Empire Perse*, 297–98; O. Tammuz, "Mare Clausum?," 151–53.

112. Yardeni, "Maritime Trade," 70.

113. *TADAE* C3.7 KR 2:23–24.

114. Natron is a salty mixture of decahydrate sodium carbonate and sodium bicarbonate that as such can be found in nature. In ancient Egypt Natron was an important ingredient for the production of the color Egyptian blue that was used while decorating Egyptian fayence.

115. E.g., in *TADAE* C3.7 GR 2:7.

116. E.g., in *TADAE* C3.7 GR 2:8.

117. Yardeni, "Maritime Trade"; Briant, *Histoire de l'Empire Perse*, 397–98; Johnson, "Ethnic Considerations," 215–16; Tammuz, "Mare Clausum?," 151–53.

118. *TADAE* C3.7 FR 1:6; FV 3:25.

119. Briant, *Histoire de l'Empire Perse*, 63–64.

TABLE 2. Clients of Phoenician Merchants According to Jar Inscriptions from Elephantine

Ethnos	Number	Names (in text)	Remarks
Phoenician	18	Abd-Baal (1)	
		Abd-Eshmun (37)	His father has a Seth name.
		Abd-Lo (12; 29)	His father has an Apis name.
		Abd-Melqart (4)	
		Abd-Petach (27; 30)	His father has a Seth name.
		Abd-Resheph (27)	
		Abd-Sikan (41)	His father has an Apis name.
		Baal-Ezer (5; 6)	
		Chawway (15b)	
		Eshmun-[...] (19)	
		Eshmun-Shalakh (7)	
		Eshmun-Yatan (3)	
		Ger-Baal (2)	
		Machrît (43)	
		Yothan (9)	
Egyptianized Phoenician	12	Abd-Ab-Seth (12; 15b; 39; 46)	
		Abd-Amun (8)	
		Abd-Osiris (1; 34b)	
		Osiris-Teny (1)	
		Paap-Ab-Seth (11a)	
		Yotan-Apis (2; 5; 16)	
Egyptian	8	Anch-Pamose (14b)	
		Chor-Wats (40)	His son has a Semitic name.
		Chepî (47)	His father has an Arabic name.
		Pet-Isis (57)	
		Si-Ptah (9)	His son has a Semitic name.
		Tsa-Hepi-Mu (11b; 21)	Both fathers have a Semitic name.
		Tsachos (34c)	

proposes an identification with Tell Ghazza on the Mediterranean coast near modern Gaza. In antiquity the site was known as Gazara.[120] All these proposals are disputable.

The main qualifier for the ships—*dwgy qnd/rtʿ* and *dwgy qnd/rtšyry*—has been left untranslated so far which is not without reason: even Porten and Yardeni dare not give a translation.[121] The language of the noun *dwgy* is still

120. Tal, "On the Identification of the Ships," 1–8.

121. In the glossary of *TADAE* C, xxx, they refer to it as a "sea-going vessel"; see also Stieglitz, "Hebrew Seafaring in the Biblical Period," 11.15, who incorrectly renders the Hebrew *sîrôt dûgāh*, "fish hooks" of Amos 4:2 with "fishing boats"; Kuhrt, *Persian Empire*, 701, "in origin a fishing boat."

TABLE 2. *(cont'd)*

Ethnos	Number	Names (in text)	Remarks
Semitic	10	Achab (34a)	
		Ach-Min (15c)	
		Akbor (15c)	Could be Yehudite.
		Chor (21)	
		Menachem (40)	
		Shamel (23)	
		Shallum (51)	
		Tippol (25)	
		Ori-Melekh (32)	
		Wa (or Ba) (11b)	
Arabic	3	Charmal (47)	His father has an Egyptian name.
		Machlam (14c)	
		Mo-Wamet (14c)	
Aramaic	6	Arqay (36)	
		Gad-Aziz (31)	
		Nabû-Barakh (33b)	
		Shamshay (53)	
		Shobay (15a)	
		Anady (15a)	
Iranian	1	Maday (55)	Probably a nickname.
Uncertain background	1	Chalpas (10)	
Uncertain reading	3	Ben-Isis (39)	
		Paal-'[. . .] (13)	
		Pasmas-Neith (8)	

unknown: it could be Greek, Egyptian, or Semitic. In the Memphis Shipyard Journal—a text excavated at Saqqara—which is dated to only a few years after the erased customs account, a noun *dwgyt*, "fishing boat," occurs about a dozen times.[122] The fragmentary state of this administrative document makes it impossible to infer any information on the character, function, and origin of the ships beyond the fact that they were used for fishing. An important observation is that this word for ship, *dwgyt*, is etymologically related to the common West Semitic noun *dg*, "fish." The same might be true for the word *dwgy*. But there is another possibility. In his analysis of the Leviathan in Psalm 104, Christoph

122. *TADAE* C3.8.

Uehlinger notes that Phoenician ships were often depicted with the head of an animal on the bowsprit, frequently a dragon or a fish—as, for instance, on the coin of Ozbaal the king of Byblos (mid-fourth century BCE).[123] His remarks suggest that ships could be imagined as animals, and animals as ships. All this raises the possibility that the noun *dwgy* could refer to Levantine ships, rather than to fishing boats. On the nouns *qnd/rtʿ'* and *qnd/rtšyry* nothing can be said beyond the assumption that both words refer to "large seafaring ships."[124]

In sum, the evidence does not falsify the idea that the ships *dwgy qnd/rtʿ'* and *dwgy qnd/rtšyry* came from Phoenicia. We simply do not know from which port they came.

Although the scroll on which the customs account was originally written was found at Elephantine, there is no proof that the text was written on the island. The scribe who wrote the text of the Sayings of Aḥiqar on the erased scroll could have used a writing material that came from elsewhere. In the customs account no name of a harbor or a quay on the Nile is mentioned. Oded Tammuz, however, argues that the not infrequent mention of *ntr'*, "natron," might hint at a port in the delta not far away from Wadi el Natrun, where in ancient times natron was quarried.[125] Since natron was only one of the commodities, this argument is not fully convincing. All in all, the text testifies to the mercantile presence of Phoenicians in Egypt, probably as far south as Elephantine. No certain connection can be made between the Phoenicians and the military or mercenaries in Egypt from this text.

3.3.2.3. A Disbursement of Wine

A much shorter text contains an account for wine dated to the last quarter of the fifth century BCE.[126] The text was originally published as *CIS* II/2:146 and was included by Arthur Cowley in his edition of the Aramaic papyri.[127] The papyrus is unprovenanced, and while it has generally been located in Elephantine, the papyrus might have been excavated at Memphis or Saqqara.[128]

The fragmentary text contains notices on the delivery of wine. To whom the wine had to be given is not mentioned in the text. Two clues, however, might be of help. A few times the noun *srw*, "dinner," is mentioned as the occasion for

123. Uehlinger, "Leviathan und die Schiffe," 499–526; on the coin, see Betlyon, *Coinage and Mints of Phoenicia*,14.

124. *DNWSI*, 1246.

125. Tammuz, "Mare Clausum?," 151; on Natron in ancient *wadi el natrun*, see Shortland, "Evaporations of the Wadi Natrun," 497–516.

126. *TADAE* C3.12.

127. Cowley, *Aramaic Papyri*, No. 72.

128. See Rohrmoser, *Götter, Tempel und Kult*, 41.

the delivery,[129] suggesting a connection with a formal meal at the house of an important person. Twice it is indicated that the wine would function as a *nqyh*, "libation," once for Ptah and once for Isis,[130] indicating a religious context, either in a private sanctuary or in a temple.

Three times the delivery of Levantine wine is mentioned: "for dinner: wine from Sidon"[131] This text does not testify to the presence of Phoenicians in either Memphis or Elephantine, but it underscores the importance of Sidonian wine for Egypt.

3.3.2.4. A Sidonian

At the SBL International Meeting in St. Andrews in 2013, Cornelius von Pilgrim presented a set of ostraca that had been found during excavation at Syene in the spring of 2013.[132] I am very grateful to him for sharing his findings. One of the ostraca—12-2-4-6/4—had an inscription of only four letters: צדני, "*ṣdny*." *Ṣdny*, "Sidonian," should be construed either as a gentilic or as a personal name derived from a gentilic. In both cases, the inscription would refer to a Sidonian. The ostracon as such is indecisive to the question in what role this person was staying at Syene.

3.3.2.5. Fragmentary Accounts

A fragmentary account from around 600 BCE lists the names of about a dozen persons who were—one way or the other—connected to silver items. The fragmentary character of the inscription does not allow any conclusions about the nature of their relationship to the silver—such as that they had to pay back a loan in silver. Among them is one person with a Phoenician name: עבססכן, "Abssikan."[133]

Another fragmentary text, dating to the second half of the fifth century, contains a few names and two gentilics.[134] The names are Aramaic, "[. . .]idri"; Egyptian, "Pasi[. . .]; Peṭese," and Babylonian, "Mushezib-Nabu." A Khwarezmian is referred to, but the name of the person is not fully preserved.[135] Lines 4–5 of the fragment read:

129. *TADAE* C3.12 ii:7, 8, 15, 22, 32.
130. *TADAE* C3.12 ii:27, 27.
131. *TADAE* C3.12 ii:9, 15, 28.
132. They will be published in a volume to be edited by Margaretha Folmer, Annalisa Azzoni, Alejandro Botta, and Ingo Kottsieper.
133. *TADAE* C3.4:4; see Porten, "Aramaic Papyrus Fragments," 26–29; the name might be a misspelling for *עבדסכן, "Abdsikan."
134. *TADAE* D3.39.
135. *TADAE* D3.39:b3. On Khwarezmians, see above (6.3).

4 [. . .]Mushezib-Nabu of the detachment of Mary⌜a . . .⌝
5 [. . .]ma, who is a Sidonian [. . .]

Mushezib-Nabu clearly was a mercenary serving in the *degel* of Marya, which was one of the detachments of the garrison.[136] It would be a premature conclusion to state that just because the nameless Sidonian is mentioned in the next line, he was part of the garrison too. The fact that line 2 refers to someone "who is over the estates," perhaps a civil officer controlling the agricultural side of the society, is an indication that the account would have listed persons with a variety of professions.

3.3.2.6. Azarbaal

A very fragmentary inscription—the text contains only the remains of two lines—mentions *ʿzrbʿl ṣydny*, "Azarbaal, a Sidonian,"[137] a common Phoenician name.[138] The purpose of the account and the role of Azarbaal cannot be inferred given the fragmentary character of the text.

3.3.2.7. An Incomplete Jar Inscription

In 1998, Hélène Lozachmeur edited a jar inscription in Phoenician script from Elephantine that contained only two letters: "[. . .]*gt*[. . .]."[139] The two letters might be part of the name of the owner or a place name. The inscription is difficult to date, but it nonetheless gives evidence of the administration of Phoenician trade in Elephantine.

3.3.2.8. Contracts and Letters

It is intriguing that among the many contracts and letters found at Elephantine no individuals from any of the Phoenician city-states are mentioned.[140] Ethnic indicators like *ṣydny* are absent from these documents, as are clear Phoenician names. Although it is difficult to argue from absence, this "Phoenician silence"

136. On the name, see Porten, Zadok, and Pearce, "Akkadian Names in Aramaic Documents," 1–12. The *degel* of Marya was one of the three detachments present at Elephantine in the last decade of the fifth century. Bactrians, Persians, and Babylonians are among the members of this detachment, see Kaplan, "Cross-Cultural Contacts."

137. *TADAE* D3.40:1.

138. Benz, *Personal Names*, 56–58, 165–68.

139. Lozachmeur, "Épigraphe sur jarre d'Eléphantine," 183–86.

140. *TADAE* A (letters); B (contracts).

might hint at the fact that although the Phoenicians were trading with Elephantine and Syene, they were not settled citizens.

3.3.3. *Conclusion on the Phoenicians*

The analysis above has made a few things clear. (1) The number of Phoenicians at Elephantine was relatively small. It does not seem that many Phoenicians were permanently settled on the island or in Syene. (2) No connections with the Persian garrison have been found. It is safe to say that the Phoenician served as merchants supplying commodities such as wine and grain to the community, as was the case over the *longue durée*. (3) No quarrels between Phoenicians and other groups at Elephantine and Syene are detected. Although it is possible that their trade interests would at times conflict with local merchants, the Phoenicians contributed to the harmonious conditions between the various ethnic groups.

3.4. Philistines

The earliest Aramaic contract from Elephantine describes an agricultural joint venture between Padi, son of Dag[an]melech, and Aḥa, son of Ḥapio. The document was drawn up in the village of Korobis, in the western part of the Oxyrhynchite nome, in 515 BCE.[141] The papyruswas found in Elephantine, however, indicating that at least one of the two parties involved also had business interests in Elephantine. Both Padi and Daganmelech are Philistine names. Aḥa and Ḥapio are Egyptians.[142] It is unclear why Padi moved to Egypt.

3.5. The Aegean Sea

There are a few indications that persons from the area we now call Greece were either settled at Elephantine or had been in business contact with the island and its surroundings.

3.5.1. *Ionians*

Greeks and Persians have been enemies throughout the existence of the Persian Empire. The sources are full of military conflicts and armed battles.[143] Greek

141. *TADAE* B1.1.

142. See Szubin, and Porten, "Aramaic Joint Venture Agreement," 67–84.

143. From the abundance of literature: Strauss, *Battle of Salamis*; Cawkwell, *Greek Wars*; Cartledge, *Thermopylae*; Garland, *Athens Burning*.

mercenaries had served in the Neo-Babylonian Empire, but this quickly ended after the Persians took over power.[144] More important is to note that the Greeks had been trading in and with Egypt. They even settled in the Nile delta.[145]

Above (§3.3.2.2), I discussed an erased customs account from 475 BCE containing notes on the administration of duties and taxes paid on cargo brought to Egypt by boat. This text referred to two types of large Ionian sea vessels, the *spynh rbh* and the *ʾswt kḥmwš spynh rbh,*[146] as well as captains with Ionian names, such as "Timokedes, son of Mikkos."[147] From the text it becomes clear that Greek merchants imported commodities such as wine and wool into Egypt during the Persian period even as far south as Elephantine.

There is no direct evidence of Greeks or Ionians living in Elephantine or Syene. An intriguing, indirect Ionian presence is attested in two of the latest Aramaic documents from Elephantine. In a document registering the sale of an apartment, the price of the property is given both in the local coinage and in Greek money: "six Ionian silver staters (סתתרי) and one sheqel."[148] An Ionian stater had about the value of a month's wages.[149] Since no individuals of Ionian descent are mentioned in the document, it is unclear why the price of the property is also indicated in this foreign coinage.

3.5.2. *Cretans*

The island of Crete was never occupied by the Persians; nevertheless an Aramaic document from 440 BCE mentions Tibrachos, a slave from Crete, and his daughter Tachmapita.[150] Whose slave he was is unclear. The document seems to indicate that Tibrachos was about to be released by his master. The name Tibrachos might be identical with Thibrachus, a Lacedaemonian commander referred to by Xenophon.[151] The other name has no parallels elsewhere.

3.6. Libyan Tribes

I turn now to persons belonging to territories that were adjacent to ancient Egypt. As far as I can see, there is one reference to the Lybian tribe of the

144. See Fantalkin and Lytle, "Alcaeus and Antimenidas," 90–117.

145. Herodotus, *Hist.* 2.178–79; see Coulson and Leonard, "Preliminary Survey," 151–68.

146. Yardeni, "Maritime Trade," 70.

147. *TADAE* C3.7 KR 2:23–24.

148. *TADAE* B3.12:5–6.14; a stater is also mentioned in a letter from Menachem to Shalluah *TADAE* B4.6:4; see Porten, "Fragmentary Aramaic Deeds of Obligation," 164–67.

149. See, e.g., Sear, *Asia and Africa*; de Callataÿ, "White Gold," 6–17.

150. *TADAE* B8.3.

151. Xenophon, *Hell.* 2.4.33.

Meshwesh, a tribe that was probably of central Berber origin.[152] A Demotic letter on a problematic delivery of grain written by Khnumemahket to the Persian official Farnava in October 486 BCE mentions an unnamed Ma or Meshwesh who functioned at the quay where the grain had to be delivered.[153] During the Third Intermediate period, the Lybian Meshwesh were in control of greater parts of Egypt. In later periods their descendants became members of the upper lower class, working as policemen and controllers on the quays. Wilhelm Spiegelberg originally read *nf-w*, "sailors." Günter Vittmann correctly proposed the reading *M-w*, which is the standard Egyptian abbreviation for the name of this tribe.[154] The role of this subordinate person is limited. He is only spoken to.

3.7. Arabs

The position of the Arab tribes, Bedouins as well as oasis-dwellers, in the Persian period is complicated. The Persians did not conquer the whole peninsula but nevertheless executed their power there. The Arabs in the northernmost part were under direct Persian control, while most of the population in the rest of the peninsula had some sort of client status that made their Persian patrons profit from the trade routes.[155] According to Herodotus, the Arabs had been friendly toward Cambyses, giving him consent to cross Arab territory on his march to conquer Egypt.[156] There is no evidence that the Persians recruited Arabs for military services. A document from North Saqqara might hint at the presence of Arabs in Egypt.[157] Line 15 of this rather damaged report contains the word *ʿrby*, which could be rendered as "Arabs" but could also be translated as "guarantors." Since the context is broken, it is difficult to make a decision here. In the next lines of the document mention is made of *nbyh*, which could be construed as a reference to Nebayoth.[158] Arguing from a parallelism, *ʿrbyʾ* could be seen here as an indicator of an ethnic group. Arabic names occur sparsely in the documents from Elephantine. Their Arabic character can only be inferred from the name form since the gentilic "Arab" is absent in the letters and legal documents.

152. See Wainwright, "Meshwesh," 789–99. They might probably be equated with the Maxyes mentioned in Herodotus, *Hist.* 4.191.

153. P. Loeb 1; Spiegelberg, *Drei demotische Schreiben*, 13–21.

154. Vittmann, "Kursivhieratische und frühdemotische Miszellen," 111–27.

155. See, e.g., Knauf, "Persian Administration in Arabia," 201–17; Retso, *Arabs in Antiquity*, 119–211; Fitzpatrick-McKinley, *Empire, Power, and Indigenous Elites*, 110–26.

156. Herodotus, *Hist.* 3.88; Hoyland, *Arabia and the Arabs*, 62–63.

157. Segal, *Aramaic Texts from North Saqqâra*, Text 29 = *TADAE* B8.1.

158. Gen 25:13 contains the tradition that *nebāyot* was one of the children of Ishmael; see also 1 Chr 1:29; the North Arabian tribe of the Nebayot was famous for its sheep breading (cf. Isa 60:7). On the history of the Nebayot, see Knauf, *Ismael*, 92–111.

TABLE 3. Societal Functions of Foreigners in Elephantine/Syene

Ethnic group	Military	Trade	Administration	Work/slaves
Arabs		×		
Bactrians	×			
Carians	?	?		
Caspians	×			
Cilicians				×
Cretans				×
Ionians		×		
Khwarezmians	×			
Libyans				×
Medians/Magians			?	?
Philistines				×
Phoenicians		×		

According to Porten two witnesses to a legal document from 440 BCE bear Arabic names. The document concerns the withdrawal of goods and was made between the Egyptian Pau, son of Pakhoi, a builder from Syene, and Mibtaiah, daughter of Mahseiah, a Yehudite from Elephantine.[159] One of the witnesses is *ʾwsnhr br d/rwmʾ*, "Awâs-nahâr, son of D/Ruma."[160] Both names have an Arabic character. The element *ʾws*, "Awâs; Uwais," meaning "small wolf," frequently occurs in all dialects of proto-Arabic,[161] as does the element *nhr*, "Nahâr," meaning "day; daytime."[162] The name Awâs-nahâr, however, is not attested elsewhere. The name of his father could be read as Duma or Ruma, both names of a North Arabian trade center from which Awâs-nahâr or his forbears might have originated. This raises the possibility that he lived in Elephantine for trade reasons. The fact that they could act as witness to a contract indicates that they had reached a certain level of acceptance in Elephantine and Syene society.

An Aramaic inscription on a jar from Elephantine reads *mḥlm br mʿwmt.*[163] According to Lidzbarski, both names are Arabic. The word *mḥlm*, "Muḥallim," occurs regularly in Safaitic inscriptions.[164] In a Qatabean inscription the cognate name *mʿwm*, "Maʿwum," occurs.[165] He probably was the recipient of the contents of the jar. Another jar inscription from the same archive reads *ḥrml*,

159. *TADAE* B2.8; see Granerød, *Dimensions of Yahwism*, 46.266–67.
160. *TADAE* B2.8:13.
161. See Lankester Harding, *Index and Concordance*, 84.
162. Lankester Harding, *Index and Concordance*, 601.
163. Lidzbarski, *Phönizische und aramäische Krugaufschriften*, 8–9, Text 14c = *TADAE* D11.4
164. Lankester Harding, *Index and Concordance*, 531.
165. Jamme, *Research on Sabaean Rock Inscriptions*, text 1066.

"Charmal."[166] In a proto-Arabic inscription the name *ḥrmlh* is attested.[167] In sum, Arabs were a very small minority on the island of Elephantine and in Syene.

3.8. Conclusion and Prospect

This analysis has yielded some interesting results. The population of Elephantine and Syene during the Persian period was multiethnic in character. People from all over the Persian Empire—and even beyond its borders—were living on the island or at the shore of the Nile or visited the area for mercantile reasons. These people acted in a variety of societal roles, as can be read from table 3. This raises a question: How did all these ethnic groups live together in Egypt under Persian hegemony? In the next chapter, I will analyze the evidence for their way of cohabitation.

166. Lidzbarski, *Phönizische und aramäische Krugaufschriften*, text 47.

167. Jaussen and Savignac, *Mission archéologique en Arabie*, 202; see Lankester Harding, *Index and Concordance*, 185.

CHAPTER 4

Pax Persica: Cooperation, Cohabitation, and Acceptance

IN THIS CHAPTER, I EXAMINE the interactions between the different ethnic groups that were living in and around Elephantine. First, I will consider the phenomenon of intermarriage. I will then discuss two texts from the archives of Elephantine, one about internal group communication and one about external group communication.

4.1. Intermarriage

The concept of endogamous marriage, or intermarriage, refers to a binding commitment between two individuals from different social groups, races, or religions. Against the tendency for endogamous marriages and the often unspoken culture expectation to find a partner within ones own community, group, or social stratum, many people opt for a lifelong partnership with a person from another group.[1] The degree of intermarriage within a specific community is an indication of its openness to the outside world. Fenced communities tend to disapprove of intermarriage. Texts in the Hebrew Bible that encourage endogamous marriages often contain a warning that exogamous relations would undermine the spirit of the community and pollute the "holy seed."[2]

4.1.1. Some Examples

Among the Yehudites in Elephantine and Syene, intermarriage was not uncommon. Although the majority of unions were clearly between individuals of the same ethnic group, the number of exogamous marriages is significant enough—about 10–15 percent—that there is no question of it being coincidence or a

1. See, e.g., Kalmijn, "Intermarriage and Homogamy," 395–421; Blau and Schwartz, *Crosscutting Social Circles*.
2. See Deut 7; Ezra 9–10.

TABLE 4. Complete Marriage Contracts in the Elephantine Papyri

Document	Groom	Bride	Date
TADAE B2.6	Esḥor s. of Ṣeḥa Egyptian	Mibtaiah d. of Mahseiah Yehudite	445 BCE
TADAE B3.3	Ananiah s. of Azariah Yehudite	Tamet handmaiden Egyptian	449 BCE
TADAE B3.8	Ananiah s. of Haggai Yehudite	Yehoishma d. of Zakkur Yehudite	420 BCE

TABLE 5. Incomplete Marriage Contracts in the Elephantine Papyri

Document	Groom	Bride	Date
TADAE B6.1	unknown	unknown	446 BCE
TADAE B6.2	unknown	unknown	450–400 BCE
TADAE B6.3	Sheloman Yehudite	Abihi Yehudite	450–425 BCE
TADAE B6.4	Hoshaiah Yehudite	Sallua Yehudite	430–400 BCE

TABLE 6. Mixed-Marriage Contract in the Elephantine Papyri

Document	Groom	Bride	Date
TADAE A4.4:5	Hoshea Yehudite	Esereshut Egyptian	410–400 BCE

singular case. The documents from Elephantine contain three complete marriage contracts. Two of them are clearly interethnic, one is endogamous (table 4). The documents from Elephantine contain four incomplete marriage contracts. Two of the marriages are clearly endogamous (table 5). In addition to these, there are various "mixed-marriages" referred to or assumed in the texts. I will discuss one clear example (table 6). Both Bezalel Porten and Hélène Nutkowicz have argued that the onomasticon from Elephantine contains a number of examples of children born to a Yehudite who were given non-Yehudite names. From this evidence they infer that at least some of the children should be seen as the offspring of a mixed marriage.[3] The other cases might be the effect of their acculturation to a multiethnic community. All in all, this survey gives the impression

3. Porten, *Archives from Elephantine*, 173–79, 188–99; Nutkowicz, *Destins de femmes à Eléphantine*.

that marriage between the various ethnic groups was not uncommon.[4] I will now discuss two very special cases.

4.1.2. The Curious Case of Ananiah bar Azariah

Among the papyri from Elephantine is an intriguing set of documents reflecting the marital life of Ananiah, son of Azariah.[5] Like his father, Ananiah was a *lḥn*. This Aramaic noun refers to a certain type of temple servant, probably a custodian.[6] The impression this evokes is that he was responsible for upkeep of the temple and its cult. In the documents from Elephantine, there is no evidence that Ananiah would have served a military function as well.

This Ananiah had drawn up a marriage-contract (or "document of wifehood" Porten classifies this textual genre) in 449 BCE.[7] This document is of importance for several reasons. The bride is Tamet, an Egyptian אמה, "handmaiden; slave girl," owned by Meshullam, son of Zakkur. Marriages to slave girls were not uncommon. As a result of the social status of Tamet, the contract is not made up between her father and Ananiah, but between Ananiah and Meshullam, her owner. A document contains a list of the personal belongings of Tamet that, however meager, formed her dowry.[8] Further on, the document contains the standard formulas in case of death or divorce. It is intriguing that Meshullam remains the owner of Tamet, despite her marriage. This fact does not concur to be the standard practice in the ancient Near East, where slave girls became free persons upon marriage.[9] The end of the document contains a small surprise. One of the stipulations of the contract concerns a boy named Pilti. From the context, it becomes clear that Pilti is a son of Tamet with Ananiah as his biological father. As son of the slave girl Tamet, Pilti also fell under the ownership of Meshullam. The contract makes clear that Ananiah accepts Pilti as his son who is now free from slavery, implying that Meshullam no longer has any rights or duties concerning the boy, except in the case of a divorce. The fact that Ananiah and Tamet had a premarital child should be interpreted within the social code

4. See also Grätz, "Question of 'Mixed Marriages,'" 194–97.

5. See Ayad, "From the Archive of Ananiah son of Azariah," 37–50; Schama, *Story of the Jews*, 19–22.

6. Porten, *Archives*, 200–202; Granerød, *Dimensions of Yahwism*, 56–58, convincigly make a comparison with Akk. *laḫḫinu* a noun that refers to an official with great responsibilities for the upkeep and maintenance of a temple, including the utensils for the ceremonies and the garments as well as the jewelrey of the divine statues.

7. *TADAE* B3.3; see, e.g., Porten, *Archives*, 205–13; Porten and Szubin, "Status of the Handmaiden Tamet," 43–64; Botta, *Aramaic and Egyptian Legal Traditions*, 59–86.87; Nutkowicz, *Destins de femmes*, 27–30.44–45; Granerød, *Dimensions of Yahwism*, 49–51.

8. *TADAE* B3.3:4–7.

9. See Porten, *Archives*, 206.

of their days. Joining in a marital bond was a private act that was generally not documented. The marriage contract was probably only made up after the birth of Pilti in order to secure the rights and duties of all parties.

Another papyrus, dated twelve years later, documents the sale of a house by Ananiah, son of Azariah.[10] The sellers were a Caspian soldier, Bagazushta, son of Bazu, and his wife Ubil. The house was situated next to the plot of land on which the temple of Yahô was built.[11] This would be very convenient for Ananiah in view of his tasks at the temple. The document presents Ananiah as the buyer; mother and son—Tamet and Pilti—are not mentioned in the document.

Three years later a new document was drawn up.[12] The text documents the gift by Ananiah to Tamet of a part of the house just mentioned: "I give you half of the large room, and the chamber of the house that I bought from Ubil and Bagazushta."[13] The document raises a set of unanswerable questions. Did the couple not yet live in the house under consideration, as Botta suggests?[14] Why would Ananiah give this room to Tamet? Were they living separate lives? Did his marriage to an Egyptian slave girl compromise his function as a *lḥn*? The document itself does not help in answering these questions, and neither do the other papyri of the "Ananiah archive." There is, however, one important clue. About the gift of the chamber, Ananiah declares, "I, Ananiah, gave it to you in affection."[15] The idiomatic expression יהב ברחמין, "to give in affection," occurs several times in contracts from Elephantine, indicating the way in which a gift was given.[16] The expression underscores that the transfer was based on the relationship between giver and receiver and distinguishes the act from a sale. It nevertheless raises two questions. Like Hebrew רחמים, Aramaic רחמין signifies "mercy" but could also have the connotation "pity." In that case, the gift could have been presented out of pity, implying that Ananiah wanted to console Tamet for something unpleasant that happened. Secondly, it could very well be that the expression יהב ברחמין can be seen as an antonym to the Aramaic verb שנא, used to indicate the failure of a marital bond and hence grounds for a divorce.[17]

10. *TADAE* B3.4; see Porten, *Archives*, 213–17; Nutkowicz, *Destins de femmes*, 287–97.
11. *TADAE* B3.4:9–10: "to the west of it is the temple of Yahô, the God."
12. *TADAE* B3.5; see Porten, *Archives*, 217–19; Nutkowicz, *Destins de femmes*, 215.
13. *TADAE* B3.5:2–3; Nutkowicz, *Destins de femmes*, 217–33.
14. See Botta, *Aramaic and Egyptian Legal Traditions*, 87.
15. *TADAE* B3.5:4; see Ilan, "Women's Archives," 175–76.
16. *TADAE* B2.10:11.14; 3.5:4.12; 3.8:41; 3.10:5.12.17; 3.11:9; 5.2:10; 5.5:2; 5.4:7.
17. See, e.g., Nutkowicz, "Concerning the Verb *śn'*," 211–25; Meinhold, "Scheidungsrecht bei Frauen," 247–59; Botta, "Hated by the Gods," 105–29; Nutkowicz, *Destins de femmes*, 114–17; Morrow, "'I Hate My Spouse,'" 7–25; Granerød, *Dimensions of Yahwism*, 49–51.295. That the verb שנא would refer to a demotion of status, as argued by Porten and Szubin, "Status of the Handmaiden Tamet," 43–64; Szubin and Porten, "Status of a Repudiated Spouse," 46–78, is a hardly defendable position.

This interpretation would indicate that although the marriage was not perfect, it should not be annulled. In sum, the expression can be seen as a clue that the gift by Ananiah should be interpreted not as a romantic act but as an indication that Ananiah continued to be responsible for Tamet. In addition to that, two things, however, become clear. First, the document makes no reference to Meshullam, the former owner of Tamet. Her social status had clearly evolved.[18] Second, the document mentions another child: Yehoishma. Her rights and that of her brother Pilti are clearly stipulated.[19]

As for the question whether his marriage to an Egyptian slave girl would compromise his function as a לחן, it should be noted that in a document dating to 402 BCE, Tamet—now called Tapamet[20]—is presented as his wife and as a לחנה זי יהו, "servitor of Yahô." This can be construed as an indication that she was fully assimilated and accepted within the community of the Yehudites. The title, however, is not conclusive for her function. As Annalisa Azzoni remarks, לחנה could also refer to the fact that she was married to a לחן.[21] Her being Egyptian cannot be construed as problematic for Ananiah's function at the temple.

The ambiguous character of the relation between Ananiah and Tamet is underscored by yet another document. In 427 BCE, Meshullam had drawn up a document for testamentary manumission.[22] The document makes clear that Tamet—now called Tapamet[23]—and her daughter Yehoishma were at that time still owned by Meshullam. The document arranges their manumission from Meshullam on his death. In this document, Yehoishma is three times refered to as "your daughter, whom you bore me."[24] This expression can be interpreted in two ways: either Meshullam was the biological father of Yehoishma, or, being born from a slave girl, Yehoishma did not fall under the legal responsibility of her biological father—presumably Ananiah—but was seen as part of the larger household of Meshullam. The document, which regulates the gift of a room to Tamet, includes a remark presenting Pilti and Yehoishma as the two children of Ananiah.[25] On the other hand, Ananiah is absent in the testamentary manumission document. All this raises more questions than answers.

In July 420 BCE, he gave a house to Yehoishma.[26] From the description, it becomes clear that this house was located adjacent to Ananiah's own house.

18. See Nutkowicz, *Destins de femmes*, 29–31.

19. *TADAE* B3.5:16–22.

20. Probably a variant or Tamet's full name; Azzoni, *Private Lives*, 92.

21. Azzoni, *Private Lives*, 92.

22. *TADAE* B3.6; see Porten, *Archives*, 219–21.

23. Probably a variant or Tamet's full name.

24. *TADAE* B3.6:4–5.6.7–8.

25. *TADAE* B3.5:18.

26. *TADAE* B3.7; see Porten, *Archives*, 225–30; Szubin and Porten, "Life Estate of Usufruct," 29–45.

In this document, Yehoishma is referred to by Ananiah as "my child, whose mother is Tamet, my wife."[27] The ambiguities in the relationships are either obviated or denied in this document. It might be, however, that Meshullam had died in the meantime and that the social status of both Pamet and Yehoishma had changed. The gift of the house to Yehoishma should be seen in connection with her marriage. In October 420 BCE, a document has been made up regulating the marriage between Yehoishma and a certain Ananiah, son of Haggai.[28] The contract is drawn up between this Ananiah, son of Haggai, and Zakkur, son of Meshullam. The absence of Meshullam, son of Zakkur, might indicate that he had died and that Zakkur, son of Meshullam, acted on behalf of the family of Yehoishma in the absence of both her biological father and her lifelong owner. Ananiah, son of Haggai, refers to Yehoishma as "your sister," indicating that Zakkur, son of Meshullam, was by then the legal representative of Yehoishma. The contract describes the dowry of Yehoishma, which is quite extensive. The absence of Ananiah, son of Azariah, is not to be seen as an indication of his death. In 402 BCE he was still alive selling property to his son-in-law, Ananiah, son of Haggai.[29]

All these documents make clear that the Yehudite Ananiah, son of Azariah, was married to an Egyptian slave girl. The documents give the impression that their relationship had its ups and downs. Through hints in text, the reader can glimpse some fissures in the marriage that, unfortunately for the historian, are not elaborated. His marriage was a curious case.

4.1.3. A Capable Woman: Mibtaiah

The documents from Elephantine contain a set of eleven papyri that can be labeled as the Mibtaiah archive.[30] This archive contains records of more than three generations of a well-to-do Yehudite family. Although the documents are mainly concerned with legal matters such as the selling of property and matrimonial affairs, they provide glimpses into the life of an extraordinary person: מפטיה בת מחסיה, "Mibtaiah, daughter of Mahseiah." It is regretable that the documents on this wealthy woman and her family are restricted to eleven papyri; the existing evidence leaves the historian curious about the events of her life not recorded. One can only hope that new documents will be unearthed.

For our purposes, the most important matter of her life is the fact that she was married twice. The details of the documents on these marriages hint at her

27. *TADAE* B3.7:3.

28. *TADAE* B3.8; see Porten, *Archives*, 221–25; Azzoni, "Where Will Yehoyišmaʿ Go?," 1–5.

29. *TADAE* B3.12; see Porten, *Archives*, 231–34

30. *TADAE* B2.1–11; see Porten, *Archives*, 235–63; Ilan, "Women's Archives from Elephantine"; Granerød, *Dimensions of Yahwism*, 295–302; Schama, *Story of the Jews*, 22–23.

great wealth and at the important position she and her family held within the community of Elephantine.

Her first husband was Yezaniah, son of Uriah.[31] This Yezaniah was a Yehudite whose father's house was adjacent to the property of Mahseiah and Mibtaiah. He thus married the girl next door. A marriage contract is not preserved. The relationship, however, becomes apparent from a few documents, especially one from around 460 BCE in which her father Mahseiah grants the usufruct of a plot of land to Yezaniah.[32] In this document, Mibtaiah is referred to as אנתתך, "your wife," indicating that the couple was married: "There is land of a house of mine, west of the house of yours, which I gave to Mibtaiah my daughter, your wife, and a document I wrote for her concerning it. . . . [33] Now, I, Mahseiah, said to you: That land build (up) and make it wealthy with her house and dwell herein with your wife."[34] The document urges Yezaniah to develop the plot of land, build a house on it, and live in that house with Mibtaiah. The document contains clear restrictions in case the marriage between Yezaniah and Mibtaiah were to dissolve. The document is signed by twelve witnesses, indicating the importance of the transaction. This plot of land is once more referred to in a document from 416 BCE, registering the withdrawal of the property.[35] In that document, the husband of Mibtaiah is named Esḥor, son of Ṣeḥa. Yezaniah had by then disappeared from the sources. It can be assumed that he died at a relatively young age.

The second non-blood-related male figure in the life of Mibtaiah was Pia, son of Paḥi. His name and that of his father is clearly Egyptian. His profession is indicated as ארדיכל, "builder; architect," of the fortress.[36] This Aramaic noun is an Akkadian loanword. Like the Akkadian *arad ekalli*, this noun refers to a person with a position of responsibility at a building project, either as a designer or as a constructor.[37] In other words, he was a person of some status. It has been assumed formerly that they were married.[38] This assumption was based on a specific interpretation of a document on the withdrawal of goods upon divorce:

> On the 14th of Av, that is, day 19 of Pachons, year 25 of Artaxerxes the king, spoke Pia, son of Paḥi, a builder of Syene the fortress, to Mibtaiah,

31. See Porten, *Archives*, 240–45.

32. *TADAE* B2.4.

33. *TADAE* B2.4:3–4; the document on the emdowment of the plot of land is *TADAE* B2.3.

34. *TADAE* B2.4:5–6; reading the second but last word of line 5 as עתר, "to make wealthy."

35. *TADAE* B2.9.

36. *TADAE* B2.8:2.

37. See *CAD A2*, 210–11, and Oppenheim, "Akk. *arad ekalli* = 'Builder,'" 227–35; Kaufman, *Akkadian Influences on Aramaic*, 50, 105–06. Note that Mibthaiah's second husband, Esḥor s. of Ṣeḥa, too was an ארדכל; *TADAE* B2.6:2.

38. See Porten, *Archives*, 245–48.

daughter of Mahseiah, son of Yedaniah, an Aramean of Syene of the detachment of Varyazata, about the suit that we made in Syene, a litigation about silver and grain and clothing and bronze and iron—all goods and property—and the wifehood document.

Then the oath came upon you and you swore to me about them by Sati the goddess. My heart was satisfied with that oath that you made to me about those goods, and I withdrew from you from this day and forever.

I shall not be able to institute against you suit or process—(against) you or son or daughter of yours—in the name of those goods about which you swore to me.

If I institute against you suit or process, or a son of mine or a daughter of mine institutes against you (suit) in the name of that oath, I, Peu—or my children—shall give to Mi[b]tahiah silver, 5 karsh[39] by the stone(-weight)s of the king, without suit or without process.

I am withdrawn from every suit or process.

Wrote Peteese, son of Nabunathan, this document in Syene the fortress at the instruction of Pia, son of Paḥi.[40]

This legal document does not support the existence of a marriage between Mibtaiah and Pia. Although some of the stipulations resemble lines in marriage contracts,[41] they do not sustain the claim of a marriage. This document regulates a trade contract between two individuals from different ethnic groups in Elephantine and Syene: a Yehudite woman and an Egyptian craftsman, both from the higher echelons of the local society. The stipulations are not unfavorable to Mibtaiah.

Mibtaiah's second husband was Egyptian. Like Pia, son of Paḥi, Esḥor, son of Ṣeḥa, was an ארדכל.[42] The marriage contract drawn up to regulate their relationship is an extensive text.[43] The various rules and litigations make clear that Mibtaiah was a woman of means. The marriage contract was a protection for her belongings and assets.[44] This second marriage gave her two sons. The names of her children—Yedaniah and Mahseiah—were familiar in her family.[45] Yedaniah was the name of one of her (half) brothers and Mahseiah was the name of her

39. Karsh is a Persian measurement for about 85 gram.
40. *TADAE* B2.8.
41. See Botta, *Aramaic and Egyptian Legal Traditions*, 128–29; Nutkowicz, *Destins de femmes*, 17.
42. *TADAE* B2.6:2.
43. *TADAE* B2.6; see Porten, *Archives*, 252–55; Nutkowicz, *Destins de femmes*.
44. Botta, *Aramaic and Egyptian Legal Traditions*, 59–60.86.
45. In a later document, the names of the parents of Yedaniah and Mahseiah are Nathan and Mibtaiah (B2.10:3). Most probably, Nathan was the second, Yehudite, name of Esḥor. There are no signs that he had converted to Yahwism; see the remarks of Porten in Porten, *Elephantine Papyri in English*, 178n2; 197n7; with Vittmann, "Arameans in Egypt," 243–44.

father. The giving of matrilineal names can be seen as a sign of her importance. The documents from this archive do not contain clues to the religious life of Mibtaiah, with one exception. On a legal document on the withdrawal of goods upon divorce, Mibtaiah satisfied the heart of her opponent, the Egyptian Pia, by swearing an oath by the Egyptian goddess Sati.[46] As I will argue below, this oath should not be seen as an indication that the Yehudite woman had adopted an Egyptian form of religion.

Mibtaiah's life was exceptional. Her assets and belongings placed her in the higher circles of the local community, in which she must have been influential. Her interactions should, however, be seen as an indication of the peaceful cohabitation of Yehudites and other ethnic groups and not as exceptional on the basis of her status.

4.2. Salutations in Letters

As noted above, several letters written by Yehudites contain greetings and blessings in which—sometimes parallel to Yahô—the gods of the other ethnicities are invoked. In the letter of a certain Giddel to his master Michaiah, Yahô and Khnum are mentioned in parallel: "I send you peace and well-being. I bless you by Yahô and Khnum."[47] This formula gives the impression that both deities were of equal importance. In addition, several letters have been found that are written by people with theophoric names containing Yahô and that still contain the blessing wishes in the plural: "May all deities seek your well-being at all times."[48] The collective language of "deities" in these letter formulas is probably not meaningful for the question of the complexity of the Yehudite pantheon in Elephantine. The supporting documents are too general and too formal.[49] The formula is also attested in non-Yehudite letters: "May a[l]l deities seek after the welfare of my brothers at all times."[50] This piece of evidence indicates that the phrase under consideration was part of the standard letter matrix of the scribes in Elephantine.

A special case is the letter written by Yarḥu to his brother Haggai:

46. *TADAE* B2.8.

47. *TADAE* D7.21; Granerød, *Dimensions of Yahwism*, 244.

48. E.g., *TADAEA* A3.7; A4.2; A4.4; D1.13. See Porten, *Archives*, 158–60; Schwiderski, *Handbuch des nordwestsemitischen Briefformulars*, 130–37.

49. See also Niehr, *Höchste Gott*, 48.

50. E.g., *TADAEA* A3.10:1 Spentadata—probably a Persian name—to "his brothers" Ḥori and Peṭemachis—both Egyptian; Porten, "Aramaic Boat Papyrus," 76–78; *TADAEA* A5.3 Paḥim—probably West Semitic or Arabic—to Mithravahisht, a Persian; the name Paḥim occurs in a Nabatean inscription, see Roche, "Introduction aux religions préislamiques d'Arabie du Nord," 119–28. In general, see Porten, "Address Formulae in Aramaic Letters," 396–415.

1. To my brother Haggai, your brother
2. Yarḥu. Peace to my brother
3. from Bêl and Nabû, Shamash and Nergal.[51]

The brothers Yarḥu and Haggai were of Yehudite origin, yet Babylonian deities are evoked in this communication. This statement contains two assumptions that can be questioned: Were the siblings Yehudite and were the deities Babylonian?

As for the "siblings," Harold Ginsberg, Pierre Grelot, and Bezalel Porten argue as follows.[52] They take the noun *'ḥ* in a nonbiological sense, meaning something like "comrade; mate; peer." Haggai for them is a Jew, while Yarḥu is construed to be a hypocorism for the Phoenician name *yrḥb'l*. Hence they present the inscription under the telling title "Greetings from a Pagan to a Jew." They see the presence of Aramaic(!) deities in the salutation as a sign of syncretism at the daily level.

The personal name Haggai is known from the Hebrew Bible and should be construed as a hypocorism for חגיה, "Yahweh is my feast."[53] The name occurs on a few dozen Hebrew seals,[54] as well as a recently published Hebrew ostracon from the seventh century BCE.[55] The inscriptions from Elephantine and Syene refer to about ten individuals with the name Haggai.[56] The letter on the *marzēaḥ* is written to Haggai.[57] The collection account that registers gifts of two sheqels for the temple of Yahô in Elephantine refers to six individuals called Haggai: to Meshullam, son of Haggai, son of Hazzul; Hazzul, son of Haggai, son of Hazzul; Nathun, son of Haggai; Haggai, son of Micah"; Hag[gai], son of Menachem [son of] Pawesi; and Yehoshama, daughter of Haggai.[58] In other documents, too, Yehudites with the name Haggai occur.[59] It can be assumed that they were all part of the Yehudite group, although this cannot be proven with certainty.

51. *TADAE* D7.30:1–3; see Lozachmeur, *Collection Clermont-Ganneau*, no. 277; I disagree with Lemaire, "Everyday Life," 360–70, who considers this ostracon to be merely a scribal exercise with no value for the history of religion; Cornell, "Forgotten Female Figurines of Elephantine," 123.

52. Ginsberg, "Greetings from a Pagan to a Jew," 491; Grelot, *Documents araméens d'Egypte*, 88; Porten in his remarks on *TADAE* D7.30.

53. Hag 1–2; Ezra 5:1; 6:14.

54. For a list, see *DCH* 3:159–60.

55. Lemaire and Yardeni, "New Hebrew Ostraca," 215–17, Ostr. 12:2. The name occurs in a shortened form *Ha-ag-ga-a* in the documents from Al Yahudu, see Alstola, *Judeans in Babylonia*, 56.

56. See already Dupont-Sommer, "Bêl et Nabû, Šamaš et Nergal," 31.

57. *TADAE* D.7.29; see Becking, "Temple, *marzēaḥ*, and Power at Elephantine," 37–47; strangely enough the *marzēaḥ* text is not taken into account by Rohrmoser, *Götter, Tempel und Kult*.

58. *TADAE* C.3.15.

59. Some of them are identical with a Haggai from the collection account. Further Yehudites by the name of Haggai can be found in the documents from the Clermont-Ganneau collection; see Lozachmeur, *Collection Clermont-Ganneau*, no.147:1; 266:4.

It is quite clear that the personal name *yrḥw* refers to the West Semitic moon god *yrḥ,* whose name occurs as a theophoric element in Ugaritic, Phoenician, and West Semitic personal names.[60] I would, however, refer to the fact Gen 10:26 and 1 Chr 1:26 list the name Ieraḥ among the decedents of Ever, which I view as an indication that Yarḥu could easily have been a Yehudite.[61]

The Aramaic noun *ʾḥ* generally has the meaning "brother," in the biological sense of the word.[62] In texts with an epistolary character, however, the noun is also used to refer to someone of equal status, a colleague, or a peer.[63] Due to the brevity of the document under consideration, the meaning of the noun *ʾḥ* is difficult to establish in each of its three attestations. All in all, I come to the conclusion that it safe to assume that we are dealing in this letter here with an internal group communication.

The salutation under consideration is not unique at Elephantine in containing the names of other deities; it is unique in the sense that four deities of Babylonian origin are mentioned.

- Bêl—as elsewhere, a mask for Marduk—was the supreme divine being of the Neo-Babylonians.[64]
- Nabû was worshiped as the son of Marduk. In origin Nabû was an Amorite deity. He was the god of wisdom and writing, especially the writing of human destiny. In Neo-Babylonian times he was enormously popular among Aramaic-speaking populations.[65]
- Shamash was the sun god and the god of justice.[66]
- Nergal is the (southern) Mesopotamian god of death, pestilence, and plague, and Lord of the underworld. Shamash and Nergal stand for opposing realms: heaven and the underworld.[67]

These four gods do not occur in any other salutation formula in letters from Elephantine. Bêl occurs in a very fragmentary letter of which "[. . .] my ⌜lord(?)⌝ Bêl [. . .] my lord [. . .] there is n⌜ot⌝" is readable.[68] Nabû is mentioned in the

60. See, e.g., Gröndahl, *Die Personennamen*, 145; Benz, *Personal Names*, 326.

61. See also Dupont-Sommer, "Bêl et Nabû, Šamaš et Nergal," 31–32.

62. Sometimes "sister."

63. See *DNSWI*, 31.

64. See Dupont-Sommer, "Bêl et Nabû, Šamaš et Nergal," 33; T. Abush, "Marduk," in *DDD*², 543–49.

65. A. R. Miljard, "Nabû," in *DDD*², 607–20.

66. E. Lipiński, "Šemeš," in *DDD*², 764–68.

67. A. Livingstone, "Nergal," in *DDD*², 621–22.

68. *TADAE* D1.22. Bêl also occurs as theophoric element in personal names from Elephantine; see Porten, Zadok, and Pearce, "Akkadian Names in Aramaic Documents," 1–12.

inscription on the sarcophagus of "She'il, the priest of Nabû."[69] The name of the deity Nergal occurs as a theophoric element in names from Elephantine such as נרגלאדן and נרגלשזב.[70] It is surprising that Babylonian gods are mentioned in this letter and not, for instance, Persian divine beings. It is a striking fact that in the entire corpus of texts from Elephantine, no Persian divine name is mentioned—with only one important exception. The Aramaic version of the Bisitun inscription found at Elephantine declares that Darius lived, acted, and ruled under "the divine favor of Ahura Mazda."[71] The absence of references to Persian deities in day-to-day correspondence and legal transactions is difficult to explain. It is hard to believe that the Persians remained silent about their religious worldview or entered into some sort of *innere Emigration*. Most probably the Persians in Elephantine adopted the veneration of the Babylonian deities Nabû, Bêl, Shamash, and Nergal, which would imply that the name for the divine was less important to them than the concept of divinity.

For reasons well known—the past is a foreign country—this assumption cannot be verified or falsified. Nevertheless, the combination of the first two deities, Bêl and Nabû, was quite common in the ancient Near East, as the following examples attest.

In an eighth-century BCE Assyrian letter from Tell Ḥalaf, the following salutation can be found: "^{d}*Bēl u* ^{d}*Nabû šu-lum ša mār*[*i-ià*] *u marti-ia liq-bu-ú*" (May Bêl and Nabû speak on behalf of the well-being of [my] so[n] and my daughter).[72] Here the two first deities are mentioned together.

In Isa 46:1, Bêl and Nabû are depicted as deities whose rule has come to an end:

> Bel has bowed down, Nebo stoops over
> Their images are consigned to the beasts and the cattle.
> The things that you carry are burdensome,
> A load for the weary beast. (Isa 46:1 NASB)

In this text Bêl and Nabû are seen as once-powerful Babylonian deities whom the Persians disposed of in their superior power. They are referred to in the context of a taunt-song probably connected with the procession of their divine images at the Babylonian New Year festival.[73]

69. *TADAE* D18:1. Nabû occurs several timesas theoporic element in personal names fro Elephantine; see Porten, Zadok, Pearce, "Akkadian Names."

70. Nergal-Iddin (*TADAE* D1.33 frg. d:2) and Nergal(u)shezib (*TADAE* B3.0:9); see Porten, Zadok, and Pearce, "Akkadian Names."

71. Kuhrt, *Persian Empire*, 141–57; Granerød, "By the Favour of Ahuramazda," 455–80.

72. Tell Halaph documents (ed. Friedrich and von Oppenheim, *Die Inschriften vom Tell Halaf*, text 117:3–4; see Dupont-Sommer, "Bêl et Nabû, Šamaš et Nergal," 33.

73. See, e.g., Machinist, "Mesopotamian Imperialism and Israelite Religion," 237–64; Petry, *Die Entgrenzung JHWHs*, 166–74; Schaudig, "Bel Bows, Nabu Stoops!" 557–72.

In the Cyrus Cylinder, the Persian king is presented as follows by the priests of the Esağila temple:

> I am Cyrus, king of the world, great king, mighty king, king of Babylon, king of Sumer and Akkad, king of the four quarters, the son of Cambyses, great king, king of Anšan, grandson of Cyrus, great king, king of Anšan, descendant of Teispes, great king, king of Anšan, of an eternal line of kingship, whose rule Bêl and Nabû love, whose kingship they desire for their hearts' pleasure.[74]

With the reference to Bêl and Nabû, the Persian king is presented as having accepted these Babylonian deities as of great importance for his empire. This gesture is underscored by the request by Cyrus that the deities for whom he had established chapels in Esağila pray for him in front of Bêl and Nabû:

> In addition, at the command of Marduk, the great lord, I settled in their habitations, in pleasing abodes, the gods of Sumer and Akkad, whom Nabonidus, to the anger of the lord of the gods, had brought into Babylon. May all the gods whom I settled in their sacred centers ask daily of Bêl and Nabû that my days be long, and may they intercede for my welfare. May they say to Marduk, my lord: "As for Cyrus, the king who reveres you, and Cambyses, his son."[75]

In this connection a remark made by Ursula Seidl needs to be considered. She observed that in the Babylonian fragment of the Bisitun inscription the name of Ahura Mazda from the Persian and Elamite versions is replaced by Bêl, which would indicate that for the Persian kings—or at least their scribes—both deities were to some degree equivalent to each other.[76]

Bêl and Nabû are referred to in a legal document from a locality at the banks of the "New Canal" in the area of Borsippa dated to 515 BCE.[77] In a promissory note concerning the delivery of thirty-five kors of dates, the debtors—who bear Babylonian names—swear by Bêl and Nabû that they will deliver within three months. Although the local context is clearly Babylonian the document is dated into the Persian period. This implies that the Persian powers apparently accepted swearing by two gods of Babylonian descent.

74. Cyrus Cylinder 20–22; Kuhrt, *Persian Empire*, 70–74; see now Finkel, *Cyrus Cylinder*, with a new translation in the appendix.

75. Cyrus Cylinder 33–35.

76. Seidl, "Ein Monument Darius I. aus Babylon," 101–14.

77. BM 27797, see Zadok, "Geography of the Borsippa Region," 407.

Bêl and Nabû are mentioned in a blessing in the Syrian section of Papyrus Amherst 63:

> All the gods will bless you.
> The Lord will bless you from Rash
>   The Lady will bless you from Siryon
> Baal will bless you from Zaphon
>   Pidraya will bless you from the Orontes
> Bêl (בל) with bless you from Babylon
>   Belet will bless you from Esağil
> Nabû (נבו) will bless you from Barsippa
>   Nanay will bless you from the sanctuary
> Will bless you throne-of-Yahô
>   and Asherah from the south.[78]

A plethora of divine beings are invoked to bless the penitent. The text gives the impression that these gods from all corners of the world and venerated by the various ethnic groups at the "oasis in the desert" are equal and interchangeable.

Another piece of evidence comes from a late Persian / early Hellenistic funerary stele found in Daskyleion in northwestern Anatolia. The inscription reads:

1. אלה צלמהזי אלנף בר אשי
2. הו עבד לנפשה הומיתך
3. בל ונבו ארחא זנה
4. יהו הער אל יעמל

I translate this as: "This is his statue which Elnaph, son of Asjahû, made for his soul. I adjure you (by) Bêl and Nabû: to whom(ever) passes by this way let no one do harm (to my tomb)."[79] It should be noted that Daskyleion was on the western edge of the Persian Empire. It was an Achaemenid administrative center, and a satrapal seat of northwestern Anatolia. Epigraphic and archaeological findings indicate that Daskyleion was populated with a variety of ethnic groups: Persians, Greeks, Lydian, and Phrygians. I construe the personal name Asjahû to refer to a member of the proto-Jewish diaspora in Daskyleion.[80] The formula

78. Pap Amherst 63 viii:1–7; see Steiner and Nims, "Aramaic Text in Demotic Script," 26–27; van der Toorn, *Papyrus Amherst 63*, 125–27.

79. Dupont-Sommer, "Une inscription araméenne inédite," 44–57; Hanfmann, "New Stelae from Daskylion," 10–13; Cross, "Aramaic Inscription from Daskyleion," 7–10; Folmer, *Aramaic Language*, 563.

80. This name is not attested in the Hebrew Bible, but occurs on an Iron Age ostracon from Tel Arad: Arad 17:3, and in a list of names: Deutsch and Helzer, *New Epigraphic Evidence*, 92–102.

"I adjure you (by) Bêl and Nabû" may contain traditional language. In a context comparable to that of Elephantine, it indicates that these deities were invoked as the divine guarantors of the Persian power.[81]

Sometimes, the pairing of Bêl and Nabû is expanded with other deities. Late calendrical texts from Hellenistic Uruk contain the description for clothing ceremonies (*lubuštu*) of Bêl, Nabû, and others.[82] From the context it is unclear whether traditional Babylonian deities or contemporary Hellenistic divinities are referred to.[83]

Finally, the veneration of the two deities—Bêl and Nabû—is continued in Babylonian Aramaic and Mandaic incantation bowls as having power over threatening spirits, as becomes clear from a spell in a Mandaic text: "I have sworn to you, O evil Eye, and I adjure you by Bêl, Nabû, and Nerig, that you be exorcised and leave this soul and house."[84]

All this implies that the four gods mentioned are not specifically presented as Babylonian deities or as the divine beings of the Aramaic contingent at Syene and Elephantine. I construe them to be a reference to the divine in general. The line in this salutation could be interpreted as a parallel to the formula "May all deities seek for your well-being at all times." I do not see this salutation as a sign of syncretism—at whatever level of religion—but as an indication of the awareness among various groups in Elephantine and Syene that, despite the difference in naming the divine, all groups accepted the existence of a divine world that could be invoked by using either general terms or specific names.

The same tendency can be detected in the Sayings of Aḥiqar. As a school text found in Elephantine, this text represents an international form of wisdom that is not bound to any one group alone.[85] The deities referred to in these sayings—"the Lord of the holy ones" (*bʿl qdšn*); "El"; "Shamash"; and "gods" (*ʾlhyn*)—are also not to be seen as bound to a specific group. The fact that scholars still quarrel about the identity of the main deity, *bʿl qdšn*—Baal-Shamayin,[86] Shamash,[87] and Hadad[88] are all contenders—indicates that it is a designation that would have been used by various groups for the head deity.

81. On Daskyleion, see Kaan, "New Discovery in Dascylium," 249–64; Abe, "Dascylium," 1–17.

82. Reisner, *Sumerisch-babylonische Hymnen*, No. 8 and 56; see Beaulieu, *Pantheon of Uruk*, 23, for the *lubuštu* ceremony.

83. See Boiy, *Late Achaemenid and Hellenistic Babylon*.

84. Morgenstern, "Mandaic Magic Bowls," 157–70; Nerig, sometimes Nirig, is the Mandaic name for the deity Nergal.

85. Niehr, *Aramäischer Aḥiqar*, 23; see §5.2 below.

86. Lindenberger, "Gods of Ahiqar," 114–16; Weigl, *Die aramäischen Achikar-Sprüche*, 73–79.

87. Lipiński, *Aramaeans*, 625.

88. Kottsieper, "El–ferner oder naher Gott?," 28; Niehr, *Aramäischer Aḥiqar*, 18–19.

All in all, the salutation under consideration can be understood as an indication of an open society in which it was acceptable to use the names of deities originating in other religious traditions in order to refer to the divine realm in general.

4.3. Trade Contacts

There are a few signs of trade between the various ethnic groups. I will not discuss them all, but only refer to a representative few.

4.3.1. Selling a House

In September 437 BCE, a house was sold.[89] As noted already in §4.1.2, the seller was a Caspian soldier, Bagazushta. The vendor was a Yehudite, Ananiah, son of Azariah—referred to above in connection with his marriage to Tamet—who is indicated here by his religious function: "a servant (לחן) of Yahô."[90] The property sold is the "house of *ʾpwly*, son of Misdaya, which is in Elephantine the fortress."[91] The house as such and its cadastral position are described in great detail. Botta has shown that the document contains all the elements of a traditional sales contract.[92] The document gives the impression that the house was as yet unfinished. It might be that *ʾpwly*, son of Misdaya, had died. The question of why Bagazushta had become the owner of the property cannot be answered. Porten assumes that *ʾpwly*, son of Misdaya ,was a Caspian too, which is uncertain.[93] If Porten is correct, Bagazushta might have acquired the house as a fellow Caspian.

4.3.2. A Loan of Grain

In a document dated to December 402 BCE contains a contract between Ananiah, son of Haggai, a Yehudite, and Pakhnum, son of Besa, an Aramean from Syene. Pakhnum is clearly an Egyptian name. It is uncertain whether this Pakhnum, son of Besa, was an Egyptian or an Aramean who had been given an Egyptian name by his parents.[94] His father's name, Besa, is of Nubian origin and means "protector," connected to the Egyptian apotropaic dwarf-god Bes.

89. Documented in *TADAE* B3.4.
90. On servitor, see Granerød, *Dimensions of Yahwism*, 56–58.
91. *TADAE* B3.4:4.
92. Botta, *Aramaic and Egyptian Legal Traditions*, 108–11.
93. Porten, *Archives*, 213–14.
94. See on this Porten, "'Egyptian Names in Aramaic Texts," 283–328.

This argues in favor of the first possibility: he was a mercenary attached to the detachment in Syene. The document itself contains the terms and obligations on a loan of grain.[95]

4.3.3. *Fragmentary Accounts*

There are several fragmentary accounts that provide evidence of interethnic trade. A fragmentary account from around 600 BCE, discussed more extensively above (§3.3.2.5) lists the names of about a dozen people connected to silver items, though the precise relationship between these individuals and the silver is not clear.[96] The list contains Israelite names—[She]lamiah and Obadiah—next to Egyptian, Babylonian, and Phoenician personal names. It is not impossible that these individuals were cooperating in a joint venture.

Another account, from the first half of the fifth century, is concerned with plots of land.[97] In it Yehoram, son of Hag[gai], is listed with seven others who have Egyptian, Babylonian, and Aramaic names. A list from the middle of the fifth century BCE—whose purpose is no longer clear—mentions "Shillem, son of . . . , and Ananiah, son of Psamshek," among twelve persons with Aramaic, Persians, and Egyptian names.[98]

4.3.4. *Contracts*

There is an incomplete document that contains a contract between the Bactrian Patu and the Yehudite Yedaniah. Since the text is broken, the character of their contract cannot be established.[99]

4.4. Oaths and Other Deities

An interesting example of cooperation between various ethnic groups can be seen in a pair of related documents (discussed in §3.1.2 above) concerning a quarrel about a piece of land between the Khwarezmian Dargamana and the Yehudite Mahseiah, son of Yedaniah. Dargamana is presented as the son of Xvarshaina, a Khwarezmian. His name as well as the name of his father is Old

95. *TADAE* B3.13; see Botta, *Aramaic and Egyptian Legal Traditions*, 58.
96. *TADAE* C3.4; see Porten, "Aramaic Papyrus Fragments," 26–29.
97. *TADAE* C3.6.
98. *TADAE* D9.10.
99. *TADAE* D2.12; see Hoftijzer, "Unpublished Aramaic Fragment," 45–48; on Bactrians, see §3.1.4 above.

Persian.[100] In Elephantine, Dargamana was a mercenary serving in the *degel* of Artabana, which contained Bactrians, Persians, and Babylonians (see also §3.1.2 above). Mahseiah, son of Yedaniah, was the father of Mibtaiah, referred to above. The name Mahseiah is borne by several members of his family, probably due to patronymy. The name is also attested in Jer 32:12 (grandfather of Baruch) and 51:59, and it is clearly Yahwistic, meaning "Yahô is a shelter." From the Elephantine documents it is clear that he and his family belonged to the Yehudite elite in Elephantine.

The first document, dated to 464 BCE, concerns a cadastral quarrel between Dargamana and Mahseiah. Since we only are informed by two documents, it is not easy to reconstruct the quarrel in detail. What is clear is that there was a dispute between these two houseowners, who held adjacent properties in a well-to-do neighborhood of Elephantine, over the ownership of Dargamana's property. The case is brought to a court presided over by Damidata, a Persian judge. This first document is presented as a withdrawal of his complaint by Dargamana.[101] The Khwarezmian was convinced that the the property he had claimed did in fact belong to Mahseiah .. What persuaded him was not the presentation of a legal document of sorts by Mahseiah but an oath sworn by the Yehudite. The judge forced Mahseiah to swear an oath: "You swore to me by Yahô and satisfied my heart about that land."[102] Thereupon Dargamana rescinds his claims and has the withdrawal of his complaint written by the scribe Itu, son of Abah.[103]

Two aspects of this text will be discussed: the practice of swearing an "oath" and the formula "to satisfy the heart." It should be noted that the legal document is written in a discursive or narrative modus, and the formula occurs three times with a finite verb, *ym't* (4; 8; 11),[104] and once with the construction noun + *l* + participle.

To swear an oath is a performative act.[105] Swearing by a deity is a precarious and daring speech act.[106] The practice of swearing an oath was well known in the

100. Tavernier, *Iranica in the Achaemenid Period*, 168: Dargamana: "Long-minded."

101. *TADAE* B2.2; see Botta, *Aramaic and Egyptian Legal Traditions*, 124–26; Siljanen, *Judeans of Egypt*, 265–67; Cornell, "Forgotten Female Figurines," 123–24.

102. *TADAE* B2.2:11–12.

103. The second document, written five years later, records Mahesiah's bequest of this property to his daughter Mibtaiah; it appears that Dargamana had again become or remained the owner of another adjacent plot: "above it [i.e., the land of Mahseiah/Mibtaiah] the house of Dargamana, son of Xvarshaina, adjoins." See *TADAE* B2.3:5–6.

104. The application of a *verbum finitum* is common in ancient Near Eastern discursive oath texts, see Conklin, *Oath Formulas in Biblical Hebrew*, 80.

105. Flowerdew, "Problems of Speech Act Theory," 79–105; Turri, "Epistemic Invariantism," 77–95; Conklin, *Oath Formulas in Biblical Hebrew*, 1–11.

106. Van der Toorn, "Herem-Bethel," 282–85; van der Toorn, "Anat-Yahu, Some Other Deities," 80–101.

ancient Near East, including pharaonic Egypt.[107] The deity is indirectly invoked as an observing witness to the case. Ancient Egyptians, Persians, Israelites, and Khwarezmians considered the divine realm to be a powerful reality. By swearing an oath by a deity, Mahseiah goes beyond a mere declaration and conveys that he is being fully truthful, since the invoked deity was expected to punish a liar.[108]

As discussed above (§2.3.7.3), swearing by the deity of another group at Elephantine was not uncommon.[109] On a legal document on the withdrawal of goods upon divorce , the Yehudite Mibtaiah, daughter of Mahseiah, satisfied the heart of her opponent, the Egyptian Pia, by swearing an oath by Sati (Satet), the deification of the flooding of the Nile.[110] Swearing by another's god should be construed not as an act of religious conversion but rather as a peaceful acceptance of others' religious values and the power of their deities.

Document *TADAE* B7.3 contains an interesting oath.[111] As noted above (§2.3.7.3), this oath text settles a quarrel between two Yehudites—Menachem, son of Shallum, son of Ho[šiah(?) . . .] and Meshullam, son of Nathan over the ownership of a she-ass. Menaḥem swears by "H[. . .], the [*god*] in the place of veneration, and by Anat-Yahô."[112] In other texts from Elephantine that refer to the act of swearing, no deities by whom the oath was sworn are mentioned.[113]

Let me return to the Mahseiah-Dargamana conflict. As a result of Mahseiah's sworn oath, Dargamana states that his heart is satisfied. This expression has its background in the terminology of the Aramaic business law and especially in documents of conveyance. The expression here is used in an active formulation: *yṭb* Ha + *lbb* + suffix: "to make good/content the heart of X."[114] This implies that Mahseiah's oath has set the uncertainties of Dargamana at ease so that he is satisfied and content. The commonly used expression—cognates of which occur in Akkadian and Demotic texts—is typically an indication of remuneration, especially in texts that describe the transfer of good. In this case, it indicates that the claimant is content and that there is no longer contention between him and Mahseiah.

Why is the god of only one party invoked in the oath? One possibility is that the oath is taken in front of the deity—or deities—of the more important partner

107. Wilson, "Oath in Ancient Egypt," 129–56; Conklin, *Oath Formulas in Biblical Hebrew*.

108. Conklin, *Oath Formulas in Biblical Hebrew*.

109. See already H. Anneler, *Zur Geschichte der Juden von Elephantine*, 39.

110. *TADAE* B2.8.

111. Recent translation in Rohrmoser, *Götter, Tempel und Kult*, 425–26.

112. Van der Toorn, "Anat-Yahu, Some Other Deities"; Mondriaan, "Anat-Yahu," 537–52; Rohrmoser, *Götter, Tempel und Kult*, 139–41. On the deity Herem-Bethel, see §2.3.6.2 above.

113. *TADAE* B7.1:6; B8.9:3–4; Lozachmeur, *Collection Clermont-Ganneau*, no. 265.

114. See Muffs, *Studies in the Aramaic Legal Papyri*, 27–194; Botta, *Aramaic and Egyptian Legal Traditions*, 125; Westbrook, "Phrase 'His Heart Is Satisfied,'" 219–24; Nutkowicz, *Destins de femmes*, 297–98.

in the quarrel. If this is correct then Mahseiah was seen as of higher social standing than Dargamana. The text does not indicate that Dargamana converted to Judaism—or its predecessor. The text confirms that it was acceptable to invoke someone else's deity as an observing witness to a human agreement and hence evidences a level of religious acceptance at Elephantine.

4.5. An Interreligious Figurine

Recently, Collin Cornell discussed a Persian-period figurine that was excavated at Elephantine in the early twentieth century.[115] This plaque depicts a naked woman with child standing at the entrance of a sanctuary.[116] The iconography of this plaque is culturally mixed. Egyptian and Levantine elements are juxtaposed.[117] Amihai Mazar suggested a Phoenician background and identified the woman on the plaque with Astarte.[118] Rohrmoser ponders the possibility that the woman depicts a deity like Anat-Yahô (Anat-Bethel) or Eshem-Bethel but ultimately argues that such an identification is impossible to confirm.[119] Cornell offers an intriguing proposal. Reading the artifact within the multiethnic context of Persian-period Elephantine, he suggests that the nameless deity on the plaque could have been invoked as different gods to different people. This would mean that the artifact could be used widely within the multiethnic community, yet another example of the interchangeability of the divine.[120]

4.6. Conclusions and Questions

The texts discussed in this chapter can be understood as hints of the mutual acceptance of the "other" in all dimensions of life in Elephantine in the fifth century BCE.[121] Phrased differently, while each group had its own ancestral myths, religious practices, and historical memories, they only partially defined the identities of the different groups. The specifics were not seen as immutable or sacrosanct. As a result of the cohabitation, the various groups negotiated a superstructure for the identity for the complex, multiethnic community as a

115. Cornell, "Forgotten Female Figurines."

116. Editio princeps: Honroth, Rubensohn, and Zucker, "Bericht über die Ausgrabungen auf Elephantine," 162–209; the object is now in the Ägyptologisches Museum in Berlin (ÄM 2156).

117. See Rohrmoser, *Götter, Tempel und Kult*, 316; Cornell, "Forgotten Female Figurines," 117.

118. Mazar, "Pottery Plaques Depicting Goddesses," 5–18.

119. Rohrmoser, *Götter, Tempel und Kult*, 321–28.

120. Cornell, "Forgotten Female Figurines," 119–25.

121. See also Schäfer, *Judeophobia*, 121.

whole, expressing a sense of solidarity not restricted to one's own group. The cultural encounter between the Yehudites of Elephantine and the other groups mentioned led to an openness toward and acceptance of the "other," not withdrawal into separate, insular ethnic communities. It is within the framework of this acceptance of the "other" that deities from different religious traditions were accepted.[122] This can be considered an aspect of the *pax persica*, to draw terminology from Maria Brosius.[123] This "pax" (peace) is a situation imposed by the power of the Persian Empire over its subjects, but also accepted by the various peoples and groups living under that umbrella. In my view the topics discussed above (such as intermarriage) are signs of that acceptance.

This almost ideal image of a multiethnic society, however, provokes two questions: Which powers made this kind of multiethnic society possible—or why did the subjects accept this Persian power? And why did the society not endure—or which historical vectors made an end to the acceptance? Both questions will be dealt with separately in the next two chapters.

122. See also Johnson, "Ethnic Considerations," 211–22.

123. See Brosius, "Pax Persica," 135–61; Brosius, *Persians*, 35.

CHAPTER 5

Control Through Education, Law, and Military Power

THE *PAX PERSICA*, AS DESCRIBED in the previous chapters, was not the result of a voluntary endeavor to forge a peaceful and harmonious multiethnic society. The situation was orchestrated and imposed by Persian power. But why was Persian power accepted by all these different ethnic groups? Why did the various ethnicities felt at ease within the *pax persica*? A simple answer would be that they had no choice, since they were dependent upon the Persian administration. The answer is more complicated when we consider the different tools the Persian used.[1] Law and military power were two state mechanism of enforcement capable of establishing and maintaining enduring harmony in the Egyptian satrapy. They will be discussed later. First, I consider how "cultural capital"—namely, scribal education—was used as another mechanism to compel loyalty and maintain peace.[2]

5.1. Two "Literary" Texts

Among the documents from Elephantine are two texts that are different from the majority of the letters, contracts, lists, etc.[3] They are the oldest known version of the Sayings of Aḥiqar—both a novella and a set of proverbs—and an Aramaic version of Darius's Bisitun inscription. I will argue that both texts were used for

1. See Gates-Foster, "'Achaemenids, Royal Power, and Persian Ethnicity," 175–93.
2. See Bourdieu, *Sur l'État*.
3. A third text is the enigmatic Tale of Hor the Son of Punesh, *TADAE* C1.2, see Porten, "Prophecy of Hor bar Punesh," 427–66. The text makes the impression of being a versio aramaica of an Egyptian tale "the stories around Setne Khamwas" about the quarrel between a king and a servant who after having been treated badly utters a spell on the "boats of the king"; Holm, "Sheikh Fadl Inscription," 193–224.

I leave aside the somewhat hypothetical assumption that the book of Job was written at Elephantine; see Knight, *Nile and Jordan*, 405; Burns, "Judith or Jael?," 12–14.

the local education of scribes in Elephantine.[4] These scribes would have been recruited from the various ethnic groups mentioned in chapter 3. I assume that these scribes, by reading and rewriting these texts, were trained in a lifestyle and a worldview characterized by the acceptance of Persian power and an openness to negotiating identity with the "other." In both cases, the subtext prescribes and instructs the reader in a moral code.[5]

5.2. Sayings of Aḫiqar as Scribal Propaganda

The oldest extant fragment of the Sayings of Aḫiqar was found at Elephantine.[6] The document consists of two parts: a narrative about the sage Aḫiqar, focusing on the topics of power and loyalty, and a collection of proverbs and sayings. The traditions on Aḫiqar were widespread across the ancient Near East. Demotic fragments from the first millennium BCE mentioning Aḫiqar are known.[7] The tale and the sayings have been translated into various languages, the latest being a recently discovered version in Neo-Aramaic.[8]

The Aḫiqar novella is set at the court of the Neo-Assyrian king Esarhaddon. Although the Aramaic name *ʾḥyqr*, "my brother is noble," is attested in a few Neo-Assyrian and Neo-Babylonian inscriptions,[9] a court official by that name

4. On scribes and scribal training in the ancient Near East, see van der Toorn, *Scribal Culture*; Hobson, "Localized Scribal Systems," 77–100; Madreiter, "Der Raum alltäglicher weiblicher Literalität," 113–41.

5. See also Granerød, *Dimensions of Yahwism*, 307.

6. *TADAE* C.1.1. Original edition: Sachau, *Aramäische Papyrus und Ostraka*. Recent translations: Grelot, *Documents araméens d'Égypte*, 427–52; Lindenberger, *Aramaic Proverbs of Ahiqar*; Kottsieper, *Die Sprache der Ahiqarsprüche*; Niehr, *Aramäischer Aḥiqar*; Holm, *Aramaic* (forthcoming). I will not discuss the complicated question of the order of the columns—see Niehr, *Aramäischer Aḥiqar*, 5—nor the role that the erased customs account could play in this discussion—see Yardeni, "Maritime Trade and Royal Accountancy," 67–78.

7. Cairo papyrus published by Sobhy, "Miscellanea," 3–5 + Pl. VII; P.Berl. 23729 edited by Zauzich, "Demotische Fragmente zum Ahikar-Roman," 180–85. On both inscriptions, see Lindenberger, *Aramaic Proverbs of Ahiqar*, 310–12; Quack, "Interaction of Egyptian and Aramaic Literature," 375–401. The fragmented P.Berl. 15658 might contain some of the Achiqar proverbs, see Zauzich, "Neue literarische Texte in demotischer Schrift," 33–38; Quack, "Interaction of Egyptian and Aramaic Literature," 376; Holm, "Memories of Sennacherib in Aramaic Texts," 299.

8. On translations and adaptations, see Niehr, *Aramäischer Aḥiqar*, 33–34; Contini and Grottanelli, *Saggio Ahiqar*; Kratz, "*Mille Ahiqar*," 39–58.

Arabic: Būlus Bahnām, *Aḥīqār al-ḥakīm*.

Ethiopic: Lusini, "Ethiopic Version of the 'Story of Ahiqar,'" 219–48.

Sogdian: Sims-Williams, *Biblical and Other Christian Sogdian Texts*, 7–111.

Neo-Aramaic: Talay, "Die Geschichte und die Sprüche des Aḥiqar," 695–712.

9. See Weigl, *Die aramäischen Achikar-Sprüche*, 1; Berlejung and Radner, "Aḫi-iaqar," 63; Oshima, "How 'Mesopotamian' Was Ahiqar the Wise?," 144–45; and in the al-Yahudu documents, see Pearce and Wunsch, *Documents of Judean Exiles*, 8–9.39; Alstola, *Judeans in Babylonia*, 112–20.

from the reigns of Esarhaddon and Assurbanipal is not known, which makes the Aḥiqar of the wisdom tradition a fictitious character.[10] The actors Esarhaddon and Sennacherib, as well as Nabušumiškun, are persons known from history. Esarhaddon and Sennacherib had been kings of the Neo-Assyrian Empire. Nabušumiškun was a son of Marduk-apla-idinna, who made a career at the Assyrian court.[11] The aim of the Aḥiqar novella, however, is not to (re)construct an episode at the palace of Nineveh. As Seth Bledsoe correctly has argued, these historical figures are remembered in the story for their symbolic role.[12] These kings, well recalled from the past by the various ethnic groups in Elephantine, form a kind of camouflage for talking about the current foreign ruler, and Aḥiqar—both novella and proverbs—should be read from this perspective.

The story starts with Aḥiqar. This childless sage had already served as scribe and advisor under Sennacherib, Esarhaddon's father. Being childless, Aḥiqar adopted his nephew Nadin and trained him for a role at the court. Esarhaddon accepted Nadin as the successor of the aged Aḥiqar. The old scribe withdrew and started a quiet life in a mountainous area. Nadin became involved in a conspiracy against Aḥiqar. The retired scribe was accused of being part of a revolt against the king. On hearing this news, the king sent an officer named *nbwsmiskn*, "Nabušumiškun," with two men to Aḥiqar in order to kill him. The retired scribe reminded Nabušumiškun that he once spared him in a comparable situation during the reign of Sennacherib and that he was rehabilitated at court after the wrath of the king had dissipated. Aḥiqar suggested to Nabušumiškun that he should hide in his own house until that foreseeable day in which the king would once again need Aḥiqar's advice and, in return for his wisdom, restore Aḥiqar to grace. Nabušumiškun responded positively to this advice. He let go of his assignment and had Aḥiqar kill one of his servants. His two companions presented that corpse at the court as an impersonation of Aḥiqar. At this point, the text breaks off. The apparent rehabilitation of Aḥiqar is not narrated in the document from Elephantine, but it is present in many of the later versions.

The name Aḥiqar is also associated with a collection of sayings and proverbs. This collection is typically dated to the eighth century BCE based on the Aramaic dialect in which it was written, which deviates from the dialect found in the

10. Already Von Soden, "Die Unterweltsvision eines assyrischen Kronprinzen," 1–31; with Niehr, *Aramäischer Aḥiqar*, 9; Kratz, "*Mille Ahiqar*," 44–45.

11. On this Neo-Babylonian name *nabû-šum-iškun*, "Nabu established the name," see Porten, Zadok, and Pearce, "Akkadian Names in Aramaic Documents," 1–12; the name also occurs in a contract from Elephantine (B2.2:19) and in Neo-Babylonian inscriptions as the name of a son of Merodakhbaladan; Von Weiher, "Marduk-apla-uṣur und Nabû-šum-iškun," 197–224; Niehr, *Aramäischer Aḥiqar*, 8; Weigl, *Die aramäischen Achikar-Sprüche*, 2.

12. Bledsoe, "Conflicting Loyalties," 239–68; see also Holm, "'Memories of Sennacherib in Aramaic Texts," 297–308; Wigand, "Politische Loyalität und religiöse Legitimierung," 128–32; Schipper, "Joseph, Ahiqar, and Elephantine," 71–84.

novella. The collection presupposes an environment that includes viticulture, cedar, steppe, and the Phoenician coast. It is therefore likely that the collection originated in the south Syrian-Lebanese area.[13] The text includes many proverbs similar to those of the biblical wisdom tradition as well as some fables reminiscent of the those in Judg 9:8–15 and 2 Kgs 14:9b. In addition, connections with the biblical book of Proverbs can be detected.[14] The proverbs of Aḥiqar can therefore be classified as an example of the international wisdom tradition of the ancient Near East.

5.2.1. Aḥiqar at Elephantine

The fact that the earliest extant manuscript of the Sayings of Aḥiqar, the ome from Elephantine, contains both the tale and the wisdom collection indicates that they were intended to be read and understood together. It should be noted that Aḥiqar is not a Yahwistic or Jewish text; it represents a more general ancient Near Eastern wisdom. The text is not what Porten supposed it to be: armchair literature for leisure reading.[15] In Elephantine it was most probably used as a school text for the training of scribes and officials of all local ethnic groups.[16] Documents from Elephantine demonstrate that there was a multitude of scribes who wrote the accounts and letters. These scribes came from a variety of ethnic groups. It is safe to assume that on the island the Persians had established a scribal school in order to train local scribes. That Aḥiqar had been on the program can only be assumed. This assumption is, however, reinforced by the number of copies uncovered at Elephantine. Among the already published documents is a heavily damaged copy in three columns whose text parallels a section of the Aḥiqar narrative,[17] and in the boxes of not yet published documents from Elephantine, now in the Ägyptisches Museum in Berlin, a few fragments of Aḥiqar are present, some of them being duplicates.[18] The aim of using Aḥiqar as a school text was not only didactic but also political. As has been argued by Ann-Kristin Wigand, the text was used to communicate a pro-Persian ideology of loyalty.[19]

13. Kottsieper, *Die Sprache der Ahiqarsprüche*, esp. 241–46; Folmer, *Aramaic Language*, 732–40; Kratz, "*Mille Ahiqar*," 47; Wigand, "Politische Loyalität und religiöse Legitimierung"; but challenged by Niehr, *Aramäischer Aḥiqar*, 14; and nuanced by Granerød, *Dimensions of Yahwism*, 309–11. As a *curiosum*, I mention the view of Parpola, "Retroterra Assiro di Ahiqar," 91–112, who proposed that the influential Neo-Assyrian queen mother Zakutu was the author of Achiqar; see also Oshima, "How 'Mesopotamian' Was Ahiqar the Wise?"

14. See Weigl, *Die aramäischen Achikar-Sprüche*.

15. Porten, *Archives*, 263. Already Anneler, *Zur Geschichte der Juden von Elephantine*, 65–66, suggested that the text was not of Jewish origin.

16. Thus Niehr, *Aramäischer Aḥiqar*, 23; C. Mitchell, "Berlin Papyrus P. 13447," 146–47.

17. Sachau Plates 40 = *TADAE* C1.1; see Niehr, *Aramäischer Aḥiqar*, 6–7.

18. Oral communication by Verena Lepper and James Moore, Berlin.

19. Wigand, "Politische Loyalität und religiöse Legitimierung."

5.2.2. Ideology in Aḥiqar

5.2.2.1. A Narrative on the Power of Retribution

The narrative circles around two themes: loyalty and retribution. Loyalty toward the court is the basic attitude that is assumed for courtiers, advisors, sages, and scribes.[20] Lack of loyalty can lead to removal from the court and its assets or to the death of the disloyal servant. Even a rumor about possible disloyalty can be fatal, as Aḥiqar discovered. Three times this theme is narrated in the Aḥiqar story. When Nadin is installed as scribe and advisor, Aḥiqar utters the wish "May he seek the good [*for me*]."[21] But Nadin soon started telling bad things about Aḥiqar, and the king, believing the gossip, sentNabušumiškun to kill Aḥiqar. Aḥiqar reminded Nabušumiškun that he had once fallen from grace and that Aḥiqar had saved his life. At the end of the story, it is Nadin who has to fear for his life. The theme of loyalty to the king is subtly intertwined with the theme of solidarity among scribes and advisors.[22] The narrator quite frankly reports the subversive actions of Aḥiqar and Nabušumiškun in protecting each other from the wrath of the king and deceiving him by presenting a dead body as if it were the body of the disloyal sage. The story shows how scribes and advisors needed to carefully maneuver between various interests and negotiate their loyalties toward the king and their peers at court; similarly the scribes in Elephantine needed to carefully balance their loyalty to Persian power with their ethnic loyalty.[23]

Recompense is another other important theme in the Aḥiqar novella. The concept of recompense refers to the religious and philosophical idea that human acts are never without consequence or effect, that good deeds will be rewarded and bad deeds punished: "that all good things come to those who make them happen."[24] In the story of Aḥiqar, this is exemplified in the reciprocity that Aḥiqar and Nabušumiškun provide each other.[25] It is even phrased with words reminiscent of the golden rule: "Now, you, just as I did for you, do for me."[26] The scribes in Elephantine who were reading and rewriting this text were presented a fine example of the principle *do ut des* (I give so that you may give).

20. See also Kratz, "*Mille Ahiqar*," 45–46.

21. Aḥiqar II 24.

22. See also Kuhrt, "Achaemenid Concept of Kingship," 156–60.

23. See Bledsoe, "Conflicting Loyalties."

24. See, e.g., Janowski, "Die Tat kehrt zum Täter zurück," 247–71; Kratz, "*Mille Ahiqar*," 45; Zaibert, *Punishment and Retribution*.

25. Kratz, "Achiqar and Bisitun," argues that in the Achiqar-narrative a "pre-cursor of the golden rule expressed in narrative form" is to be found, see Bledsoe, "Conflicting Loyalties," 34.

26. Aḥiqar IV 51–52; see Granerød, *Dimensions of Yahwism*, 317–18; this moral code to treat the other as you yourself would like to have been treated, is an almost universal element in moral reflections, see the essays in Neusner and Chilton, *Golden Rule*; Gensler, *Ethics and the Golden Rule*; Kratz, "*Mille Ahiqar*," 58.

5.2.2.2. *Wisdom as an Education in Loyalty and Modesty*

The proverbs in the Sayings of Aḥiqar promote the values of loyalty, prudence, modesty, and adaptation.[27] This might imply that the educated and upper classes of the various ethnic and/or religious groups in Elephantine were trained in a lifestyle and a worldview characterized by the acceptance of Persian power and an openness to negotiate identity with the "other." I will present a selection of such sayings below.

Loyalty to the king and his representatives is an important feature in the saying[28] "Do not ignore the word of a king; let it be healing [for] your [heart]."[29] With Porten and Yardeni, I construe the verb *ksh*—literally, "to cover"—to mean "ignore" here.[30] Hiding or veiling the word of a superior made it powerless. In the next lines, the advice to not ignore the king is elaborated: "Sweet is the word of the king, (but also) sharper and stronger than a double-edged knife."[31] To avoid harm to himself, a servant best executes the command eagerly. Royal rage is also portrayed in this saying as swifter than lightning. The section closes with a warning in the form of a rhetorical question: "[H]ow can wood contest with fire, flesh with a knife, man with a k[ing]?"[32]

Another value expressed in the sayings is modesty. One of the proverbs advises verbal discretion and hence trustworthiness:

> A good vessel cover[s] a word in its heart,
> but one th[at] is broken let it go outside.[33]

The scribe and the royal servant are proverbially compared to a vessel. Vessels are easily broken when not handled correctly. The readers are warned against greed: "[Do not multiply] wealth and do not lead astray the heart."[34] Although

27. See also Folmer, "De Achikar Traditie," 73–83; Wigand, "Politische Loyalität und religiöse Legitimierung."

28. Granerød, *Dimensions of Yahwism*, 318–20.

29. Aḥiqar VI 6 (84); see Weigl, *Die aramäischen Achikar-Sprüche*, 110–16, who refers to some parallels from the biblical book of Proverbs; Kratz, " *Mille Ahiqar*," 49–51; Wigand, " 'Politische Loyalität und religiöse Legitimierung," 132–33.

30. Porten and Yardeni, *TADAE* C, 37; Kottsieper, *Die Sprache der Ahiqarsprüche*, 210; *pace*: *ANET* 428; Lindenberger, *Aramaic Proverbs of Ahiqar*, 85.

31. Aḥiqar VI 6 (84); Wigand, "Politische Loyalität und religiöse Legitimierung," 132–33.

32. Aḥiqar VI 15 (92); see Lindenberger, *Aramaic Proverbs of Ahiqar*, 87–88; Weigl, *Die aramäischen Achikar-Sprüche*, 152–57; Wigand, "Politische Loyalität und religiöse Legitimierung," 133–34.

33. Aḥiqar VI 16 (93); Lindenberger, *Aramaic Proverbs of Ahiqar*, 95; Weigl, *Die aramäischen Achikar-Sprüche*, 185–90, who refers to a parallel in Sir 21:14: "A fool, on the other hand, has a mind like a jar with a hole in it; anything he learns is soon lost."

34. Aḥiqar IX 51 (137); Lindenberger, *Aramaic Proverbs of Ahiqar*, 134; Weigl, *Die aramäischen Achikar-Sprüche*, 318–20.

the Aramaic noun *ḥyl* can also refer to "(military) power," in parallelism with the noun *lbb*, "heart," in the sense of inner-empathy, the meaning "wealth" is to be preferred.[35] The parallelism hints at modesty: too many earthly possessions will lead one away from one's tasks and from empathy. The value of modesty is indirectly promoted in the following broken section:

> With one who is more exalted than you
> do not make [. . .]
> With one who is more impu[dent] and mightier than you
> ⸢do not . . .⸣.[36]

This implies that a servant always has to be aware of his position in the fabric of society. A clearer invitation to modesty is found in the following saying: "Do not consider what is too great."[37]

The theme of retribution also occurs frequently, mainly as a warning not to act desperately in bad times or take revenge.[38] A beautiful example is:

> If the wicked seizes the corners of your garment,
> leave (it) in his hand.
> Then submit to Shamash.
> He [will] take his and give it to you.[39]

The servant reading this text is clearly warned not to take revenge but to seek the favor of the righteous sun god. In the context of legal procedures, the act of seizing the garment of a superior is an expression of humility. An indicted person could, by grabbing the garment of a judicial officer, express his subservience and acclaim presence in the courtroom. The saying advises one not to obstruct an accused person from doing this but to bring the case before the god of righteousness.[40]

35. See Lindenberger, *Aramaic Proverbs of Ahiqar*, 134; Weigl, *Die aramäischen Achikar-Sprüche*, 318–19.

36. Aḥiqar X 58–59 (142–44); Weigl, *Die aramäischen Achikar-Sprüche*, 349–58; Ayali-Darshan, "Sequence of Sir 4:26–27," 441–43; it is tempting to fill in the gaps and construe the remark in the following line that the "other" will add your portion to his possessions as a punishment of immodesty.

37. Aḥiqar X 62 (147); with Niehr, *Aramäischer Aḥiqar*, 48, contra *TADAE* C, 45; the saying is reminiscent of Ps 131:1: "I do not concern myself with great matters or things too wonderful for me"; see Weigl, *Die aramäischen Achikar-Sprüche*, 360–65.

38. Granerød, *Dimensions of Yahwism*, 315–16,

39. Aḥiqar VII 27 (107–8); Lindenberger, *Aramaic Proverbs of Ahiqar*, 174–75; Weigl, *Die aramäischen Achikar-Sprüche*, 243–47; Granerød, *Dimensions of Yahwism*, 316.

40. See Stone, "Grasping the Fringe (Part 1)," 36–47; *pace* Weigl, *Die aramäischen Achikar-Sprüche*, 245, who interprets the phrase as the expression of a *Loyalitätsgestus*.

A clear example of retribution is the following saying:

If good goes out from the mouth of [a] pe⸢rson⸣
  […]
And if bad goes out fr⸢om⸣ their mouth.
  gods will make it bad for them,
but when the eyes of the gods are on a person
  […].[41]

Although the text is broken, both positive and negative retributions are implied here. Michael Weigl, for instance, augments that "then it is good" should be read in the last line between the brackets. In doing so, a nice parallelism with "to make it bad" is present.[42] This augmentation is supported by the comparative material, for instance:

Trouble pursues the sinner,
  but the righteous are rewarded with good things.[43]

For a scribe at Elephantine this double saying functions as a warning to be careful what one says.

The final aspect I want to call attention to is the desired attitude of a servant toward a superior. This is spelled out in a section of which only a few lines have remained. Quite readable is the saying:

If your master will deposit water (with) you to guard (it),
  [do not] drink […][44]

This saying expresses the idea that reasonability pays off.[45] To the scribes and servants in Elephantine this would have meant that they should not abuse goods entrusted to them by a superior for their own interests.

41. Aḥiqar XI 82 (171–72); Lindenberger, *Aramaic Proverbs of Ahiqar*, 113; Weigl, *Die aramäischen Achikar-Sprüche*, 422–30; Granerød, *Dimensions of Yahwism*, 315; note the thematic parallel with Ps 141:3: "Set a guard over my mouth, YHWH; keep watch over the door of my lips"; and Sir 22:27: "Who will put a guard on my mouth and an effective seal upon my lips so that I don't fall because of my speech and so that my tongue doesn't destroy me?"; see Weigl, *Die aramäischen Achikar-Sprüche*, 91–92.

42. Weigl, *Die aramäischen Achikar-Sprüche*, 422–23.

43. Prov 13:21.

44. Aḥiqar XIII 99 (191); Weigl, *Die aramäischen Achikar-Sprüche*, 513–15.

45. Weigl, *Die aramäischen Achikar-Sprüche*, 513–15.

5.2.3. Conclusion on the Sayings of Aḥiqar

The above analysis reinforces the view of Bledsoe that the Sayings of Aḥiqar functioned as a text communicating a morality of loyalty toward Persian power.[46] By reading and writing this text, the scribes at Elephantine internalized the idea that rebellion against Persia would lead to nothing other than one's ruination. In addition, Bledsoe makes an interesting remark on the wisdom character of the text. According to him, both the narrative and the proverbs contain a deeper meaning. Although the king is supposed to be the source of justice, the text is aware of the inscrutable fickleness of rulers. Bledsoe reads this theme in light of the daily practice in Persian-occupied Egypt, in which good behavior was no guarantee for royal favor.

By way of an example, he refers to the parable of the bear and the lambs:

> The bear went to [the] lamb[s]
> and said "Come here and I will be quiet."
> The lambs answered and said to him
> "Carry away what you [will] carry from us
> We [. . .]."
> For it is not in the hands of a per⌜son⌝
> (to) lift their feet and put them down
> apart from the gods.
> For it is not in your hands to lift your foot
> to put it down.[47]

The bear in this parable can be read as a reference to higher powers, while the sheep symbolize the audience and readership of the Sayings of Aḥiqar: scribes and servants under Persian rule. The point of the parable is that the sheep can only acquiesce in the fate brought by the capricious longing of the leaders for more and more.[48] The message of Aḥiqar seems to be that there is futility in resisting the king, and that a wise scribe or servant must maneuver between the tides of royal fickleness.

Ann-Kristin Wigand has made an important observation on the composition of the Aramaic in this text. In her view, the character of the Aramaic of

46. Bledsoe, "Conflicting Loyalties"; Kratz, "'*Mille Ahiqar*,'" 52; Wigand, "Politische Loyalität und religiöse Legitimierung."

47. Aḥiqar XI 81 (168–71); text added with Weigl, *Die aramäischen Achikar-Sprüche*, 416; see Niehr, *Aramäischer Aḥiqar*, 49; Granerød, *Dimensions of Yahwism*, 313–14.

48. Bledsoe, "Conflicting Loyalties," 261–62; see also Weigl, *Die aramäischen Achikar-Sprüche*, 416–21.

the sayings indicates that the kernel of that part must have been older than the narrative that is written in the Imperial Aramaic of the Persian period. She then assumes that in the Persian period the sayings were redacted by including some sections that have to do with the theme of the "loyalty to the king." In the same redaction, or shortly thereafter, the narrative was added in order to function as a hermeneutical key to help the scribes such as those at Elephantine understand the sayings and to read them through the lens of loyalty.[49]

5.3. The Function of the Aramaic Version of the Bisitun Inscription[50]

After he had consolidated his rule over Persia, Darius I erected a monumental inscription accompanied by images at the slopes of Mount Bisitun in the present-day Iranian province of Kermanshah.[51] The images are a clear expression of the overwhelming power the Persian king had over once-rebellious people. Viewing the rock relief must have left an impression on all his subjects. Darius I is placed at the intersection of the horizontal and vertical axes. On the vertical axis the king is between the good god Ahura Mazda and the evil rebel Gaumāta. The deity looks benevolently toward the king. On the horizontal axis he stands between two heroic Persian soldiers and a group of defeated rebels in chains representing the various regions that rebelled. The inscriptions surrounding the images contain a text in three languages: Old Persian, Elamite, and Babylonian.[52]

The inscription consists of two parts. After a short autobiography in which Darius claims to be a descendant of Achaemenes,[53] it narrates in great length and in many details the suppresion of Gaumāta's revolt and the successful campaigns of the Persian king against a great variety of rebellious subjects who had been supporters of "the lie."[54] The inscription ends with a series of blessing for all those who will be loyal to the king.[55] The message of the inscription is clear:

49. Wigand, "Politische Loyalität und religiöse Legitimierung."

50. Opening words of the Old Persian version of the Bisitun inscription: *Adam Dârayavauš xšâyathiya vazraka xšâyathiya xšâyathiy*, "I am Darius, the great king, king of kings"; Darius I DB § 1; translation: Kuhrt, *Persian Empire*, 141.

51. Old Persian Bagastana means "the abode of the gods/divine"; for the ideology of the inscription, see Lincoln, *Religion, Empire, and Torture*.

52. On trilinguaism in Achaemenid texts, see Finn, "Gods, Kings, Men," 219–75. A copy in Babylonian was found along the procession-way in Babylon; two fragments: BE 3627 and Bab. 41446; see Seidl, "Ein Monument Darius I," 101–14.

53. Darius I DB § 1–5; translation: Kuhrt, *Persian Empire*, 141.

54. Darius I DB § 6–58; translation: Kuhrt, *Persian Empire*, 141–48. "The lie" is a demonising reference to Gaumāta.

55. Darius I DB § 59–75; translation: Kuhrt, *Persian Empire*, 148–51; the language of "blessings and curses" is probably an echo of the Neo-Assyrian treaty terminology.

thanks to the favor of Ahura Mazda, the great god, Darius righteously rules the world.[56] He is to be seen as the center of the earthly realm, the one to whom all nations have been rendered subservient. A rebellion against this king will be futile and pointless in view of the powers of Darius I and the divine support for his deeds.

5.3.1. Bisitun at Elephantine

A copy in Aramaic of Darius's Bisitun inscription was found in Elephantine.[57] This text was—like the Sayings of Aḥiqar—presumably used for scribal education.[58] In reading and writing this text, the intelligentsia from Elephantine coming from a variety of ethnic and/or religious groups were trained in Persian imperial ideology, especially in the idea that revolting against the central power was futile. One way or another, they had integrated this ideology within their own identity, as can be proven by the fact that the Yehudites and the other ethnicities never revolted against Persian power or cooperated with Egyptians in their struggle for independence.

The Bisitun inscription from Elephantine is written on papyrus. The text is rather damaged, but a few things are clear. Generally, the text follows the order of the Old Persian and Elamite source texts. The text can be seen as an accurate and grammatically sound translation into Imperial Aramaic. Nevertheless, a few differences may be observed.

5.3.1.1. Variants

The most important difference is that the Elephantine version is not illustrated. The text is not accompanied by the impressive image of Darius known from the Bisitun rock-inscription. The Aramaic text hence lacks the multimodality of the original inscription.[59] It is in this strictly textual form, more subtle than the monumental Bisitun inscription, that it became part of the scribal culture. The reader is not compelled to read it in the context of an impressive visual portrayal of a victorious Persian king, but is left to form his own mental image

Another important difference is the insertion of a passage toward the end of the Aramaic version:

56. See Granerød, "By the Favour of Ahuramazda," 455–80.

57. *TADAE* C2.1; Greenfield and Porten, *Bisitun Inscription of Darius the Great*; see also Mitchell, "Berlin Papyrus P. 13447," 139–41; Wigand, "'Politische Loyalität und religiöse Legitimierung," 141–46.

58. See Mitchell, "Berlin Papyrus P. 13447," 146–47.

59. On this concept, see Bateman, *Multimodality and Genre*; Bonfiglio, "Visualizing Literacy," 293–319; see also Finn, "Gods, Kings, Men."

> [Darius, the king, thus says: Whoever yo]u are, O king who will be after me, a man who lies [. . .] from great lies. Withdraw [. . .] A li[a]r who lies [. . .] make known how you are made and how your conduct is. ⸢. . . *in*⸣ your e⸢a⸣r one may say. Hear what one would in public. ⸢. . . d⸣o. What a poor man will do. Moreover before you [. . .] your well-being be remiss. Your [. . .] not what I did. To [. . .] you do not hide this. Ahura Mazda will bl⸢ess you . . . ab⸣undant and your days will be long-lasting. But if you do not conceal it, Ahura Mazda will ⸢curse . . .⸣.[60]

Porten and others construe this insertion as a paraphrase of a text on royal qualities that is found in two virtually identical copies—one on the tomb of Darius I at Naqsh-i Rustam and the other in the vicinity of Persepolis ascribed to Xerxes.[61] This piece of royal propaganda praises the moral and bodily qualities of the Persian king, who is wise, righteous, and strong. The king does not act whimsically; he is in control: "What things develop in my anger, I hold firmly under control by my thinking power. I am firmly ruling over my own impulses."[62] This line is probably more propagandistic in character than a reflection of reality. The Darius text ends with a few lines that are not present in the Xerxes text:

> Young man, make in a large measure known of what kind you are, which are your gifts, of what kind your conduct is. Let not that seem best to you which one whispers in your ear. Rather, listen to what is said openly.
> Young man, let not that seem very good to you what the freeborn man does. Rather, look at what he who is not freeborn does.
> Young man, do not achieve your goal. Neither be unfitting in your prosperity.
> A negligent man will not prosper, and in his country he will not live.[63]

Although the insertion in the Aramaic Bisitun from Elephantine is a rather broken text and cannot be seen as a direct translation, the intertextual links with the

60. *TADAE* C2.1 XI 64–73.

61. *TADAE* C, 59; see also Greenfield and Porten, *Bisitun Inscription*, 5–16; Mitchell, "Berlin Papyrus P. 13447," 140. The texts referred to are DNb and XPl; translation: Kuhrt, *Persian Empire*, 503–5; Lecoq, *Inscriptions de la Perse achéménide*, 221–24.259–61; see Sims-Williams, "Final Paragraph of the Tomb-Inscription," 1–7; Wiesehofer, *Das antike Persien*, 43; Kuhrt, "Achaemenid Concept of Kingship"; Tavernier, "Achaemenid Royal Inscription," 161–76; Jonker, "Achaemenid Understanding of Law and Justice," 24–41.

62. DNb and XPl §2b.

63. DNb §9:50–60; translation according Tavernier, "Achaemenid Royal Inscription," 167; Mitchell, "Testament of Darius," 363–80; Wigand, "Politische Loyalität und religiöse Legitimierung," 145–46.

version at Naqsh-i Rustam are striking.[64] The insertion is rephrased and directed toward a successor of Darius I. To the people in and around Elephantine, it must have been clear that Darius II, then the ruling monarch, was meant. In line with the context of the final part of the Bisitun inscription, the ideology presented in this addition is the motif of good versus bad behavior: blessing for the loyal, but curse for the disloyal. According to Wigand, this addition functions as a hermeneutical clue in the Aramaic Bisitun: it presses the scribes at Elephantine to read the whole of the Bisitun inscription through the lens of loyalty.[65] To the people at Elephantine the message must have been clear: remain loyal to the successor of Darius.[66]

An interesting difference between the Aramaic on the one hand and the Old Persian, Elamite, and Babylonian versions on the other is found in the treatment of the month names in table 7.[67] The Old Persian and Elamite calendars had been in use in what is now Iran from the dawn of the local civilization up to the middle of the fifth century BCE. The calendars were based on the lunar cycle and served the agricultural year through a system of intercalation based on the solar cycle.[68] It is intriguing to see that in the Elamite version of the Bisitun inscription uses Persian month names and not the traditional Elamite names. This adaptation is a sign of cultural dependency. By the middle of the fifth century BCE, the Old Persian calendar faded away due to assimilation to the Babylonian culture.[69] In view of internal communication and trade relations, the adaptation of the Babylonian calendar was a logical step in the construction of the Persian Empire.[70]

The Aramaic month names were—like the Israelite and Phoenician names—adopted from the Babylonian system.[71] This implies two things. First, the Babylonian/Aramaic calendar system was an international phenomenon in the fifth century. It is therefore impossible to construe these month names in the Elephantine version of Bisitun as purely Yehudite and restricting the readership of the

64. The Aramaic adverb *prtr*, "openly," in line 54 is clearly a loan from Old Persian *paratar*, "openly."

65. Wigand, "'Politische Loyalität und religiöse Legitimierung," 145–46.

66. See Mitchel, "Testament of Darius," 363; Jonker, "Achaemenid Understanding of Law and Justice," 25.

67. Only names that are present in the Aramaic text are listed; Lecoq, *Inscriptions de la Perse achéménide*, 190, notes Du'ūzu as a variant in the Aramaic of DB §11; this section, however, has no counterpart in the Elephantine text; Lecoq probably was confused by the Babylonian version; the Aramaic version most probably is a translation of the Babylonian text, see Mitchell, "Berlin Papyrus P. 13447," 140; Kosmin, "New Hypothesis," 1–10, recently supposed that one of the functions of the Bisitun inscription was its synchronization of the Persian and Babylonian calendars.

68. See Stern, *Calendars in Antiquity*, 170–74.

69. Stern, *Calendars in Antiquity*, 174.

70. On the Babylonian calendar, see Stern, *Calendars in Antiquity*, 71–123.

71. Porten, "Calendar of Aramaic Texts," 13–32; Stern, "Babylonian Calendar," 159–71.

TABLE 7. Months Names in the Various Versions of the Bisitun Inscription

Text	Old Persian	Elamite	Babylonian	Aramaic
§27	Thûravâhara	Thurvarna	Ayyāru	*ʾyr*; Iyyar[a]
§28	Thâigarca	Thaigarrizisna	Simānu	*sywn*; Siwan[b]
§30	Thûravâhara	Thurvarna	Ayyaru	*ʾyr*; Iyyar[c]
§38	Âçiyâdiya	Hašiyatiyaš	Kislīmu	*kslw*; Kislew[d]
§41	Thûravâhara	Thurvarna	Ayyāru	*ʾyr*; Iyyar[e]
§42	Garmapada	Garmapada	Du'ūzu	*t*[*mwz*]; Iyyar[f]
§45	Anâmaka	Hanamakaš	Ṭebētu	[*ṭbt*]; Thebet[g]

[a]*TADAE* C2.1 V 13.
[b]*TADAE* C2.1 V 16; addition by Porten and Yardeni probably based on the Babylonian version.
[c]*TADAE* C2.1 V 22.
[d]*TADAE* C2.1 VII 33.
[e]*TADAE* C2.1 VII 43; addition by Porten and Yardeni probably based on the Babylonian version.
[f]*TADAE* C2.1 VII 46; addition by Porten and Yardeni probably based on the Babylonian version.
[g]*TADAE* C2.1 VII 56; addition by Porten and Yardeni probably based on the Babylonian version.

text to Yehudites alone.[72] All the other ethnic groups must have been familiar with this naming of the months. Second, the use of Babylonian-derived month names in the Elephantine version of Bisitun can be read as a sign of communality between the various ethnic groups.

Within the broader scope of the Aramaic documents from Elephantine, two calendars are in use: the Babylonian and the native Egyptian.[73] Many documents use both dating systems side by side, indicating that the Persians adopted to local customs.[74]

The Aramaic Bisitun text from Elephantine contains other minor differences. A few might be attributed to writing errors by a novice scribe. In §38 the revolt of the province Margiana is narrated.[75] The Aramaic text, however, reads [. . .]*prtw*, "Parthia," probably influenced by *bprtw*, "in Parthia," in §37.[76] In the Old Persian text, §40 opens with "King Darius says: A certain man named Vahyazdâta dwelt in a city called Târavâ in a district in Persia called Vautiyâ." The personal name Vahyazdâta is rendered in the Aramaic version as *wydzt*,

72. Stern, "Babylonian Calendar."
73. Stern, "Babylonian Calendar."
74. Botta, *Aramaic and Egyptian Legal Traditions*.
75. Margiana, Old Persian *marguš*, was a region within the Bactrian satrapy. It was situated in present-day Turkmenistan around the oasis of Merv.
76. *TADAE* C2.1 VII 30.

"Vahyadazta,"[77] an error based on metathesis. The topographical name Târavâ is rendered as *prt*[*w*, "in Parth[ia," probably influenced by the preceding sections. In adition to these there are a few mistakes in numbers. §25 relates a campaign against rebels in Media. The Babylonian version has a supplement to the Old Persian text—"on the twenty-seventh day of the month Anamaka the battle was fought by them"—by reading "they killed 3,278 and took captive 4,329 alive."[78] The Aramaic version includes the addition but contains a scribal error by stating that 5,872 persons were killed.[79] In §27, on a campaign against Armenia, the Babylonian version has an addition: "They killed 546 and took 520 persons alive." The Aramaic version has rendered the number with 5,041 ⸢+5 ??? . . .⸣. Again, a scribal error can be assumed.[80] In §28, the Babylonian version has a comparable addition. This time, the Aramaic version correctly rendered the number of people killed as 472.[81] The same holds for the number 2,034 in the addition in §29, a campaign against Urartu. The Aramaic version left out Izala, the rather obscure location where the battle took place.[82] In §30, the Babylonian version has the addition "They killed 2,045 and took 1,558 persons alive." The Aramaic version renders: "They killed 2,046 and took 1,578 persons alive."[83] These simple writing errors underscore the hypothesis that the Aramaic Bisitun inscription was used in the training of local scribes.

5.3.1.2. Rebellious and Overpowered Satrapies

The Bisitun inscription is a display of the overpowering might of Darius. The language is probably hyperbolic at times, but the twofold ideology is clear: do not rebel against the power of Persia and remain loyal: then you will be blessed. It is interesting to have a look at the question of which of the various ethnic groups attested at Elephantine are also mentioned as rebellious in the Aramaic Bisitun text. It turns out that only the Medians/Magians are attested in both texts. Throughout the Aramaic Bisitun text, Gaumāta the Magian is mentioned as the archrebel. Specific mentions are found at §25 = *TADAE* C2.1 4.1–7, which relates a campaign against rebels in Media, and §31 = *TADAE* C2.1 1.25–28, which relates a campaign against rebels in Media. The fact that only Medians are mentioned can be seen as a result of the poor preservation of the document.

77. *TADAE* C2.1 VII 36.
78. See Kuhrt, *Persian Empire*, 154.
79. *TADAE* C2.1 IV 6.
80. *TADAE* C2.1 V 13, Kuhrt, *Persian Empire*, 154.
81. *TADAE* C2.1 V 17.
82. *TADAE* C2.1 V 19–21; on the toponym Izala, see Radner, "How to Reach the Upper Tigris," 273–305.
83. *TADAE* C2.1 V 23.

In the Old Persian, Elamite, and Babylonian versions, two other ethnic groups present at Elephantine are mentioned: Babylonians (§§18–20; 50) and Egyptians (§21). The other groups are not labeled as inimical in the Bisitun inscription. This does not imply that they had always been loyal, however.

The mention of all the rebels from all corners of the Persian Empire must have left a clear impression on the scribes at Elephantine. In combination with the insertion mentioned above on "blessing" and "curse," a moral code of loyalty toward the Persian power was imprinted on them that probably generated a sense of solidarity with the other ethnic groups.

5.3.2. *Conclusion on the Aramaic Bisitun Text*

Different from the Sayings of Aḥiqar but with the same aim, the Aramaic text of the Bisitun inscription functioned as a means of controlling the minds of the peoples who were settled at Elephantine and its environs.[84]

5.3.3. *The Bandakas Were What They Read and Wrote*

The Old Persian version of the Bisitun inscription refers to the concept of *bandaka*. Unfortunately, the sections that contain that word are absent in the Aramaic version from Elephantine due to the condition of the papyrus. The concept of *bandaka* is a reference to an obedient servant who acts in favor of Persian power.[85] The scribes at Elephantine were "reading with their pen."[86] In doing so they inscribed themselves as *bandakas* of Persian power. This belief system was then controlled by the law and the presence of the Persian army.

The famous dictum "you are what you read" is attributed to Oscar Wilde. Whether that attribution is correct or not, it is obviously true that what people read not only tells much about who people are but also indicates that our belief systems are molded and formed by what we read. Social-science studies have made clear that what people read is formative for their opinions, as books, magazines, internet reports, and newspapers can lead but also mislead.[87]

84. See also Granerød, *Dimensions of Yahwism*, 320–23; Wigand, "Politische Loyalität und religiöse Legitimierung."

85. See, e.g., Herrenschmidt, "Designation de l'empire," 33–65. This concept stands in the background of the remark in Neh 9:36–37, where the postexilic community construes themselves as "servants," see Mitchell, "Achaemenid Persian Concepts," 291–306.

86. I adopted this phrase from Mertens, "Lezen met de pen," 187–200 ("reading with the pen").

87. See, e.g., Becnel and Moeller, "What, Why, and How They Read," 299–307; Davis, "Moving Beyond the Single Mediated Arena Model," 167–86; Leung, Wong, and Farver, "You Are What You Read."

5.4. Law

As part of the Egyptian satrapy, Elephantine fell under Persian law. Unfortunately, not much is known about the character of their legal system or the specifics of their regulations. A canonized Persian law has not been found. Interestingly, on the recto of the Demotic Chronicle is a narrative that describes how Darius I, after taking control over Egypt, took measures concerning the legal system in Egypt:

> He wrote to his satrap in Egypt in year 3, saying:
>
> > Have them bring to me the scholars [. . .] among the soldiers, priests, and scribes of Egypt [. . .]. They are to write the law of Egypt from the olden days until year 44 of Pharaoh[88]
>
> [. . .]
>
> He wrote matters [. . .] in the manner (?) of the code of Egypt.[89] They wrote a copy in Assyrian writing and in documentary writing.[90]

I will not enter into the debate whether this text could be used as an argument for or against a Persian *Reichsautorisation* (imperial authorization). The text clearly is a piece of propaganda conveying the good intentions of the Persian king and stresses the idea of continuity between his rule and that of his predecessors. The absence of concrete regulations and the qualifier "in the manner (?) of the law of Egypt" might be seen as indications that Darius I kneaded the traditional Egyptian law into a pro-Persian mold.[91]

That the Persianized Egyptian system was in operation can be concluded from the fact that various Aramaic texts from Elephantine refer to a *dyn*, "judge."[92] Two judges are mentioned by name: (1) Damidata who presided over the cadastral quarrel between Dargamana and Mahseiah.[93] (2) A "⌈. . . *Pi*⌉sina, the judge" is referred to in a letter asking for the transport of money and goods to Memphis.[94] Although the letter is incomplete, it can be deduced from the

88. Probably Ahmose.

89. With Nims, "Term Hp, 'Law, Right,'" 243–60, I construe the Demotic word *hp* as a reference not to civil law but as referring to the "the code accepted within a group."

90. Demotic Chronicle, ed. Spiegelberg, *Die sogenannte demotische Chronik*, recto C:1–16; translation Kuhrt, *Persian Empire*, 125. "Assyrian writing" being Aramaic and "documentary writing" Demotic, see Kuhrt, *Persian Empire*, 126; Lee, *Authority and Authorization of Torah*, 56–71.

91. Rohrmoser, *Götter, Tempel und Kult*, 50–52.

92. *TADAE* B2.2:13; 2.3:24; 3.1:13.19; 3.2:6; 3.12:28; 4.6:14; 5.1:12; 8.4:2; 8.10:2

93. *TADAE* B2.2; see Botta, *Aramaic and Egyptian Legal Traditions*, 124–26; see §4.6 above.

94. *TADAE* A3.8; see van der Toorn, "Previously, at Elephantine," 266–67; van der Toorn, *Becoming Diaspora Jews*, 128–36. Pisina is also mentioned in the letters *TADAE* A3.6 and A4.2, where he is not presented as a judge.

personal names in it that it was part of inner-Yehudite communication. In the letter it is stated that an amount of ten karsh of silver was paid by the Yehudites to [*Pi*]sina. The context of the letter is unclear. Van der Toorn argues unconvincingly that the letter should be read in the context of the theft of a *'bnṣrp*, "precious stone."[95] Various contracts show that a common sense of law was present, apparently accepted by all ethnic groups. Botta has argued that the majority of the legal decisions are based on local Egyptian legal traditions.[96] He is able to trace various legal formulas back to Egyptian legal practice. Some formulas—such as *ṭyb lbby*, "my heart was satisfied"—have a Mesopotamian background. Although Botta is right in stating that there has been more Egyptian influence in the legal practice than thought before,[97] the more general impression of the legal practice in Achaemenid Egypt is that of a world power applying generally accepted legal ideas and adapting them to local circumstances.[98]

How the law functioned in a specific case can be seen in the following letter written by Arshamesh, the Persian satrap, to Artavant,[99] the commander of the garrison, asking for the punishment of eight slaves belonging to Ankhoḥapi who ran away from their master:

> From Aršama to Artavanta. I send you (wishes for) much peace and strength! And [now]: (he) whose name is [Ps]amšek, son of ʿA(n)khoḥap[i], my servant, has complained in this (place). He says thus:
>
> > When I was coming [t]o [my] lord ⸢... the sla⸣ves of ʿA(n)khoḥapi my father whom I [was bringing (?)] after me to my lord, (who were): (he) whose name is Psamšekḥasi [son of PN, 1; PN, son of PN]TWY, 1; ʿA(n)khoḥapi, son of P[šenpe]berekhef, 1; Aḥer[ṭais, son of Psamšek, 1; Pšubaste, son of Ḥor[i, 1; PN, son of Tja]ḥapiemou, 1; Psamšek, son of Waḥpreʿmakhi, 1; [PN]Y, son of Waḥ[preʿ, 1.]
> >
> > (In) all, 8 men. They took my goods and fled from me. Now, if it (seems) good to my lord, let (word) be sent to Artavanta (that) [when] those [slaves] I shall present before him, the punishment that I shall order for them, it shall be done to them.
>
> Now, Aršama says [thus]:
>
> > That [P]samše[kḥasi] and his companions, the slaves of ʿA(n)khoḥapi, whom P[s]amšek shall present before you th[ere], you are to order the

95. See *TADAE* A4.3. I will argue below why van der Toorn's argument is unconvincing (see §6.1.2).

96. Botta, *Aramaic and Egyptian Legal Traditions*.

97. Muffs, *Studies in the Aramaic Legal Papyri*, 2003; Yaron, *Introduction to the Law*.

98. This is corroborated by the analysis of Simonson, "Demotic Parallel," 242–64, who concluded that Aramaic term *hnṣl* is equal to Demotic *ṯy*.

99. On this Iranian named person, see Fried, *Priest and the Great King*, 89–90.

> punishment that Psamšek shall [issue] for them (as) an order to carry out; that (punishment) shall be done to them.[100]

This document makes clear that a disruption of the fabric of society was not acceptable.

The law—as controlled by the Persians—functioned as a mechanism for adjudicating local disputes on land tenure, commodities, and marriage contracts. As such, the system contributed to the mutual acceptance of the various ethnic groups. It even stimulated it.

5.5. Military

The Persian had invaded and occupied Egypt by military force. The Aramaic documents from Elephantine witness the presence of a Persian-led military force on and around the island.[101] It can be assumed that this military presence was to be found throughout Egypt, though primarily concentrated in the border regions. The purpose of the Persian military presence was twofold: to guarantee Persian rule and to safeguard Persian trade interests. The documents from Elephantine do not relate military conflicts. This does not indicate that there were no such conflicts or that the military presence was wholly sufficient to avoid all sorts of strife. This would be too peaceful an image. There were Egyptian struggles for independence and at times fierce Persian military reaction, as I will discuss in chapter 7.

5.6. An Inadequate Analogy

The three mechanisms of control discussed in this chapter—an ideology imprinted through scribal education, a locally adapted international law, and the presence of the military—were all instrumental to keeping the *pax persica*. In the end, all this led to a multiethnic population that was loyal to Persian rule and capable of a solidarity that crossed the boundaries of ethnicity.

Historical analogies are always dangerous and delicate, since the circumstances between two or more cultural systems never fully align. Next to elements that are comparable stand features that are fundamentally different. Nevertheless, I would like to propose an analogy with postwar Yugoslavia.[102]

100. *TADAE* A6.3.

101. On the organisation of the Persian military presence at Elephantine, see Rohrmoser, *Götter, Tempel und Kult*, 47–49.

102. See, e.g., Carter, *Marshal Tito*; Hudson, *Breaking the South Slav Dream*; Rubinstein, *Yugoslavia and the Nonaligned World*.

In 1945, Josip Broz Tito became prime minister and later president of the Republic of Yugoslavia, helped by the Soviet Union and with the support of Western diplomatic and military forces. The Soviets wanted a communist nation within their sphere of influence, and the Western allies feared Balkanization, the fragmentation of a state or region into a multitude of rivaling nations. Tito ruled Yugoslavia with a smiling face and an iron fist. His ideology of the "third way" (nonalignment in the East-West rivalry)—present in every schoolbook written in the official Serbo-Croatian language but not in the local vernaculars—together with a fierce military presence held the country together. During Tito's reign, ethnic and religious diversity was suppressed. When he died in 1980, the country broke apart into seven independent nation-states, each with its own language, and the religious and ethnic differences exploded into violence.[103]

This analogy raises the question: To what degree was the gradual disappearance of Persian power a factor that led to the disintegration of interethnic solidarity at Elephantine? The next two chapters attempt to address this question. In chapter 6, I look for signs of this disintegration, and in chapter 7 I consider the reasons why the Persians withdrew from Egypt.

103. See, e.g., Borneman, *Death of the Father*; Ramet, *Balkan Babel.*

CHAPTER 6

Disruptions of the Interethnic Solidarity

THE *PAX PERSICA*, AS DESCRIBED in the previous chapters, was challenged and disrupted in the last twenty-five years of Persian hegemony over Egypt. In this chapter, I will discuss four incidents from Elephantine that give evidence of this process of dismantling.

6.1. A Stone of Contention

There is a slightly enigmatic letter written by Mauziah, son of Nathan, from Abydos, to the leaders of the Yehudite community at Elephantine.[1] The letter is not dated, but the mention of Vidranga, the garrison commander, dates the document to the final decades of the fifth century BCE. A cursory reading of the letter gives the impression that he was a Yehudite imprisoned in connection with the theft of a precious stone. For a better understanding, the letter must be set in context.

6.1.1. Compromised Trade

Recently, van der Toorn has offered an intriguing interpretation of the letter.[2] He places the letter just mentioned, A4.3, within the context of a small archive of letters all related to the same chain of events. He reads in these letters references to Yehudite trade operations that involved the alleged theft of the precious stone mentioned. The Egyptians used this theft to pit the Persians against the Yehudites and get them to punish the Yehudites with a heavy financial penalty: 120 karsh of silver. This amount is mentioned in letter A4.4, which van der Toorn sees as referring to a second investigation into the case of the stolen precious

1. *TADAE* A4.3.
2. Van der Toorn, "Previously," 255–70; van der Toorn, *Becoming Diaspora Jews*, 128–36.

stone.[3] The payment of the penalty would have finally settled the case. The other four letters would then—according to van der Toorn—give information on the diplomatic moves around the incident, the malicious role of Vidranga, and the acts of the Persian Pisina, probably the judge in this case. Van der Toorn offers a coherent picture of the chain of events. It could have happened this way, but I have my doubts.

Since the reconstruction of what happened does not impact the final point I would like to make in this section, I will not go into too much detail but only indicate a few weaknesses in his argument:

1. The six letters were not found together on the island, but at different spots, which makes it more difficult to construe them as a coherent archive.
2. Van der Toorn's argument relied on the assumption that there had been a Yehudite trading company of sorts stationed at Elephantine. In the known inscriptions, I do not see such a trading network. Although I do not exclude the possibility that some Yehudites participated in trade activities, I still think that their main task was in the military.
3. There is not a complete correspondence between the Yehudite names in the various letters.
4. Vidranga, mentioned in A4.3, does not occur elsewhere in the archive. Van der Toorn inserts the name into the letter from Hosea to his brother Pilṭi.[4] This addition, however, is a wild guess without any basis in the document.
5. In A4.3:4, the letter on the stolen stone, it is stated that the contested object was found *byd rkly*ʾ, "in the possession of the merchants/traders." Without argument, van der Toorn assumes that these traders were "Jewish traders."[5] An ethnic marker, however, is absent in the text, leaving open the possibility that Phoenician or Greek traders had been the evildoers.
6. The *ʾbnṣrp*, "precious stone," is only mentioned in A4.3, but never in one of the other documents. Even a stone of whatever sort does not occur in the other five letters.

Although I agree with van der Toorn that the document under consideration refers to conflicts arising between the Egyptians, on the one hand, and the

3. Van der Toorn, "Previously," 267–70; see, however, Becking, "Burglars, Diplomats, or Victims?," 223–28.

4. *TADAE* A3.6:2; see van der Toorn, "'Previously," 262.

5. Van der Toorn, "Previously," 259; I leave aside the question of the translation of the uncommon Aramaic noun *rkl*. Van der Toorn follows the traditional interpretation that connects this noun to Hebrew *rōkēl*, "trader." In my view a connection with *rkl* II, "to slander; lie in wait," should at least be considered.

Yehudites, seen by the Egyptians as footmen of the Persian oppressor, on the other,[6] I am not convinced by his proposal to read all six letters as a coherent archive. I will therefore present my view on the events based only on the document A4.3.

6.1.2. A Thick Description of a Compromising Theft

Based on the document, I offer the following "thick description" of the chain of events in this letter. Adopting ideas of the philosopher Gilbert Ryle, the cultural anthropologist Clifford Geertz coined the term "thick description" to describe a way of doing ethnography that goes beyond the mere presentation of human behavior by construing this behavior in its broader social, religious, cultural, and economic contexts, among others.[7] It should be noted that any thick description is an interpretation of human behavior and hence is open for criticism.

Mauziah was a Yehudite soldier from Elephantine.[8] His name occurs in several documents. He is, for instance, the scribe that drew up the contract between Ananiah, son of Haggai, and Zakkur, son of Meshullam.[9] He was the son of Nathan, son of Ananiah and Tamet, the Egyptian handmaiden.[10] He was also among those who signed the petition for the rebuilding of the temple of Yahô.[11]

One of the duties of these soldiers was to safeguard the caravans carrying tribute for the Persians.[12] When the caravan he escorted arrived at Abydos, north of Elephantine, Mauziah was arrested by Vidranga. A *ʾbnṣrp*, "precious stone,"[13] was stolen and found *byd rklyʾ*. The Aramaic noun *rkl* is traditionally construed as referring to merchants, connected to the Hebrew *rōkēl*, "trader."[14] In my view, an alternate connection with the Hebrew verb *rkl* II, "to slander; lie in wait," should at least be considered. This verb is attested twice in the Hebrew text of

6. See already Kaplan, "Sojourner in the Land," 410
7. Geertz, "Thick Description," 3–30.
8. The assumption by van der Toorn, "Previously," 256, and van der Toorn, *Becoming Diaspora Jews*, 129–30, that he was the "secretary-treasurer of the Jewish community" is not based on evidence.
9. *TADAE* B8.3.
10. *TADAE* B3.3; see §4.1.1–2 above with Porten, *Archives*, 205–13; Porten and Szubin, "Status of the Handmaiden Tamet," 43–64; Botta, *Aramaic and Egyptian Legal Traditions*, 59–87; Nutkowicz, *Destins de femmes*.
11. *TADAE* A.4.7=8; see Porten, *Archives*, 193.
12. As suggested by Porten, *Archives*, 41.
13. The noun is not easily understood. It is often rendered with "dyer's stone; dyed stone"; Porten, *Archives*, 41; *TADAE* A, 58; *DNSWI*, 976; van der Toorn, "Previously," 258, and van der Toorn, *Becoming Diaspora Jews*, 129. Since the Aramaic verb *ṣrp* refers to the act of purifying, it would be better to construe the item as a purified or precious stone probably of a red color.
14. As attested several times in Ezek 27.

Sirach, where it takes the meaning "decoy."[15] This opens the possibility that the precious stone was found in the possession of people who had been waiting in an ambush to attack the convoy. Either way the Aramaic noun is construed, the stone should have been in the hands of the caravan drivers. Vidranga arrested Mauziah probably on the accusation of either theft of the stone or negligence of his duties as a guardsman.[16] It is unknown whether Mauziah was found guilty or not. His arrest might well have been an act of anti-Yehudite behavior on the part of Vidranga. Perhaps indicative of this is Mauziah's outcry: "To you it is known that Khnum is against us since Hananiah has been in Egypt until now!"[17] Mauziah assumes that the leadership of the Yehudite community at Elephantine must have been aware that the priests of Khnum had taken an anti-Yehudite stance ever since Hananiah became in charge of Yehudite affairs under the satrap Arshames.[18] According to Ingo Kottsieper, the openly pro-Yehudite politics of the Persian administrator Hananiah irritated the Khnum priests. One of the pro-Yehudite actions of Hananiah is reflected in the so-called Passover Letter regulating a fixed date for an unmentioned Yehudite festival.[19]

Mauziah had friends in high places. Two Egyptians—Ḥori and Ṣeḥa, both servants of the high-ranked Anani—intervened on his behalf and negotiated his release. Freedom, however, has its price. That is the reason why Mauziah writes to the Yehudite leadership in Elephantine. Yedaniah, Uriah, and the priests of Yahô are asked to pay Ḥori and Ṣeḥa when they return to Elephantine. That payment will also help to maintain good relations with the local Persian authorities in Elephantine.

Reconstructing this situtation is admittedly a somewhat subjective exercise, given the limitations in our evidence, and some readers might prefer van der Toorn's interpretation over my own. It is clear, however, that by the end of the fifth century the interethnic relations in Elephantine were less friendly than before.

6.2. A Conflict Between Egyptians and Yehudites

Another letter, which van der Toorn attributes to a small archive of letters all related to the same chain of events, presents a conflict between Egyptians and

15. Sir 11:29–30.

16. See Fried, *Priest and the Great King*, 96–97.

17. *TADAE* A4.3:7; Kottsieper, "'Die Religionspolitik der Achämeniden," 154–55.

18. On Hananiah, see Porten, *Archives*, 130; Joisten-Pruschke, *Das religiöse Leben*, 75; Kratz, "Judean Ambassadors," 421–44; van der Toorn, "Ezra in Egypt?," 602–10; van der Toorn, *Becoming Diaspora Jews*, 120–24.

19. P.Berl. 13464; *TADAE* A4.1; see §2.3.1.1 above.

Yehudites, with the Persians in the role of arbiter.[20] This text can be dated to 410 BCE. The letter is written by an unknown person to Yedaniah, Mauziah, and Uriah.[21] The letter opens after the prescript: "Now, every day that [...] he complained to the investigators.[22] One Zivaka,[23] he complained to an investigator [...] we have since the Egyptians gave a bribe to them.[24] And from (the time) that [...] of the Egyptians before Arshames, but thievishly act."[25] The character of the quarrel between the Egyptians and the Yehudites is unclear. It is, however, important to note that "they"—probably the Egyptians—tried to bribe the Persian officer, which put the Yehudites temporarily at a disadvantage. The dispute took place in a period when Arshames was absent. The Yehudites complain, "Had we revealed our wrath[26] to Arshames before this, this(!) wou[ld] not [have been done to us ...]."[27] The Persian satrap is presented here as a guarantor of the fortunes of the Yehudites. His absence, however, enabled the escalation of the conflict. The remainder of the letter is an expression of hope that Pisina will pacify the relations.[28] The outcome of the conflict is the imprisonment of two Egyptians: Ṣeḥa and Ḥori, probably the persons who bribed the Persian officer.[29]

6.3. Burglary in Times of Turmoil

Among the texts connected by van der Toorn to the incident of the theft of a precious stone is an enigmatic Aramaic letter that lists a set of Yehudite females

20. *TADAE* A4.2; see Fried, *Priest and the Great King*, 90–92; Joisten-Pruschke, *Das religiöse Leben*, 162–67; Rohrmoser, *Götter, Tempel und Kult*, 2014, 386–88; van der Toorn, "Previously," 263–65.

21. Van der Toorn, "Previously," 263–65, proposes that Hoshea, son of Nathan, would be the auther of this letter. This proposal is only based on his assumption that a group of letters formed a coherent archive.

22. The Iranian loanword פתפרס refers to an "investigator; or examiner"; see Eilers, *Iranische Beamtennamen*, 24–26.

23. The name זיכה, "Zivaka; Ziwka," is either an An Iranian name—see Kornfeld, *Onomastica Aramaica aus Ägypten*, 106, or of Indo-European origin; see Sanskrit *śivaka*, "belonging to Shiva/Ziva."

24. The verb שחד, "to bribe," already occurs in Old Aramaic, see *KAI* 224:28.

25. *TADAE* A4.2:2–5.

26. With Grelot, *Documents araméens d'Egypte*, 389; and Rohrmoser, *Götter, Tempel und Kult*, 387, I construe the Aramaic expression גלי ענף as a reference to "wrath," since in West Semitic languages the "nose" generally stands for the emotions; contra Porten, *Elephantine Papyri in English*, 128; van der Toorn, "Previously," 264.

27. *TADAE* A4.2:8; Arshamesh fuctions as a representation of Persian power, as is clearly seen in his role protecting the Yehudites.

28. Pisina is referred to as a judge in *TADAE* A3.8.

29. *TADAE* A4.2:14–15. Strangely enough, in the letter *TADAE* A4.3—discussed above—they are presented as helpers of the Yehudites.

and males loosely connected with the theft.[30] The letter has been translated by Porten as follows:

> **1**[To my brother PN, your brother Islaḥ.
> *It is well for me here*]. May the gods seek after your welfare at all times.
> And now, [... **2** ...] PN son of PN went to Syene and did/made ... [... **3** ...]
> Behold, these are the names of the men wh]o were imprisoned in [Ele]phantine: Berechia, Hose⸢a, ... **4** ...⸣, Pakhnum.
> Behold, this is the names of the women who were f[ound at the gate **5**in Thebes and seized as p]risoners:
> Rami wife of Hodo,
> Esereshut wife of Hosea,
> Pallul wife of Islaḥ,
> Reia [wife/daughter of PN]
> **6**Tubla daughter of Meshullam (and) Kavla her sister.
> Behold the name of the men who were found at the gate in Thebes and were seized [as prisoners]:
> **7**Jedaniah son of Gemariah,
> Hosea son of Yathom,
> Hosea son of Nattum,
> Haggai his brother,
> Ahio son of Micai⸢ah.
> *They left*⸣ **8**the houses into which they had broken in at Elephantine and the goods that they took they surely returned to their owners. However, they mentioned to [their] owners [silver], **9**120 karsh. May another decree no more be delivered to them here.
> Greetings, your house and your children until the gods, let ⸢me⸣ behold ⸢your face in peace⸣.
> **10**⸢To (*sealing*) my brother PN son of⸣ Gaddul, your broth⸢er⸣ Islaḥ son of Nathan.[31]

The text is not *prima facie* clear. Porten classifies it as a "report of imprisonment of Jewish leaders."[32] Lindenberger labels it a text on "riot and rebellion." In his opinion, the letter "speaks of riots and looting at Elephantine, naming several men and women arrested there and at Thebes. Some of the names are Jewish, some Egyptian, and some of uncertain affiliation."[33] The text is seen as a report

30. *TADAE* A4.4; see Fried, *Priest and the Great King*, 97–98; Schama, *Story of the Jews*, 24; van der Toorn, "'Previously," 267–70.

31. Porten, *Elephantine Papyri in English*, 134–35.

32. In *TADAE* A4.4; Porten, *Elephantine Papyri in English*, 134.

33. Lindenberger, *Ancient Aramaic and Hebrew Letters*, 60–61, quotation from 55.

on a burglary in Elephantine, though it is uncertain which roles the individuals mentioned in the text played.

Recently, Caryn Tamber-Rosenau argued for a different interpretation of this text. In her view, the six women referred to in lines 5–6 were not simply accompanying their husbands or fathers on a business trip to Thebes. According to Tamber-Rosenau, they had a much more official role: they were female diplomats, sent to the court in Thebes ask the authorities to sort out the problems that had arisen.[34] Her proposal is intriguing and corroborates the observations of other scholars that women in Elephantine fully participated in the community.[35] Both ancient Near Eastern and ancient Egyptian texts bear witness to the fact that women could play a role in diplomacy.[36] There is likewise abundantly clear evididence that at Elephantine, too, women could fulfil public roles within the broader community.[37] The Collection Account lists a number of women who contributed two sheqels to the temple of Yahô in Elephantine.[38] This indicates that women could contribute to religious causes on their own. Of great importance in this connection is the role played by Mibtaiah, daughter of Maḥseiah, as described above.

In the report, three toponyms are mentioned: *swn*, "Syene" (line 2); [*y*]*b*, "[Ye]b; [Eleph]antine" (line 2); *n*', "No; Thebes" (line 6).[39] This implies that the acts referred to in the report, took place at different localities. One way or another, the text relates a burglary and its judicial aftermath. Elephantine had its own local juridical apparatus. Various texts refer to a "judge." Thebes was a provincial administrative center.[40] By implication, its judicial apparatus was more powerful than that of Elephantine. The report under consideration gives the impression that the burglary case from Elephantine was brought to court in Thebes. There are two possible reasons for that transfer: the judicial apparatus at Elephantine was in disarray as a result of the troubles caused by Vidranga and the priests of Khnum, or the case was so important that it had to

34. Tamber-Rosenau, "Female Diplomats in Jewish Elephantine?," 491–510; on the function of "gates" see May, "City Gates and their Functions."

35. See, e.g., Johnson, "Social, Economic and Legal Status of Women in Ancient Egypt," 82–97; Botta, "'Aspects of the Daily," 63–84; Azzoni, *Private Lives of Women*.

36. Tamber-Rosenau, "Female Diplomats in Jewish Elephantine?," 500–502; see especially the Neo-Assyrian documents *ABL* 886 = *SAA* XVII,73; *SAA* XVII, 68; see also Dubovský, *Hezekiah and the Assyrian Spies*, 109–17.

37. Tamber-Rosenau, "Female Diplomats in Jewish Elephantine?," 502–7.

38. *TADAE* C3.15.

39. In ancient Egyptian, Thebes is named *niwt-'imn*, "city of Amun"; this name is reflected in the Hebrew Bible as נא־אמון, "No-Amon" (Nah 3:8) and נא, "No" (Jer 46:25; Ezek 30:14–16); the Assyrian inscriptions of Esarhaddon and Ashurbanipal name Thebes *ni-'*; the Aramaic indication *n'* also occurs in *TADAE* A4.2:6.

40. Not the capital of the satrapy Mudrāya as Tamber-Rosenau, "Female Diplomats in Jewish Elephantine?," 496, suggests.

be brought before a higher court. There is no evidence of a judicial disruption in Elephantine in the last decades of the Persian rule. The payment to be made by the sentenced—120 karsh of silver—is rather large. The amount corresponds to eight to ten years of average family income.[41] This leads me to the conclusion that the second scenario just mentioned is the most probable one.

The report contains three lists of people:

1. A probably incomplete list of individuals who were imprisoned in Elephantine[42]
2. A list of six women who—according to Porten—were found as prisoners at the gate of Thebes[43]
3. A list of five men who were found at the gate in Thebes[44]

A few remarks are to be made. the first and second lists contain names of differing linguistic backgrounds. Most of them are clearly Hebrew, some have a more general West Semitic character, and some are Egyptian, like Pakhnum and Esereshut.[45] The names in the third list, however, are all Hebrew. The linguistic classification of a name, however, is not always conclusive for determining the ethnic background of the person bearing that name.

The precise nature of these groups is not clearly evident. Of the first group, it is said that they were *ʾsyrw*, "imprisoned," in Elephantine. The reason for their incarceration is not given. I would offer the possibility that they were the burglars who had stolen goods from houses in Elephantine. With regard to the second group, Porten made a misstep by filling the lacuna in the text at the end of line 4 and the beginning of line 5 with a phrase from line 6: "the women who were f[ound at the gate in Thebes and seized as p]risoners."[46] In the text only the word *ʾ]syrn*, "p]risoners," is extant. Strangely enough, that word is absent in line 6. By interpolating these lines, Porten made a connection between the two groups and gave them comparable or parallel functions in the incident. It should be noted that Tamber-Rosenau's proposal is based on this addition.[47] As for the second group, their role is unclear. It is far from certain that they had been to Thebes. The word *ʾ]syrn*, "p]risoners," suggests that they were in one way or another connected to the burglars. They could be victims or villains. The third

41. See Lindenberger, *Ancient Aramaic and Hebrew Letters*, 60.
42. *TADAE* A4.4:3–4.
43. *TADAE* A4.4:5–6.
44. *TADAE* A4.4:7.
45. See, e.g., Azzoni, *Private Lifes*, 108; Tamber-Rosenau, "Female Diplomats in Jewish Elephantine?," 496.
46. *TADAE* A4.4; Porten, *Elephantine Papyri in English*, 134–35; adapted by van der Toorn, "Previously," 267.
47. Tamber-Rosenau, "Female Diplomats in Jewish Elephantine?," 496.

group can be located at the *bbb' bn'*, "in the gate," of Thebes. Of them, it is said that they were *'tḥdw*, "seized; taken as prisoners."[48] This is the only instance in the Aramaic documents from Elephantine where this word is attested, thus making it difficult to establish the exact meaning. The additions by Porten—"seized [as prisoners]"—hint in the direction, suggesting that these men were imprisoned while—correctly or incorrectly—being accused of the burglary.

The three groups are not connected by family ties. As Tamber-Rosenau correctly argues, the women in the second group cannot be seen as the wives or daughters of the men in the third group. These women were certainly not accompanying their husbands or fathers on a business trip.[49] The only exception could be Esereshut, wife of Hosea. She could be related to one of the Hoseas in the third group, but in view of the fact that Hosea is a quite common name in Elephantine, this is far from decisive.

The third group is located *bbb' bn'*, "in the gate," of Thebes. The Aramaic noun *bb* is an Akkadian loanword, corresponding to Canaanite *š'r*.[50] In the Hebrew Bible, the gate of a city was also the spatial territory where judicial affairs were settled.[51] Some scholars have proposed translating *bb* with "court."[52] Porten adopted the idea that *bb* could be interpreted as a court, but did not translate it as such.[53] Tamber-Rosenau rejected the proposal on the basis of two arguments: the documents from Elephantine make clear that judicial matters were settled in various courts,[54] and the idea of the gate as a court is connected to a more tribal society like ancient Israel and cannot be transposed onto the highly developed bureaucracy of the Persian Empire.[55] Nevertheless, she treats the "gate of Thebes" as a space for judicial ordeal.

In my view, the "gate of Thebes" should be construed for what it is: a boundary marker between the world within the city and the world without. Such a boundary was controlled and guarded. On the question of why they went to Thebes, I see at least two possible scenarios. It has often been suggested that these men belonged to the leadership of the Yehudite community in Elephantine.[56]

48. Itp. of the verb *'ḥd* // *'ḥz*, "be taken; seized." See Muraoka and Porten, *Grammar of Egyptian Aramaic*, 16; *DNWSI* I, 37.

49. Tamber-Rosenau, "Female Diplomats in Jewish Elephantine?," 498–99.

50. See Kaufman, *Akkadian Influences on Aramaic*, 40–41; note that in the Aḥiqar story the Akkadian loan construction *bbb hykl'*, "in the gate of the palace," occurs (Aḥiqar 17.23), see M. L. Folmer, *Aramaic Language*, 740; the noun *ša'ar* is attested in the Hebrew Bible; see also EA 244:16; Phoenician and Punic; on the function of "gates," see May, "City Gates and their Functions."

51. Ruth 4, for instance.

52. E.g., Lindenberger, *Ancient Aramaic and Hebrew Letters*, 60.

53. Porten, *Elephantine Papyri in English*, 133.

54. See also Nutkowicz, "Note sur une institution juridique," 181–85.

55. Tamber-Rosenau, "Female Diplomats in Jewish Elephantine?," 495.

56. E.g., by Porten, *Archives*; Grelot, *Documents araméens d'Egypte*, 126; Porten, "Archive of Jedaniah," 165–77; Granerød, *Dimensions of Yahwism*, 33; van der Toorn, "Previously."

"Yedaniah, son of Gemariah," for instance, occurs in a leading role in the correspondence on the rebuilding of the demolished temple of Yahô.[57] On the basis of that observation, this group has been seen as a delegation of the Yehudites seeking to soften the relations.[58] I would propose a different reading: the third group should be seen as a party that, in the aftermath of the large-scale burglaries in Elephantine, fled to Thebes. They could have been the burglars on the run or the victims looking for a save place. On their flight they were "captured" when entering the city of Thebes.

The evidence seems to support the intepretation that they were burglars on the run, but it does not make clear why they were captured in the gate of Thebes. My thick description of the event would be as follows:

- During the tense period leading up to the destruction of the Yehudites' temple by Vidranga and the priests of Khnum, a large-scale burglary took place.
- Who trespassed the privacy of whom is unknown, but either way the act is a sign of growing animosity between at least two ethnic groups in and around Elephantine.
- A small group of probably multiethnic origin was imprisoned in Elephantine.
- A group of women stood one way or the other in connection with the imprisoned and or the burglars.
- A group of Yehudite men sought refuge in Thebes, for reasons unknown.
- A judicial authority adjudicated the case.[59]
- 120 karsh of silver had to be payed, probably the monetary valueof the stolen goods.

The function of the women (the second group) in this process is unclear. Until new evidence is found, their role will remain buried in the dust of the past. What is clear is that in the years preceding the demolition of the temple of Yahô, animosity between the groups was growing. In the case of this large theft, the Persians were still able to exercise their power. A few years later, things had changed.

6.4. The Crisis Around the Demolition of the Temple of Yahô

One of the most well-known events from Persian-period Elephantine is the demolition of the temple of Yahô by the priests of Khnum in cooperation with

57. E.g., *TADAE* A4.10:1.
58. Grelot, *Documents araméens d'Egypte*, 126.
59. I will resist the temptation to see Pisina as the judge who ruled the case.

Vidranga, the local governor, and the attempt to rebuild that temple by the Yehudite community. This set of events is documented in a small collection of letters and memoranda from Elephantine.[60] It is referenced in the following texts:

- A report on the demolitions made in Elephantine by the priests of Khnum and Vidranga during the absence of the Persian satrap Arshames.[61]
- The first version of a letter by Yedaniah, a leading Yehudite from Elephantine, to Bagohi/Bagavahya, the governor of Judah, asking for recommendations for rebuilding the temple of Yahô in Elephantine.[62]
- A second, slightly revised version of this letter by Yedaniah to Bagohi/Bagavahya asking for recommendations for rebuilding the temple of Yahô in Elephantine.[63]
- A memorandum by Bagohi/Bagavahya and Delaiah giving permission to rebuild the temple and to resume the meal offerings and the incense burning in it.[64]
- A memorandum in which a group of leading Yehudites are offering contributions of silver in case the temple were to be rebuilt and the meal offerings and incense burning to be resumed; it also implies that there will no longer be burnt-offerings of sheep, oxen, and goats in the rebuilt temple.[65]

Three basic facts can be discerned from a reading of these documents. First, local Egyptians connected to the temple of Khnum, in conspiracy with the Persian governor, demolished the temple of Yahô in Elephantine; second, this act took place when the Persian satrap Arshames was absent from the area; and third, the Yehudites were seeking support for the rebuilding of their sanctuary.

This set of events has been described and interpreted in terms of a religious conflict. Most scholars argue within the framework of a clash between the priests of Khnum and the leaders of the Yehudite community with their veneration of the deity Yahô.[66] Others assume political motives at the background:

60. Unfortunately, the events can not be corroborated with evidence from outside Elephantine.

61. *TADAE* A4.5; Porten, *Elephantine Papyri in English*, 136–39. Below, I will argue that Porten and others—e.g., Granerød, *Dimensions of Yahwism*, 28—incorrectly construe this document in its entirety to be a draft version of the request for support written by the Yehudite community to political and religious leaders in Samaria and Jerusalem.

62. *TADAE* A4.7; Porten, *Elephantine Papyri in English*, 141–46.

63. *TADAE* A4.8; Porten, *Elephantine Papyri in English*, 147–49.

64. *TADAE* A4.9; Porten, *Elephantine Papyri in English*, 150–51.

65. *TADAE* A4.10; Porten, *Elephantine Papyri in English*, 152–53.

66. Cowley, *Aramaic Papyri*, xvii; Porten, *Archives*, 284–96; Schäfer, *Judeophobia*, 121–35; Kottsieper, "Die Religionspolitik der Achämeniden,"155; Vittmann, *Ägypten und die Fremden*, 92; Meinhold, "Vergleichbar-/Unvergleichbarkeit des Wiederaufbaus der Tempel," 35–59; Von Pilgrim, "Tempel des Jahu und 'Straße des Königs,'" 303–17; Kratz, "Second Temple of Jeb and of

Vidranga was a weak character who could easily be bribed by Egyptian freedom fighters.[67] Mark van de Mieroop offers a down-to-earth explanation: the temple of Khnum needed more space, and the temple of Yahô just stood in the way.[68] An unconvincing proposal has been given by Angela Rohrmoser. In her view, the initiative for the demolitions came from the Persians. Following Pierre Briant,[69] she argues from a demotic legal code dated to the Roman Era[70] that the Persians could have had property rights for the area where the temple of Yahô was built.[71] The legal connection is tenuous, though, as Briant already indicated.[72] Next to that, Rohrmoser blurs the concepts of "initiative" and "implementation."[73] As will be argued below, the priests of Khnum took the initiative, while the wicked Vidranga took care of the implementation after having been bribed by the priests of Khnum.

According to the interpretation of these events as a religious conflict, the sacrifice of animals by the Yehudites would have been a bone of contention for the priests of Khnum. Their deity was represented in language and stone as a ram-headed god.[74] Porten argues that the priests of Khnum had recently built a Khnumeum—a burial place for sacred rams—near the border of the temple precincts. Porten assumes that the offering of lambs by the "Jews of Elephantine" so close to this Khnumeum fueled the religious zeal of the priests of Khnum.[75]

Religion was an important factor in daily life in ancient communities, and it often functioned as a clear boundary marker. Although the importance of religion should not be underappreciated, it should be noted that other dimensions of life, such as the social, the economic, and the political, also played important roles. A concentration on the religious aspects of the events just mentioned will lead to a "thin description."[76] The aim of this chapter is to "read" this string of events in their religious, social, and historical context. I will, therefore, read these documents with two tools in mind: Clifford Geertz's concept of "thick description" and the presence of "clues" in the texts.

Jerusalem," 247–64; Kratz, "Zwischen Elephantine und Qumran," 135–38; Kaplan, "'Sojourner in the Land," 410; Fitzpatrick-McKinley, "Preserving the Cult of Yhwh," 426–28.

67. Anneler, *Zur Geschichte der Juden von Elephantine*, 42, 135; Van Hoonacker, *Communauté Judéo-araméenne à Éléphantine*, 38.

68. Van de Mieroop, *History of Ancient Egypt*, 309.

69. Briant, "Une curieuse affaire à Èlephantine," 115–35.

70. Codex Hermopolis West: ed. Mattha and Hughes, *Demotic Legal Code*; Donker van Heel, *Legal Manual of Hermopolis*.

71. Rohrmoser, *Götter, Tempel und Kult*, 255–65.

72. Briant, "Une curieuse affaire," 524.

73. Rohrmoser, *Götter, Tempel und Kult*, 255.

74. On Khnum and his veneration in Elephantine, see Badawi, *Der Gott Chnum*; Otto, "Chnum," *Lexikon der Ägyptologie* 1 (1974): 950–54.

75. Porten, *Archives*, 286; Schäfer, *Judeophobia*, 129, 133–35.

76. See Geertz, "Thick Description."

The concept of "thick description" has already been explained above (see §6.1.2), but the term "clues" as I use it requires some clarification. The Italian historian Carlo Ginzburg noted a difference between "traces" and "clues" in documents, artifacts, and other fragments that relate to the past.[77] Any piece of evidence on the past contains "traces" of human behavior in times gone by. These traces can be reformulated by historians as the propositions that form the skeleton of their constructions of the past. "Clues" are a specific kind of "traces." They contain references to the past that go beyond the direct context of the given piece of evidence. In his study on inquisitorial archives from the early sixteenth century, for instance, he found remarks not only on the specific person under trial, but also "clues" on the connection between these inquisitorial procedures and doctrinal developments in demonology. Before presenting my thick description of the chain of events, I will read the documents carefully, looking especially for "clues."

6.4.1. A Report on Demolitions

TADAE A4.5, a papyrus document discovered and published prior to the French and German excavations at Elephantine, is intriguing for several reasons. On the recto of the papyrus is an Aramaic text written in two columns, in contrast with all other letters from Elephantine, which were written in one column. The fact that the recto of the document was inscribed with two columns might therefore be an indication of its genre. On this basis, the text should perhaps be construed as an official report rather than a letter. Presently, five lines of each column of the recto are readable; a few lines on the top and bottom of each column has been lost. The verso of the papyrus contains an inscription in one column that was written in a different hand than the text on the recto. The fourteen legible lines of text give the impression of a draft for a letter. There is no salutation, but the lines of the inscription are characteristic of a letter. There is no colophon in either text, so they cannot be dated and the names of the scribes/authors are unknown. In view of these observations, I will treat the two texts separately.

6.4.1.1. The Recto

The recto of the inscription reads as follows:

> [. . .] we grew, (some) detachments of the Egyptians rebelled. We did not leave our posts. ⌜. . . of⌝ damage was not found with us.
>
> In year 14 of Darius the [ki]ng, when our lord Arshames had gone to the king, this is the evil act that the priests of Khnum, the god, [di]d in

77. Ginzburg, *Clues, Myths and the Historical Method.*

> Elephantine the fortress in agreement with Vidranga who was Chief here: They gave him silver and goods.
>
> [. . .]
>
> And now, that wall (stands) built in the midst of the fortress.
>
> There is a well that is built with[in] the f[or]tress and water it does not lack to give the troop drink so that whenever they would be stationed in the garrison (there), they would drink the water from [th]at well. Those priests of Khnum stopped up that well.
>
> If an inquiry would be made by the judges, the police, and hearers who are appointed in the province of Tshetres, it will be [known] to our lord in accordance with this which we say. Moreover, we are separated [. . .][78]

The text mentions a variety of groups. The first is the Egyptians. The text reports that "detachments of the Egyptians rebelled." The Aramaic noun *dgl* used here is a standard Persian term to indicate a group of foreign soldiers that were under one banner (see discussion in §2.3.7.2).[79] The texts from Elephantine refer to "detachments" of various ethnic groups. Presumably, there was also an Egyptian *dgl*. The mercenaries in this group rebelled against Persian power. Another group of Egyptians indicated is the "priests of Khnum." They committed the "evil act" of demolition, which will be discussed below. They had forged a coalition with Vidranga who was recently promoted to the role of *frataraka* at Elephantine and was put in charge during the absence of Arshames.[80] In order to get his support, the priests of Khnum bribed him with silver and goods.[81]

The second is the Persians. Three Persians are mentioned in the text: King Darius (II), in whose fourteenth regnal year the "evil act" took place; "our lord, Arshames," the governor who was not present in the time of the incident; and the aforementioned *frataraka* Vidranga.

The third is an unspecified group that presents themselves in the first-person plural ("we") and who cast themselves as loyal to the Persian Empire. The identity of this group is difficult to establish from the document itself. Porten construes them as a leading group of the "Jews of Elephantine."[82] His view, however,

78. *TADAE* A4.5 Col. I and II; translation based on Porten, *Elephantine Papyri in English*, 136–38 (with modifications); Fried, *Priest and the Great King*, 91, 98–99.

79. A *dgl* was built up from several, at least two, groups. These groups can be compared with the later Roman group under a *centurion*. In the relatively peaceful circumstances of Elephantine these groups might have consisted of sixty to eighty persons, which means that a *dgl* consisted of at least 120 to 160 persons. See Porten, *Archives*, 28–35; *DNWSI*, 240–41 [with lit.]; Knauf, "Elephantine und das vor-biblische Judentum," 181–82; Rohrmoser, *Götter, Tempel und Kult*, 47–49.

80. *Frataraka* is a function of lesser rank than the governor Arshames; Schäfer, *Judeophobia*, 122.

81. Lindenberger, "What Ever Happened to Vidranga?," 135.

82. Porten, *Archives*, 284–89; see also Granerød, *Dimensions of Yahwism*, 28, 86, 305–7.

is based on the assumption that the papyrus under consideration is to be seen as one coherent document, a draft version of a request for support written by the Yehudite community to political and religious leaders in Samaria and Jerusalem.

The "evil act" is indicated with the Iranian loanword *dwškrt*, "crime; evil act."[83] In Persian royal inscriptions, the related adjective *duškarta* qualifies deeds performed in disloyalty to the Persian rule.[84] The use of the word in the report is a clue for understanding the deeds of demolition as disloyal acts. In the recto document, the following acts are reported:

- Demolition of parts of the *ywdn' zy mlk'*, "the granary of the king." The Aramaic noun is a Persian loanword: **yau-dāna*, "grain-house."[85] This granary was most probably part of the local administrative building complex and functioned for the collection of taxes *in natura*.[86] I construe this demolition as a clue: a vital element of the Persian administration was attacked.
- Building of a wall. A wall was built in the middle of the fortress. With Porten, I am of the opinion that this wall had a defensive function: it separated the area around the temple of Khnum from the rest of the fortress.[87] I read this act as a clue to a shift in mentality. During most of the Persian occupation of Elephantine, the various ethnic groups lived together in harmony, accepting one another's customs and intermingling in mixed marriages. The building of the wall is a clear break from this mentality and a step toward a separate Egyptian identity.
- Cutting off the water supply. The text on the recto refers to the existence of a well on the island that supplied the garrison with water. Part of the "evil act" was the fact that the priests of Khnum stopped the well. In doing so, they deprived the soldiers in the garrison of fresh water vital for their existence.[88]
- The text on the recto does not mention the temple of Yahô.[89] There are two ways to explain this absence. Its demolition might have been described in

83. See *DNWSI*, 244; cf. Old Persian *duškarta*, "evil-done"; see Tavernier, *Iranica in the Achaemenid Period*, 418; Rohrmoser, *Götter, Tempel und Kult*, 394–95; Granerød, *Dimensions of Yahwism*, 48.

84. Darius II: DSe 31; Xerxes: XPh 42: "And there was something else, that had been done wrong (*duškartam*), that too I put right."

85. Avestian *yauua*, "grain," and Av. *dāman*, "house," see Tavernier, *Iranica in the Achaemenid Period*, 441; Rohrmoser, *Götter, Tempel und Kult*, 395, surmises that the word refers to a silo in which food for the garrison was kept.

86. Porten, *Elephantine Papyri in English*, 137.

87. Porten, *Elephantine Papyri in English*, 137; Rohrmoser, *Götter, Tempel und Kult*, 253–54, 259–65.

88. Rohrmoser, *Götter, Tempel und Kult*, 259–65.

89. Lindenberger, "What Ever happened to Vidranga?," 135; Granerød, *Dimensions of Yahwism*, 86, incorrectly assume that the recto text would mention the demolition of the temple of Yahô.

> the lines now missing. On the other hand, the demolition was, in the mind of the reporter, not as important as the other attacks.

All in all, the inscription refers to a set of "evil acts" targeted toward vital elements of the Persian administration, apparently aimed at destabilizing Persian rule.

This all happened when Arshames was absent. The document does not give the reason why the satrap went to the king. Arshames probably visited the Persian king to pay his respects and to report personally on the situation in Egypt.[90] Whether this was a regular visit or a journey caused by local circumstances and developments is a matter of speculation. Another possibility, suggested by Peter Schäfer, is that Arshames left Egypt to campaign for Darius II in the early years of his reign.[91] Regardless of the precise interpretation, this statement can be read as a "clue": the temporary absence of the most important Persian official in southern Egypt created a partial power-vacuum that was used by local Egyptians to plan their "evil act." Apparently, the balance in the complex system was dependent upon the presence of the Persian figurehead.

In sum, this document presents the "evil act" as a willfully disloyal attack by Egyptians against vital elements of the Persian administration. The rebellion was orchestrated by the priests of Khnum and abused the temporary power-vacuum to destabilize the political infrastructure. The demolition of the temple of Yahô is not seen as the central target in the "evil act." A question that rises—and that cannot be answered from the evidence of this document alone—is whether the act was a unique incident or should be seen as just one of many such anti-Persian acts.

6.4.1.2. The Verso

On the verso is an Aramaic text written in a different hand, implying that the text should not be construed as the continuation of the report on the recto.[92] The inscription is puzzlingly incomplete. I will try to translate what I can read:

1. [. . .] the [. . .] who are in Elephantine the f⌜ortress . . .⌝
2. [. . .] of our distress became great [. . .]
3. [. . .] was not found in [. . .]
4. [. . .] to bring meal offerin⌜g . . .⌝
5. [. . .] to serve there before Yahô, the g⌜od . . .⌝

90. Granerød, *Dimensions of Yahwism*, 89–90.

91. Schäfer, *Judeophobia*, 123.

92. *Pace* Porten, *Elephantine Papyri in English*, 136–39; Fried, *Priest and the Great King*, 99.

6. [. . .] in which [. . .]
7. [. . .] to them one brazier [. . .]
8. [. . .] the fitting they took for [their] own [. . .]
9. [. . .] if it be good to our lord in an abundant way [. . .]
10. [. . .] we of the force [. . .]
11. [. . .] our lord, may a [decree] be issued [. . .]
12. [. . .] we. If it be [. . .] to [our] l⸢ord . . .⸣
13. [. . . pro]tect the items that [. . .]
14. [. . .] the [. . .] that they demolished to [. . .]

Notes on the translation:

1. The letters *d/rḥpny'* probably form the final part of a Persian loanword indicating a cast of Persian officials.
2. The word *'nḥnh* could be seen as the pronoun "we";[93] alternatively, it could be construed as a form of the noun *'nḥ*, "distress,"[94] with a suffix indicating that the increased despair of the "we" group.
14. The noun "temple," added by Porten,[95] might fit the context, but it is not present in the text.

It is not easy to interpret this inscription. The text is not dated. The genre of the text is unclear: Is it a letter or a report? Formal elements, such as a salutation, are absent. The presence of the word *mr'n*, "our lord" (lines 9, 11, and 12), in a section that apparently reads as a plea, might, however, indicate that the text was in one way or another meant to reach this addressee, "our lord." The identity of this master is not easily inferred from this text as such. Moreover, it is unclear who the "we" mentioned throughout the text actually are. The expression "to serve there before Yahô" (line 5) might contain a clue as to the identity of this group. This indicates that they are most likely to be identified as (some of) the Yehudites of Elephantine. A closer look at the text, in combination with reading it in the context of the other documents listed above, might, however, reveal a few clues.

It is remarkable to observe that some of the expressions in the beginning of the verso document resemble the phraseology of the beginning of the report on the recto: "[. . .] of our distress became great [. . .]" (line 2 // recto line 1); "[. . .] was not found in [. . .]" (line 3 // recto line 2). This might be construed as

93. Thus Porten, *Elephantine Papyri in English*, 138.

94. The noun is attested in the Sfire Treaty Inscription, *KAI* 222 B:39; see Lipiński, *Studies in Aramaic Inscriptions and Onomastics* 1, 43.

95. Porten, *Elephantine Papyri in English*, 139; adopted by Rohrmoser, *Götter, Tempel und Kult*, 396.

an indication that the verso text would in one way or another refer to the same event as the recto text.

Some words in the verso text occur also in the petitions written by Yedaniah to Bagohi/Bagavahya, the governor of Judah, asking for a recommendation to rebuild the temple of Yahô in Elephantine.[96] (1) The noun *'šrn'*, "fittings,"[97] (line 8) occurs in the petition. Both versions report that various wooden items from the temple of Yahô, including the *'šrn'*, had been burned during the demolition of the temple.[98] The verso text gives the impression that they were stolen and subsequently burned.[99] (2) The indefinite pronoun *mnd'mt'*, "thing(s); item(s),"[100] is also attested in both petitions, albeit in a different context. The word occurs in the section on the demolition of "the temples of the gods in Egypt," in which it is claimed that in those days "not a thing was damaged" in the temple of Yahô.[101] (3) The verb *ndš*, "to destroy; to demolish," is present several times in the petitions. The verb describes the destruction of the temple and its various components, such as the five stone gates.[102]

In light of these similarities, it seems obvious to construe the text as a report or a request—or a draft of such a text—regarding the demolition of the Yehudite temple. If this is correct, the demolition of the Yehudite temple would have been another element in the "evil act."

The question remains: Who was the intended receiver of the request or the report? The text itself gives a clue. As noted above, the word *mr'n*, "our lord" (lines 9, 11, and 12), refers to the addressee of the text. Who, however, was *mr'n*? From the documents listed above, two candidates present themselves. The first possibility is that both versions of the petition are directed to *mr'n bgwhy*, "our lord Bagohi," then governor of the Persian province Yehud. It is very likely, then, that this *mr'n* can be identified with the Persian officer in Jerusalem referenced in the recto text. This would implicate that the recto text was a draft

96. *TADAE* A4.7; Porten, *Elephantine Papyri in English*, 141–46; *TADAE* A4.8; Porten, *Elephantine Papyri in English*, 147–49.

97. An Old Persian loanword: **uščarana*, "material." The noun refers to materials for construction or repair, mostly made from wood. See, e.g., Ezra 5:3, 9; Tuland, "*'Uššayyā'* and *'Uššarnâ*," 269–75; Granerød, *Dimensions of Yahwism*, 86. In a text from Elephantine authorizing the repair of a boat rented by a group of Carians the noun refers to the wooden coating of the vessel; *TADAE* A6.2:5.

98. *TADAE* A4.7:11 // *TADAE* A4.8:11.

99. Interestingly, the noun *'trdwn*, "brazier," does not occur in the two versions of the petition. This Old Persian loanword, **ātṛvadana*—see Tavernier, *Iranica in the Achaemenid Period*, 461—which indicates "a container for hot coals," is not attested elsewhere in the documents from Elephantine. The item might have been part of the inventory of the temple that had been looted by the troops of Naphaina: "But the gold and silver basins and (other) t[h]ings which were in that temple—they all took and made their own," *TADAE* A4.7:11–13 // *TADAE* A4.8:11–12. The noun is a cognate of Hebrew *'āḥ*, "fire-pot; brazier," mentioned at Jer 36:22–23.

100. See Folmer, *Aramaic Language*, 440, 478–79.

101. *TADAE* A4.7:14 // *TADAE* A4.8:14.

102. *TADAE* A4.7:9–10 // *TADAE* A4.8:8—9.

version of the later petition.[103] The second possibility is that this is the same *mr'n* mentioned in lines 7, 12, and 13 of the memorandum recording the offerings of silver by Yehudites for the rebuilding of the temple.[104]. This document is clearly part of the phase of negotiations after Bagohi and Delaiah indicate their support for the rebuilding of the temple.[105] Scholars have offered several different identifications for this "lord."[106] In accordance with the scholarly discussion, I would like to offer three arguments for identifying him with Arshames, the Persian governor, after his return to Elephantine. (1) The topography of the document is local: only Elephantine is mentioned, and Jerusalem and Samaria are not referred to. (2) The noun *mr'n* is not clarified by a name, which suggests this figure's identity as a master would have been undisputed. Within the community of Elephantine, no other "master" besides Arshames would fit this description. (3) The *mr'n* is addressed in conditional clauses comparable to the ones used in the verso text—for instance, *hn mr'n* [. . .], "if our lord [. . .]" (line 7). Although the identification cannot be proven beyond doubt, the possibility that *mr'n* in the verso text refers to Arshames is stronger than an identification with Bagohi.

All in all, I arrive at the following hypothesis. The demolition of the Yehudite sanctuary was—though not the focal target—part of the "evil act" by which the priests of Khnum wanted to destabilize Persian power in Elephantine. The Yehudites, as well as the other mercenaries, were seen as the accomplices of the Persian occupation. After the return of the Persian governor, the Yehudites made a request to their Persian overlords for the rebuilding of their sanctuary in order to be able to make offerings to Yahô, their god.

6.4.2. Two Versions of One Petition

Two almost identical copies of a letter written by Yedaniah from Elephantine to Bagohi have been found.[107] Presumably, these letters were duplicates of the official letter sent to Jerusalem and Samaria. The text is a well-written and

103. Porten, *Archives from Elephantine*, 289–93.

104. *TADAE* A4.10; Porten, *Elephantine Papyri in English*, 152—53.

105. *TADAE* A4.9; Porten, *Elephantine Papyri in English*, 150–51; Granerød, *Dimensions of Yahwism*, 86–87.

106. Arshames: Grelot, *Documents araméens d'Egypte*, 418; Granerød, *Dimensions of Yahwism*, 44; G. Granerød, "'Canon and Archive," 354. Rohrmoser, *Götter, Tempel und Kult*, 411, proposes a variant: an official subordinated to Arshames.

Bagohi: Cowley, *Aramaic Papyri*, 124.

Schäfer, *Judeophobia*, 132–33, is undecided on the question of the addressee.

107. *TADAE* A4.7 // *TADAE* A4.8; see Lindenberger, "What Ever Happened to Vidranga?," 134–57; Porten, "Settlement of the Jews at Elephantine," 454–56; Fried, *Priest and the Great King*, 100–102; Grabbe, *History of Jews and Judaism*, 1:210–12; Kratz, "Second Temple of Jeb"; Rohrmoser, *Götter, Tempel und Kult*, 397–407; Cornell, "Cult Statuary in the Judean Temple at Yeb," 1–19; Siljanen, *Judeans of Egypt*, 231–37.

well-ordered report composed in courteous language and ending in a request.[108] Yedaniah gives a detailed report of the demolition of the temple of Yahô in Elephantine and the cultic statue in it,[109] leading to a rather short but clear request for permission to rebuild the temple. I would like to make a few remarks on this often-discussed petition.

Bagohi, or Bagoses, was the Persian governor over Samaria and Yehud around 400 BCE.[110] He was the figurehead of Persian power in these areas, who was accepted by Yedaniah with the application of the title *mr'n*, "our lord." Although Bagohi was not formally the master over the Elephantine Yehudites—Arshames was—in addressing him this way, Yedaniah accepts the power of Bagohi over the Yahwists in Samaria and Jerusalem.[111]

Yedaniah offers a detailed depiction of the demolition. By mentioning all the features in and around the sanctuary that were destroyed or looted and stating that the temple was "demolished to the ground," Yedaniah communicates the complete ruination of the sanctuary.[112] In contrast to all these details, the letter is silent about the other aspects of the "evil act." It does not menton the demolition of the parts of the the granary of the king (*ywdn' zy mlk'*), the building of the wall, or the cutting off of the water supply. This selection hints at the worldview of Yedaniah and his peers: to them the destruction of the temple of Yahô was probably of greater importance than the attack on the elements vital to Persian rule in Elephantine.

Yedaniah, as could be expected, assesses the demolition in a negative way. He labels Vidranga as "evil."[113] The destroyers of the temple—directed by Nafaina, a troop leader and son of Vidranga—are seen as "those who sought evil."[114] The actions of the priests of Khnum and their accomplices are referred to as the "time when this evil was done to us."[115] The Persian loanword *dwškrt*, "crime; evil act," however, is not used in the petition. Two Semitic words are used: Vidranga is called *lḥy'*, "evil,"[116] and the act is seen as *b'š*, "bad; evil." This phraseological difference is one more indication that the petition was written by a person different than the scribe of the recto report.

Yedaniah stresses the effect of the destruction of the temple on the daily life of the community. Since the "evil act," a variety of mourning rites were

108. On the courteous language, see Fales, "Aramaic Letters and Neo-Assyrian Letters," 451–69.

109. See Cornell, "Cult Statuary in the Judean Temple at Yeb."

110. See Klinkott, *Der Satrap*, 456–58.

111. See Granerød, "Canon and Archive," 353–54.

112. *TADAE* A4.7:9 // *TADAE* A4.8:8.

113. *TADAE* A4.7:6–7 // *TADAE* A4.8:6.

114. *TADAE* A4.7:16–17 // *TADAE* A4.8:15–16.

115. *TADAE* A4.7:17–18 // *TADAE* A4.8:16 [augmented].

116. This word is used in Aramaic to describe one's depreciation of a person; see for instance Aḥiqar 9.130; see Rohrmoser, *Götter, Tempel und Kult*, 278–80.

enacted: donning sackcloth, fasting, no longer anointing, and abstaining from wine.[117] These mourning rites are well known in the Hebrew Bible, but it would be premature to conclude that the Yehudites were acting out Israelite rites: those rites were, with local variation, common in the ancient Near East.[118] Olyan has correctly remarked that such mourning rites are not restricted to the period of coping with sorrow after the death of a beloved; they could also be performed in other situations of great personal or communal disturbance.[119] The mourning rites described by Yedaniah can be construed as forms of nonpetitionary mourning associated with a calamity.[120] The rites are a bodily expression of a mental state and not so much a prayer acted out.

The desperation of the Yehudites was increased by two failures. First, while Vidranga and all who had conspired with him had been punished by death,[121] the temple had not yet been rebuilt by the local authorities.[122] Second, the Yehudites had sent an earlier letter to the priestly authorities in Jerusalem with the request for support in their endeavors to rebuild, but they had not received an answer.[123]

All this is leading to a request. In comparison to the petition in its entirety, the request is rather short and formulated in polite language. The request is introduced with a conditional clause *hn mr'n ṭb*, "if it be good to our lord."[124] This phrase occurs elsewhere in letters and requests from Elephantine—for instance, in the memorandum recording Yehudites' silver offerings for rebuilding the temple.[125] The aim of this obsequious language is to please the powers that be and certainly not affront them, paving the way for a positive reaction.

Yedaniah obeisantly pleads, "Regard your obligees and your friends who are here in Egypt."[126] The expression "obligees and friends" refers to the

117. *TADAE* A4.7:20–22 // *TADAE* A4.8:18–20.

118. See Pham, *Mourning in the Ancient Near East.*

119. Olyan, *Biblical Mourning*; see also Rohrmoser, *Götter, Tempel und Kult*, 227–39; Granerød, *Dimensions of Yahwism*, 78–79.

120. Olyan, *Biblical Mourning*, esp. 98–10.

121. On this section and the humiliating death of Vidranga by a set of dogs "tearing out the guts between his legs," see especially Fales, "Aramaic Letters and Neo-Assyrian," 468–69; Lindenberger, "What Ever Happened to Vidranga?,"137–48; Schäfer, *Judeophobia*, 123; Rohrmoser, *Götter, Tempel und Kult*, 282–85.

122. *TADAE* A4.7:15–17 // *TADAE* A4.8:13–16.

123. *TADAE* A4.7:17–19 // *TADAE* A4.8:16–18; a copy or a draft of this first letter has been preserved. Rainer Albertz has convincingly argued that an answer from Jerusalem could not have been written since Bagoses had closed the temple in order to punish the fratricide of Jochanan, the priest, who killed his brother Joshua, the high priest appointed by Bagohi, while he was serving in the temple as is narrated in Josephus, *Antiq.* 11.297–301; see Albertz, "Controversy about Judean versus Israelite Identity," 483–504.

124. *TADAE* A4.7:23 // *TADAE* A4.8:22.

125. *TADAE* A4.10.

126. *TADAE* A4.7:23–24 // *TADAE* A4.8:23.

administrative peers of Bagohi who are in Egypt.[127] The aim of the request is clear: Yedaniah kindly asks Bagohi to put some diplomatic pressure on Arshames by sending a letter of recommendation for the rebuilding of the temple.

The penultimate section of the petitions contains a clear example of *quid pro quo*.[128] If Bagohi acts favorably on the request, offerings will be made in his name on the new altar in the temple of Yahô, the Yehudite community will pray for his well-being, and he will receive a *ṣdqh* before Yahô. This Aramaic noun *ṣdqh* is not easily translated or understood. In this context, the noun has a specific, developed meaning and should not be rendered with just "righteousness." With Basile Aggoula, I prefer the translation "share; portion."[129] The word then refers to the concept that Bagohi will have a "righteous share" in the temple of Yahô, implying that he will profit from the temple's economy.[130]

All in all, the petition makes clear that the Yehudites were aware of coreligionists in Samaria and Jerusalem, that they understood the balance of power in that Persian province, that they could use the Persian administration in Jerusalem and Samaria as a lever to reach their aims in Elephantine (i.e., the rebuilding of their temple), and that they knew that every agreement has its price, hence their offer to Bagohi of both immaterial and material goods in return for his approval.

6.4.3. The Memorandum by Bagohi and Delaiah

This document presents itself as a *zkrn*.[131] The noun literally means "an object that must be remembered." It can be rendered as "charter" or "memorandum." Like *dikrônāh* in Ezra 6:2, *zkrn* refers to the written version of an oral communication.[132] The senders of this communication are Bagohi and Delaiah, both high-ranking Persian officials in Samaria, if not both governors.[133] The anonymous messenger reports in the first person what Bagohi and Delaiah had said to him. It is unclear to whom the memorandum was addressed. Was the Persian administration the addressee, or was the message directed toward Yedaniah? In view

127. See Porten, *Elephantine Papyri in English*, 145; Granerød, *Dimensions of Yahwism*, 44.

128. The label "bakshish," as proposed by Sachau, *Drei aramäische Papyrus-Urkunden aus Elephantine*, 36; Meyer, *Der Papyrusfund von Elephantine*, 85, for this act is too strong, see Vogelstein, "Bakshish for Bagoas?," 89–92; Granerød, *Dimensions of Yahwism*, 136–40.

129. Aggoula, "Studia Aramaica, II," 64.

130. This interpretation of the noun also applies for its occurrences in two Aramaic stela (*KAI* 226:2; 228 A:15) and in the warning of Nehemiah against his opponents that Sanballat and his accomplices will not have a "share" in Jerusalem (Neh 2:20).

131. *TADAE* A4.9:1, 2; see Grabbe, *History of Jews and Judaism*, 1:211.

132. See *DNWSI*, 331; Porten, *Elephantine Papyri in English*, 150; Greenfield, "Aspects of Archives in the Achaemenid Period," 277; Granerød, *Dimensions of Yahwism*, 87.

133. Delaiah was one of the sons of Sanballat; see Dušek, *Manuscripts araméens*, 319–31.

of the power relations, the first possibility is more likely, although Yedaniah was an interested party, as Liz Fried has argued.[134] The text reads as follows:

> Memorandum. What Bagavahya and Delaiah said to me. Memorandum. Saying:
>
> Let it be for you in Egypt to say before Arshames about the altar-house of the God of Heaven, which was formerly—before Cambyses—built in Elephantine, the fortress, which Vidranga, that wicked (man), demolished in year 14 of Darius the king:
>
> Decision:
>
> to (re)build it on its site as it was formerly.
>
> The meal offering and the incense they shall offer upon that altar just as formerly was done.

The message of this memorandum is clear. The Persian authorities support the pursuit of the Yehudites to rebuild their temple.

A few elements about this document are remarkable. First, the Yehudite sanctuary in Elephantine is not called a *ʾgwrʾ*, "temple," as in the petition, but a *byt mdbḥʾ*, "altar-house," and it is also notable that the deity is not referred to as Yahô but as the God of heaven.[135] The expression "altar-house" was until recently not attested in known Aramaic inscriptions. In an inscription written in lapidary Aramaic script excavated at Tell Gerizim, the comparable phrase *byt dbḥʾ*, "house of sacrifice," occurs.[136] What clue is given here? Do Bagohi and Delaiah avoid the word "temple" in an attempt not to affront those who are responsible for the temples in Jerusalem or on Mount Gerizim? Or do they avoid this word in order to communicate to the Persian administration that the sanctuary of the Yehudites was no more than the "altar house" of one of the many ethnic groups in and around Elephantine? It is very likely that the expression *byt mdbḥʾ*, "altar-house," was simply an extrapolation from the term *mdbḥʾ* used in the petition, and that no greater strategic or political views are implied.

Second, it is intriguing to see that Bagohi and Delaiah adopted the "continuity" argument. In the petition, Yedaniah had claimed that the temple of Yahô already existed in the days of the kings of Egypt and that their temple was the only one not destroyed by Cambyses when he conquered Egypt.[137] From a historical point of view, this claim meets some serious challenges. On the

134. Fried, *Ezra*, 259; her view that A4.9 would contain the minutes of a meeting stands contrary to all we know about Persian administration in the satrapies.

135. *TADAE* A4.9:3; Granerød, *Dimensions of Yahwism*, 107.

136. Magen, Misgav and Tsfania, *Aramaic, Hebrew and Samaritan Inscriptions*, text 199; see Hensel, *Juda und Samaria*, 57; compare 2 Chr 7:12.

137. *TADAE* A4.7:13–14 // *TADAE* A4.8:12–13.

basis of the description of Cambyses's rule by Herodotus (biased though it is), one can only infer that Cambyses continued the religious policy of his father Cyrus and did not destroy temples in Egypt.[138] There is no evidence that could confirm Yedaniah's claim. On the other hand, the claim contains a clue as to the religious identity of the Yehudites: they construed themselves as not just one of the many ethnic groups, but an ethnic group with a long pedigree in the garrison of Elephantine and a history of loyalty to Persian power.[139]

Third, the "evil act" is presented as the work of Vidranga. The priests of Khnum are not referenced in this document. Informed as they are by Yedaniah, Bagohi and Delaiah see Vidranga as the evil genius behind the affair. The author expresses the Yehudites' negative view of him by describing him as *lḥy'*, "evil" (line 6), using the same term as in the petition.

Fourth, when expressing their support for the rebuilding of the sanctuary for Yahô, Bagohi and Delaiah refer specifically to the resuming meal and incense offerings: "And the meal offering and the incense they may offer upon that altar just as formerly was done."[140]It is significant that Bagohi and Delaiah omit any reference to *ʿlwh*-offerings—that is, the sacrifice of animals—which Yedaniah had promised to resume in the petition to Bagohi: "And they will offer the meal offering and the incense, and the holocaust on the altar of Yahô in your name."[141] There is a huge discussion on the possible reasons for this. Three positions are defended:[142]

1. The animal sacrifices are left out in order not to affront the priests of Khnum. Their deity is always depicted as a ram-headed god, and the offering of rams by the Yehudites might once again trigger their religious zeal.[143]
2. The animal sacrifices are left out in order not to affront the Persians, who, according to Zoroastrian teaching, abhorred blood sacrifice.[144]
3. The animal sacrifices are left out in order not to affront the priests of the temple in Jerusalem, who, according to the Deuteronomistic views, were serving in the only temple in which the cult of YHWH was seen as legal.[145]

138. Herodotus, *Hist.* 4; see also Kuhrt, *Ancient Near East* 2:662–63.
139. Granerød, *Dimensions of Yahwism*, 214–27.
140. *TADAE* A4.9:9–11.
141. *TADAE* A4.7:25–26 // *TADAE* A4.8:24–25.
142. As outlined by Kottsieper, "Die Religionspolitik der Achämeniden," 169–75; Granerød, *Dimensions of Yahwism*, 140–47.
143. Porten, *Archives from Elephantine*, 289–93; Schäfer, *Judeophobia*, 132–33; Herrera, "P. 13497. 'Ofrecerán la oblación y el incienso,'" 421–49. Rohrmoser, *Götter, Tempel und Kult*, 244–51, has argued convincingly against this view: there were too less sheep in and around Elephantine.
144. Koch, "Iranische Religion," 11–29.
145. Frey, "Temple and Rival Temple," 173–80.

With Gard Granerød, I am of the opinion that none of these three explanations is convincing. I share his view that the "veto on animal sacrifice" functioned to appease the satrap Arshames.[146]

The memorandum can be seen as a clue that leading circles in Jerusalem and Samaria were willing to support the interests of their coreligionists in faraway Elephantine. The support was probably based not on sentimental values but on a weighing of political interests and possibilities.

6.4.4. An Offer of Payment by Leading Yehudites

This document is only partially preserved.[147] The lower-left corner is lost, and above that the document is damaged, making the middle part of the inscription difficult to read. The text contains 14 lines. Before line 1 there is a clear blank, as there likewise is after line 14. The absence of a formal salutation indicates that the text could be construed as a draft for a letter.[148] The text consists of two elements: a list of five Yehudites and a conditional promise of payment to the "house of our lord."

The five Yehudites listed are well known from other documents dating to the final part of the fifth century BCE: Yedaniah, son of Gem[ariah]; Mauziah, son of Nathan; Shemaiah, son of Haggai; Hosea, son of Yathom; and Hosea, son of Nattun. They can easily be construed as members of the leading circles of the Yehudite community. This is underscored by the fact that they present themselves as "heredi[tary property hol]ders" in Elephantine, which also indicates that they were seen as important citizens in the community as a whole.[149]

The absence of a salutation makes it difficult to identify the addressee of this draft. Yet the text contains two clues. In line 1 the five Yehudites present themselves as *'bdyk*, "your servants," and the conditional promise is clearly addressed to *mr'n*, "our lord" (lines 7, 12, and 13). Above, I have argued that this "lord" was most likely the Persian satrap Arshames. This would imply that the Persian satrap residing in Memphis was the intended receiver of the text and its promise.

The conditional promise contains two important features: "If our lord [...] and our temple of Yahô be rebuilt in Elephantine the fortress as it was former[ly

146. Granerød, *Dimensions of Yahwism*, 145–47.

147. *TADAE* A4.10; Porten, *Elephantine Papyri in English*, 152–53; Grabbe, *History of Jews and Judaism*, 1:211; Rohrmoser, *Götter, Tempel und Kult*, 409–11.

148. Porten, *Elephantine Papyri in English*, 152; contra Kraeling, *Brooklyn Museum Aramaic Papyri*, 110; Kottsieper, "Die Religionspolitik der Achämeniden," 169, who assume that the text was a "bribery-offer" handed over secretly.

149. *TADAE* A4.10:6. The expression "hereditary property holders" occurs four times in the Aramaic documents from Elephantine and indicates a position of prestige within the community; see Szubin and Porten, "Ancestral estates," 3–9; Szubin and Porten, "Testamentary Succession at Elephantine," 35–46; on the leading Yehudites, see Granerød, *Dimensions of Yahwism*, 33–34, 38–41.

bu]ilt—and sheep, ox, and goat are [n]ot brought there as burnt offering but [. . .] incense and meal offerings—and should our lord mak⌜e⌝ a statement [. . .] we shall give the house of our lord s⌜ilver . . .⌝ a thousand ardabs of barley."[150] The kernel of this is the promise that the Yehudites mentioned will make payment if the temple of Yahô is to be rebuilt. The condition mentions the purpose of the rebuilding: the continuation of the cult. There is, however, one important restriction made: animals will no longer be used in offerings. Sheep, oxen, and goat are explicitly mentioned as animals that will no longer be burned on the altar (line 10).[151] Above, I discussed several possible reasons for this restriction, but unfortunately this document des not contain the clues needed to solve this riddle. The fact that the restriction is explicitly mentioned can be seen as an indication that the restriction was probably the outcome of negotiations that are no longer traceable. It should be noted that the restriction was implicitly mentioned in the memorandum of Bagohi and Delaiah (see above). Its acceptance by the Yehudites can be construed as a sign of their willingness to return the status quo ante, with balance in the community between the various groups.[152]

It is intriguing to read that the Yehudites were willing to pay "sil⌜ver . . . and⌝ a thousand ardabs of barley" *ʿl byt mrʾn*, "to the house of our lord" (lines 13–14). This means that they did not directly pay the workers rebuilding temple. The payment to "the house of our lord" can be interpreted in two ways: the Yehudites had to pay "baksheesh"[153] to the Persian administration, or the payment for the rebuilding was organized through the Persian administration, and the gift mentioned was part of the payment by the Yehudites. Either way, "our lord" would have benefitted personally from the transaction.

6.5. A Thick Description

All this leads to the following construction of the past.[154] In ancient Egypt during the fifth century BCE, the unease with Persian occupation was growing. Step by step, the dream of an independent Egypt became stronger.[155] As a result,

150. *TADAE* A4.10:7–14; an Ardab is a measure of capacity of about 22 liters.

151. The three kinds of animals are referred to in regulations in Lev 7:23; 17:3; 22:27; Num 18:17. It is, however, most likely that the Yehudites did not possess a written copy of these in whatever phase of their redaction.

152. Porten, *Elephantine Papyri in English*, 153.

153. The later Middle Persian noun *baksheesh* is used here as an anachronism for "bribe; tip."

154. With Lorenz, *Konstruktion der Vergangenheit*, I prefer the concept of "construction" over the more classical idea of a "reconstruction." We must keep in mind that everything we say about the past is formulated in the presence.

155. This process will be described in chapter 7.

the aversion to loyal mercenaries, like the Yehudites, grew.[156] Time and again, the Egyptians tried to forcefully break Persian domination. After the death of Artaxerxes I and the crisis that followed in which Xerxes II, Sogdianus, and Darius II battled for the throne,[157] Persian power was weakened, and the administration began to lose its grip over the vast empire. The *pax persica*—the relatively peaceful coexistence of different ethnic groups across a vast empire—was threatened, especially in regions far away from the center of power. As argued above, in fifth-century BCE Elephantine, various ethnic groups lived together in relative harmony. Mercenaries from all parts of the empire were serving in the border garrison, and merchants from Phoenicia and Greece were trading their wares. The presence of these mercenaries in Elephantine safeguarded the *pax persica.* [158] but as conditions changed and the Egyptians began striving for independence, these foreign mercenaries came to be viewed as part of the Persian yoke, as accomplices to the Persian suppression of their political ambitions.

In 410 BCE the Persian satrap Arshames, who was residing in Memphis, went to visit the king. The temporary absence of the satrap, who as head administrator served as an enforcer of Persian power and protected the empire's interests, created a local power vacuum. The priests of Khnum in Elephantine, who, in one way or another, were connected to the Egyptian strive for independence, took the absence of the satrap as an opportunity to reach their ambitions. They bribed the recently appointed *frataraka*, Vidranga, who on his turn instructed his son Naphaina, an army commander, to do the "evil act." Various vital and symbolic elements of Persian rule in Elephantine were attacked: the granary of the king was demolished, a dividing wall was built within the town, a well supplying water to the garrison was stopped, and the temple of the Yehudites was demolished. In light of these other anti-Persian acts, the devastation of the temple of Yahô cannot be seen as an isolated act, let alone one simply based in a property dispute between two adjacent sanctuaries.[159]

Later on, loyal servants of Persian rule communicated the extent of the "evil act" to the satrap. Arshames acted promptly to stop this Egyptian uprising: Vidranga was imprisoned and deprived of all his belongings, and his conspirers were all killed. Arshames had exemplarily stopped the Egyptian uprising. He did not, however, order the reconstruction of the ruined temple of Yahô.

At that point, the leading Yehudites took the initiative by writing a petition to the political and religious leaders in Samaria and Jerusalem. When they received no response, they once more wrote a petition, now to the Persian governor

156. Lindenberger, "What Ever Happened to Vidranga?," 153; Schama, *Story of the Jews*, 25.

157. See S. Zawadzki, "The Circumstances of Darius II's Accession," *Jaarbericht Ex Oriente Lux* 34 (1995–96): 45–49.

158. See chapter 3.

159. Pace Kratz, *Historical and Biblical Israel*, 138–39.

Bagohi in Samaria. In well-chosen words they explained to him the miserable state of their sanctuary, without mentioning the other parts of the "evil act." They requested support for their plans to rebuild the temple, and Bagohi—in cooperation with Delaiah—assented. In a memorandum to Arshames, the leading Yehudites promised to pay "their lord" silver and goods in case the temple were to be rebuilt.

There are no official documents relating the reconstruction of the Yehudite sanctuary. The fact that the temple was rebuilt, however, can be inferred from two documents dated to 404 and 402 BCE.[160] The latter document, a deed concerning the sale of a property, clearly indicates that the property of Ananaiah, son of Azariah, and Ananaiah's wife, Tapamet, was situated across the street of the temple of Yahô. There are also no documents in which the permission of the Persians to rebuild is documented. It is nevertheless certain that the Persians accepted the request of the loyal Yehudites in order to have them on their side in the troublesome times of Egyptian uprising.[161]

The demolition of the Yehudite temple was only one part of the Egyptian attack. Arshames succeeded in suppressing the Egyptian revolt, albeit temporarily. After a dozen years the Egyptians succeeded in freeing themselves from the Persian yoke and became independent again, though not for long.

6.6. Concluding Question

The texts discussed in this chapter make clear that toward the end of the fifth century BCE the reciprocal acceptance between the various ethnic groups in and around Elephantine slowly dissipated. It should be noted that all four incidents discussed were quarrels between Egyptians and Yehudites. Problematic encounters between other ethnic groups in and around Elephantine are not documented in the texts known to us. To be able to understand this shift, we must consider other historical circumstances in fifth-century BCE Egypt. That will be done in the next chapter.

160. *TADAE* B3.10 and 12; see Schäfer, *Judeophobia*, 123–24; Rohrmoser, *Götter, Tempel und Kult*, 265–67; Granerød, *Dimensions of Yahwism*, 90–92; Siljanen, *Judeans in Egypt*, 237–38.

161. Porten, *Archives*, 295; Bledsoe, "Conflicting Loyalties," 251.

CHAPTER 7

"Khnum Is Against Us Since Hananiah Has Been in Egypt": On Two Historical Movements in the Fifth Century BCE

MAUZIAH, SON OF NATHAN, in his letter reporting his imprisonment and later release in the case of the stolen precious stone, hints at a reason for the upcoming tension between the various ethnic groups in and around Elephantine. In his opinion, Hananiah's coming to Egypt caused a major disruption to intergroup solidarity.[1] Hananiah—*ḥnnyh*—is known as the author of the so-called Passover Letter, dated to 419 BCE. With this letter some calendrical issues of Yehudite religion were arranged with imperial approval.[2] Although nothing is known about comparable arrangements for other ethnic groups, it can be assumed that this official recognition of the Yehudite religion—or at least parts of it—disturbed the balance between the various ethnic groups.[3] In particular, the priests of Khnum and the Egyptians on the island probably disapproved of this—in their view—preferential treatment.[4] There is, however, no direct evidence for this assumption; it can only be inferred from the later disruptions. Moreover, Hananiah is not attested in other documents from Elephantine. His role, function, and biography remain in the twilight of the past. We can only guess at his position in the Persian bureaucracy.

Nevertheless, the observation by Mauziah, son of Nathan, seems to hit the nail on the head, although I am of the opinion that the distortion of the *pax persica* was not the result of a single event or the coming of an individual to Egypt at the level of a single event. In this chapter, I would like to present two historical movements, both of which were, in my opinion,instrumental for the shift(s) in mentality. The first movement is not based on hard evidence and hence is a daring proposal of a speculative character. The second movement is based in various sources.

1. *TADAE* A4.3; see §6.1 above.
2. P.Berl. 13464; *TADAE* A4.1; see §2.3.1.1 above.
3. See Becking, "Centre, Periphery, and Interference," 65–78.
4. Thus Kottsieper, "Die Religionspolitik der Achämeniden," 150–78; van der Toorn, "Ezra in Egypt?," 602–10; van der Toorn, "Previously," 258; Van der Toorn, *Becoming Diaspora Jews*, 120–24.

7.1. From the Oasis in the Desert to the Land of the Pyramids

The argument for my speculative proposal starts with an observation made above (§2.3.6.2). The names of the deities Eshem-Bethel, Ḥerem-Bethel, Anat, and Bethel occur not only in Aramaic documents from Egypt dating from the Persian period but also in Papyrus Amherst 63. This papyrus was found in Egypt, though its specific provenance is unknown, and the Demotic text can be dated to the late fourth century BCE. The contents, however, reflect a syncretistic form of religion from an earlier age.[5] According to van der Toorn, the text consists of five sections.[6] The first three sections can be connected to ethnic groups: Babylonians (col. i–v), Syrians (col. vi–xi), and Israelites (col. xii–xiii).[7] I would prefer to label the third section as Israelite, and not as Samarian as suggested by van der Toorn.[8] As argued in the previous note, column xii 1–11 is better seen as part of the Syrian section. This challenges the idea that the conquest of Samaria is reflected in these lines. In the rest of the Israelite section, no references are made to Samaria, Judah, or Israel. In the Palmyra section, mention is made of š'm{|}r_2⌜r_2⌝[y]'n (שמרר[י]ן), "Samar[ia]ns."[9] In the same sub-canto the following lines are found:

> From where are the [pe]ople of your argot?
> —I come from [J]udah,
> my brothers have been brou[ght]
> from Samaria.
> A man is bringing now
> my sister from Jerusalem.[10]

The mention of both Jerusalem and Samaria in this section is an indication that the ethnic group behind section 3 of Papyrus Amherst should not be considered

5. See Heckl, "Inside the Canon and Out," 359–79; van der Toorn, *Papyrus Amherst 63*; van der Toorn, *Becoming Diaspora Jews*.

6. For now, I adopt the delimitation by van der Toorn, knowing that it is open to challenge and refinement.

7. The absence of the delimitor sp.C at the end of column xi might be an indication that col. xii:1–11—a mockery by the victors over a destructed city—could be the final part of the Syrian section and hence should not be treated as a reflection on the conquest of Samaria by the Assyrians. On the delimitor sp.C, probably s'k | p'r'š'H, סך פרשא, "end of section," see Vleeming and Wesselius, "'Betel the Saviour," 136; van der Toorn, *Papyrus Amherst 63*, 6.

8. Van der Toorn, *Papyrus Amherst 63*.

9. P. Amherst 63 xvii:2; van der Toorn, *Papyrus Amherst 63*, 204; van der Toorn, *Becoming Diaspora Jews*, 70–71.

10. P. Amherst 63 xvii:3–4; Heckl, "Inside the Canon and Out," 362–63; Steiner and Nims, "Aramaic Text in Demotic Script," 64; Holm, "Nanay and Her Lover," 1–37; van der Toorn, *Papyrus Amherst 63*, 204; van der Toorn, *Becoming Diaspora Jews*, 70–71.

to be only Samarians. The fourth section (col. xiv–xvii) is situated—according to van der Toorn—in a ḫlt's's | tm'r, חלץ תמר, "fortress of palms," identified by him with Palmyra.[11] His reading, however, is far from certain. In their 2017 online edition, Richard Steiner and Charles Nims propose the reading b.ḫrt.s.^{m} $\overline{\text{sy}}$.r^{m} (בחרץ סיאל), "into gold, divine Sheep."[12] I will therefore abandon van der Toorn's identification "fortress of palms" as the location from which a multiethnic community later migrated to Egypt, carrying with them the traditions later to be written as Papyrus Amherst 63. For that reason, I choose to identify this group as the one from the "oasis in the desert," where the various groups assembled and mixed. This fourth section has a clear syncretistic subtext and clearly bears witness to the peaceful coexistence of the groups mentioned. The fifth section (col. xviii–xxiii) is a kind of appendix containing the "tale of two brothers"—that is, a narrative on the fate of the Neo-Assyrian king Assurbanipal and his brother Shamash-shum-ukin.[13] Since the Aramaic of Papyrus Amherst 63 does not contain Persianisms or Persian loanwords—as, for instance, the majority of the Elephantine documents and the Aramaic sections in the biblical books of Ezra and Daniel do—and since the text does not refer to Egypt,[14] it can safely be assumed that the text stems from a period between the end of the reign of Assurbanipal[15] and the Persian conquest of the ancient Near East.[16]

The text of Papyrus Amherst functioned as a symbol for unifying the various ethnic groups living in the oasis in the desert. The text indicates that the deities of these groups were all understood to be manifestations of the deity named *mry*, מר, "lord," the Aramaic noun for a divine being comparable to Baal or Adon, which is attested throughout the text. The text, however, was not found in this oasis in the desert—whether Palmyra, Tayma,[17] or Jericho[18]—but somewhere

11. P. Amherst 63 xvi:7; van der Toorn, *Papyrus Amherst 63*, 18–37; van der Toorn, *Becoming Diaspora Jews*, 73–80.

12. Steiner and Nims, "Aramaic Text in Demotic Script," 59; corroborated by Tawny Holm in a private letter, December 2018; see her forthcoming edition, *Aramaic Literary Texts*.

13. First edition by Steiner and Nims, "Ashurbanipal and Shamash-shum-ukin," 60–81; see now Zaia, "My Brother's Keeper," 19–52.

14. With the exception of xx:4 where in a list of tribute, mention is made of "wonderful linen from Egypt."

15. Since the Tale of Two Brothers in Papyrus Amherst 63 is obviously dependent on the description of the deeds and doings of Ashurbanipal in his Royal Inscriptions, a date in the seventh century of this fifth section can be assumed; see Kottsieper, "Die literarische Aufnahme assyrischer Begebenheiten," 283–89; van der Toorn, *Papyrus Amherst 63*, 37.

16. See also van der Toorn, *Papyrus Amherst 63*, 37–39.

17. This oasis was part of the area controlled by the Qedarites and was a center for Arabian trade routes. The Neo-Babylonian king Nabonidus stayed in the oasis for many years; see Beaulieu, *Reign of Nabonidus King of Babylon*. In the late classical period, a group of Jews lived in Tayma; see Newby, *History of the Jews of Arabia*.

18. In the Hebrew Bible, Jericho is referred to as עיר התמרים, "city of palms," Deut 34:3; Judg 1:16; 3:13; 2 Chr 28:15; the city was an important station on the trade routes coming from Arabia.

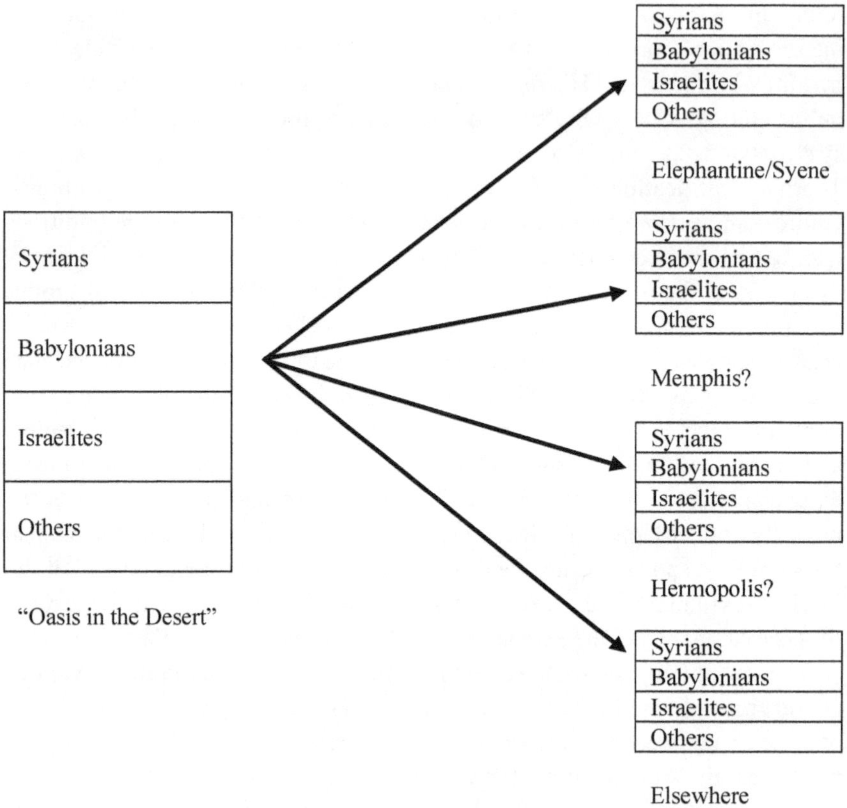

FIGURE 1. Diagram on the Migration of People from the Oasis in the Desert to the Banks of the Nile.

in Egypt. This raises the question how this text ended up in the land of the Nile. Van der Toorn entertains the idea that greater parts of the community at the oasis in the desert migrated to Egypt after the Persians came to rule over the ancient Near East. They took with them the text that would later be recorded in Papyrus Amherst 63 either as a manuscript or as an oral tradition. In his opinion, the Judeo-Arameans at Elephantine derived from this migration of Israelites, Syrians, and Babylonians at the end of the sixth century BCE.[19]

Although this proposal luminously explains the transition to Egypt, the thesis is in need of specification. First of all, it should be noted that the location where

19. Van der Toorn, *Papyrus Amherst 63*, 37–39; van der Toorn, *Becoming Diaspora Jews*. The idea of a migration had already been argued by Steiner, "Aramaic text in Demotic Script," 362–63, based, however, on an incorrect identification of syn', סין, with Syene in pap Amherst x:14.

the papyrus was found in Egypt is still unknown. The papyrus was purchased on the antiquities market in the second half of the nineteenth century and not discovered in a controlled archaeological excavation. The assumption that the papyrus was found at Elephantine or Syene is an interesting but indemonstrable proposal. It could have been discovered at any place in Egypt. In addition to that, as indicated above, the deities Eshem-Bethel, Anat-Yahû, and Ḥerem-Bethel are not mentioned in the Aramaic documents before 520 BCE.[20] If the people from the oasis in the desert had migrated in the early years of Persian dominance, we should expect these deities to be mentioned in earlier documents.

This brings me to the assumption that some of the people from the oasis in the desert migrated to Elephantine and Syene shortly before 520 BCE. Other parts of the group probably settled at other locations along the Nile as visualized in figure 1. It is tempting to connect the coming of Hananiah to Egypt with this assumed migration, but it is unproveable. Hananiah is mentioned in only two Aramaic documents from Elephantine: in the so-called Passover Letter[21] and in a side comment in the letter by Mauziah reporting about the assumed theft of a precious stone and its aftermath.[22] Nothing else is known about Hananiah. He might have been sent on a mission to southern Egypt comparable to Ezra's and Nehemiah's to Yehud.[23] Or he might have just come as an ordinary migrant. Independent of his background, it is remarkable that his coming to Elephantine coincides temporarily with both the assumed migration from the oasis in the desert and the deterioration of interethnic relations in Elephantine especially between the Egyptians and the mercenaries. In any case, the assumed migration would have led to the growth of the Yehudite community and distorted the balance between the various ethnic groups on the island and in Syene.

The Israelite section of Papyrus Amherst 63 contains three hymns:[24]

- xii 11–19 probably a precursor of the biblical Psalm 20[25]
- xiii 1–10 a song celebrating the joy of the New Moon Festival[26]
- xiii 11–17 a hymn on Yahô as divine and empathic warrior[27]

20. See §2.3.6.2.
21. P.Berl. 13464; *TADAE* A4.1; see §2.3.1.1 above.
22. See *TADAE* A4.3; see §6.1 above.
23. As suggested by van der Toorn, "Ezra in Egypt?," 602–10; van der Toorn, *Becoming Diaspora Jews*, 120–24.
24. See van der Toorn, *Papyrus Amherst 63*, 66–68 (text and translation), 165–75 (commentary); van der Toorn, *Becoming Diaspora Jews*, 69–73.
25. See Vleeming and Wesselius, "Aramaic Hymn," 501–9; Nims and Steiner, "Paganized Version of Psalm 20:2–6," 261–74; van der Toorn, "Celebrating the New Year," 634–37, 645–49 (with extensive literature); van der Toorn, "Psalm 20 and Amherst Papyrus 63," 244–61.
26. Van der Toorn, "Celebrating the New Year," 637–43.
27. Van der Toorn, "Celebrating the New Year," 643–45.

According to van der Toorn, these three hymns belong together. He reads them as parts of a New Year Festival. In his view, the elements of the new wine, the new moon, and the enthronement in the heavenly council together hint at the celebration of an autumnal New Year.[28] His view is interesting but based on an overinterpretation of the hymns. Wine—*y'yn'* (יין)—is mentioned in the second song,[29] but it is not presented as *new* wine, and there is no explict connection with the theme of harvest. The song only states, "They have mixed the wine in our jars!" Line 7 mentions *b'ḥdyš'n'* (בחדישן), "at our New Moon Festival."[30] The New Moon Festival was celebrated monthly in Canaan and ancient Israel.[31] Van der Toorn too quickly assumes a connection with the Ugaritic New Moon Festival and the "beginning of the wine" in the twelfth month to argue that the song in Papyrus Amherst 63 is connected with a New Year Festival.[32] Even if a connection to that festival could be made, it should be noted that the new moon of the twelfth month should not be confused with the start of the new year, which would be the new moon of the first month. The theme of enthronement is altogether absent in these lines.The hymn on Yahô as a divine warrior is simply praising God for his incomparability. The song presupposes the existence of other gods, but it does not mention them or the divine council.

Although van der Toorn's suggestion is unconvincing, it is plausible that the three hymns mentioned were introduced by the Israelites from the oasis in the desert into the cult of the temple of Yahô in Elephantine. I would like to round off this section with two very speculative remarks, one on the *marzēaḥ* institution and one on the provenance of the Aramaic Aḥiqar.

As noted above, one of the Aramaic documents from Elephantine refers to the *marzēaḥ* institution.[33] Porten and Yardeni date the text to the first quarter of the fifth century BCE.[34] Since two out of the three persons mentioned in the *marzēaḥ* text also occur in the Collection Account,[35] it might be better to date the *marzēaḥ* text to the last quarter of the fifth century BCE. The institution of the *marzēaḥ* was often, but not always, connected with the cult of the dead

28. Van der Toorn, "Celebrating the New Year." A New Year's festival is mentioned in the Babylonian section, pap Amherst 63 v:1–17; see Steiner, "Liturgy of a New Year's Festival."

29. Pap Amherst xiii:6.

30. See van der Toorn, *Papyrus Amherst 63*, 171, who refers to a variety of other possible translations.

31. See, e.g., Ps 81:4. There exists much literature on this Canaanite/Israelite festival; see, e.g., Goldstein and Cooper, "Festivals of Israel and Judah," 19–31; Keel, *Goddesses and Trees*.

32. See van der Toorn, *Papyrus Amherst 63*, 172; for the Ugaritic festival, see Pardee, *Ritual and Cult at Ugarit*, 56–65.

33. *TADAE* D.7.29; see §2.3.4 above.

34. In their edition in *TADAE* D, 177; adapted by Alavoine, "*Mrzḥ* est-il un banquet funéraire?," 11.

35. *TADAE* C.3.15 mentions Haggai and Yigdal. A daughter of Ashian is mentioned in the fragmentary remains of a contract that id difficult to date; *TADAE* D.2.4.

and the veneration of the ancestors, but it always included a banquet with an abundance of wine.[36] In Papyrus Amherst 63, a *q'r₂'₂* (קראה), "festive banquet," is mentioned on two occasions. The Syrian section mentions a banquet held for Bethel and his lady, during which a beauty contest takes place.[37] The song celebrating the joy of the New Moon Festival in the Israelite section is set at an abundant banquet for Yahô, who is depicted as drinking together with the people.[38] Although "banquet" and *marzēaḥ* are not fully equal, almost all *marzēaḥ* celebrations included a banquet. The description of the banquets in Papyrus Amherst 63 do not deviate very much from what is known about the meals at a *marzēaḥ*. Hence, it might be that the people from the oasis in the desert, after they migrated to Elephantine and Syene, introduced the *marzēaḥ* institution locally. This is, I admit, a very speculative thought.

Even more speculative than the *marzēaḥ* connection is the following proposal. When reading through Papyrus Amherst 63, I noticed that the Aramaic in this document is quite similar to the kind of Aramaic that is found in the text of the Saying of Aḥiqar from Elephantine. This raises an interesting possibility: Could it be that the Aramaic Aḥiqar was introduced to Elephantine by the people who migrated from the oasis in the desert? This is an audacious hypothesis that requires further investigation, but it is beyond the scope of the present monograph.

In this connection, a remark should be made about the festivals of Passover and Matzot.[39] Granerød correctly observed that in the older document, D7.6, the celebration of Passover is set in the context of the family, while the so-called Passover Letter discusses the celebration of an unknown festival—probably Matzot—in the context of the official religion.[40] This shift might, in my opinion, have been caused by the influx of the people who migrated from the "oasis in the desert. At the same time, this shift can be labeled anachronistically as a form of confessionalism. This is a concept borrowed from the Reformation, in which new and old congregations reformulated the traditional lived religion using formulaic language in order to make clear the boundaries between the various Reformed and Catholic groups. Adhering to the phrasing of the confessional documents became more important than personal faith.[41] The official, formulaic language of the so-called Passover Letter might indicate the Yehudites' need of reframing

36. See Alavoine, "*Mrzḥ* est-il un banquet funéraire?"; McLaughlin, *Marzēah in the Prophetic Literature*; Na'aman, "Four Notes," 215–22; Amadasi Guzzo and Zamora, "Phoenician *Marzēaḥ*," 187–214.

37. P. Amherst 63 ix:7; see van der Toorn, *Papyrus Amherst 63*, 132–41.

38. P. Amherst 63 xiii:2.10; see van der Toorn, "Celebrating the New Year," 637–43; van der Toorn, *Papyrus Amherst 63*, 169–72.

39. See §2.3.1.1 above.

40. Granerød, "Canon and Archive," 356.

41. Kaplan, *Calvinists and Libertines*, 5–13.

the traditional, lived religion through this sort of demarcation. This would imply tensions within the group and fissures within the broader community.

In sum, I argue that a group of Israelites from the oasis in the desert came to Elephantine and its environs and enlarged the Yehudite community there. In bringing their form of Yahwism—influenced as it was by the syncretistic situation in the oasis in the desert—they challenged and changed the form of Yahwism at Elephantine, probably to the aversion of the priests of Khnum. An inadequate analogy can be seen in the early years of the Dutch Republic. In the aftermath of the Spanish conquest of the city of Antwerp (1585 CE), many Protestants from that city, as well as from the territory of present-day Belgium, took refuge in what is now the Netherlands. They brought their skills with them, which was one of the reasons for the blossoming Dutch Golden Age in the seventeenth century. They also brought with them their pietistic form of Protestantism, which eventually led to a change in the profile of Dutch Protestantism—from more liberal to orthodox, culminating in the anti-liberal decisions at the Synod of Dordrecht (1518–19).[42] The changes at Elephantine around 420 BCE can be construed as a distant parallel to this historical development.

7.2. Egypt's Struggle for Independence

From the early days of the reign of Cambyses, Persian rule in Egypt was contested. In this section, I will discuss five major rebellions against the Persians.[43] It is not always fully clear what led to the Egyptian uprisings. Besides the struggle for political independence, two intertwined factors were of great importance: taxations and food shortages. In §1.5 above, I indicated the burden of Persian taxes skimming the economic surplus. Donald Redford has pointed out the Persians' ongoing neglect of the interests of the original Egyptian populations that resulted in food riots.[44] It is perhaps superfluous to say that the people from the various ethnic groups who served as soldiers in the Persian army were construed by the rebellious Egyptians as the accomplices of the Persians.[45]

7.2.1. Psammetichus III

After Cambyses had defeated the Egyptian king Ahmose, the son of the latter started a revolt against the new Persian ruler. Herodotus tells a lengthy and

42. See Kaplan, *Calvinists and Libertines*; Israel, *Dutch Republic*, 1998; Parker, "Two Generations of Discipline," 215–31.

43. For an outline of the Egyptian rebellions, see Rottpeter, "Initiatoren und Träger," 9–49.

44. Redford, "Origin and Termination," 149–57.

45. See Redford, "Origin and Termination."

detailed story on the fate of Psammetichus III and his unsuccessful rebellion.[46] The Persian military campaign to Egypt is related with only a few words in Darius's Bisitun inscription, and mainly as a prelude to the rebellion by Gaumāta: "Thereupon Cambyses went to Egypt. When Cambyses had departed into Egypt, the people became hostile, and the lie multiplied in the land, even in Persia and Media, and in the other provinces."[47] According to Herodotus, Cambyses locked the Egyptian king in the outskirts of the city in order to break his spirit. Cambyses first had the daughter of Psammetichus pass by dressed as a slave girl and later on had his son killed as a reprisal. On both occasions, Psammetichus, unlike Egyptians incarcerated with him, did not burst out in tears of anger but instead bowed himself to the ground as a gesture of respect.[48] When, however, Psammetichus saw an impoverished companion, he broke into loud weeping, striking his head and calling on his companion by name. When questioned by the king through an intermediary messenger, Psammetichus answered: "Son of Cyrus, my private grief was too great for weeping; but the unhappiness of my companion deserves tears—a man fallen from abundance and prosperity to beggary come to the threshold of old age."[49] This answer moved Cambyses, and the Egyptian king was brought to live at the court at Memphis for the rest of his life.[50] Psammetichus, however, was not at ease with this role as a puppet and again rebelled against Persia, though unsuccessfully: "But as it was, Psammetichus plotted evil and got his reward; for he was caught raising a revolt among the Egyptians; and when Cambyses heard of it, Psammetichus drank bull's blood and died. Such was his end."[51] It should be noted that Cambyses, shortly after conquering Egypt, took some measures leading to budget cuts for several Egyptian temples.[52] Details about the character of the rebellion and the art of the Persian response are not given by Herodotus except for the bloody end of Psammetichus, who probably committed suicide.[53] The rebellion shows that Persian rule was from its beginning not generally appreciated in Egypt.[54]

46. See Herodotus, *Hist.* 3.14–15; translation: Kuhrt, *Persian Empire*, 113–14; see Kuhrt, *Ancient Near East*, 662; Serrano Delgado, "'Cambyses in Sais," 31–52.

47. DB §10.

48. See Harrison, "Upside Down and Back to Front," 161–72.

49. Herodotus, *Hist.* 3.14.10–11.

50. There is an interesting parallel in the Hebrew Bible, 2 Kgs 25:27–30, although the amnesty for Jehojachin is rooted in the Akitu, or New Year festival, and not in the personal pity of the emperor; see Patton, *Hope for a Tender Sprig*.

51. Herodotus, *Hist.* 3.15.4.

52. Demotic Chronicle Verso D:1–17; translation: Kuhrt, *Persian Empire*, 125–26; see §1.3 above.

53. "Drinking the blood of the bull" was the fabled cause of the death of Themistocles in 459 BCE (cf. Aristotle, *Eq.* 83–84 and Plutarch, *Them.* 31); the blood was supposed to coagulate and choke the drinker (Aristotle, *Hist. An.* 3.19); see How and Wells, *Commentary on Herodotus*, 284. The expression could well be an euphemism for suicide; see Marr, "Death of Themistocles," 159–67.

54. See also Kuhrt, *Ancient Near East*, 646–62; Sternberg-el Hotabi, "Die persische Herrschaft in Ägypten," 124–15; Lloyd, "Egyptian Attitude to the Persians," 185–98.

7.2.2. Petubastis IV

The Bisitun inscription of Darius I refers to rebellions throughout the empire: "King Darius says: While I was in Babylon, these provinces revolted from me: Persia, Elam, Media, Assyria, Egypt, Parthia, Margiana, Sattagydia, and Scythia."[55] This raises the question of the character of the Egyptian revolt against Darius I and its suppression. Within the Bisitun inscription, no mention is made of a campaign by Darius to Egypt. Excavations at Amheida in the Dakhla oasis have made clear that in 520 BCE Persia was confronted with a rival king, Petubastis IV, a descendant of the Saite pharaohs.[56] At the remains of a gateway to the local temple, three correlated hieroglyphic inscriptions were found:

1. Horus, who controls the Two Lands; the Two Ladies [Son of Neith?] who illuminates the temples; Horus of Gold . . . (lost); [King of Upper and Lower Egypt, Lord of the Two Lands] Who-delights-the-heart-of-Re; Son of Re, Lord of Appearances, Petubastis, beloved of Ptah of Memphis (South of His Wall).
2. [King of Upper and Lower Egypt, Lord of the Two Lands], Lord of Rituals, Who-delights-the-heart-of-Re; Son of Re, Lord of [Appearances, Petubastis]; he has made (it) as a monument for his father Thoth the Twice Great, the Lord of Amheida, so that he may be given [life].
3. Petubastis living forever.[57]

The presence of the full throne names of Petubastis in these inscriptions reveals that he was seen as king by the Egyptians, at least in Memphis[58] and the western oases. As discussed above (§1.3), Kaper connects this story of the lost army of Cambyses with the rebellion of Petubastis. In doing so, he identifies the Libyan tribe of the Ammonians with the groups supporting Petubastis. The aim of Cambyses's campaign was to quell Petubastis's revolt, but the army was ambushed and was lost in a sandstorm, never to be seen again. The conflict was not resolved when Cambyses died "on the way home," but it lasted deep into the reign of Darius. Recently, based on a complex chronological argument, Wijnsma has argued that Darius I brought Egypt under Persian control only in 518 BCE.[59]

55. DB §21.

56. See Kaper, "Petubastis IV in the Dakhla Oasis,"; Wijnsma, "Worst Revolt of the Bisitun Crisis," 157–73.

57. See Kaper, "Petubastis IV in the Dakhla Oasis," 127–34.

58. Possibly the *nšn ꜥ3*, "great rage," mentioned in the Autobiography of Udjaḥoresnet 33–34.40–41; see Kaper, "Petubastis IV in the Dakhla Oasis," 138.

59. Wijnsma, "Worst Revolt of the Bisitun Crisis."

There is no evidence about the background of this rebellion. No reasons for the acts of Petubastis are known, but his behavior is another sign of Egyptian discord with their Persian overlords.

7.2.3. Psammetichus IV

In August 492 BCE, Darius was defeated in the battle of Marathon. The Persian army was surprised by the tactics of the Athenians and their martial craftsmanship.[60] In evaluating Marathon, Darius decided to return to the traditional Persian strategy of using massive number of soldiers in a campaign. To reach that goal and to overpower Greece, he had to recruit large numbers of soldiers, countless horses, and a load of armaments from all corners of the empire.[61] This massive enlistment led to trouble—for instance, in Egypt, where the retraction of forces and arms lead to a rebellion: "In the fourth year the Egyptians, whom Cambyses had enslaved, revolted from the Persians; thereupon Darius was even more eager to send expeditions against both."[62] According to Cruz-Uribe, this revolt could well be connected to the rebellion of Psammetichus IV.[63] This king is mentioned in Demotic ostraca from Diospolis Parva, Hut-Sekhem, nowadays Hiw in Egypt.[64] In these documents, Psammetichus IV receives a royal name, indicating that he was seen as a ruler. Darius started a campaign against Egypt shortly before his death in 486 BCE.[65] It was only in the reign of Xerxes that the rebellion was suppressed: "After being persuaded to send an expedition against Hellas, Xerxes first marched against the rebels in the year after Darius's death. He subdued them and laid Egypt under a much harder slavery than in the time of Darius, and he handed it over to Achaemenes, his own brother and Darius' son."[66] Details about the campaigns of Darius I and Xerxes are absent.[67] The Demotic ostraca from Diospolis Parva indicate that the area had a flourishing agriculture. The threat of losing the fruits of this land to the Persians might have been the origin of the rebellion.

60. See Herodotus, *Hist.* 6.112–16; translation: Kuhrt, *Persian Empire*, 234–35; Green, *Greco-Persian Wars*, 43–74; Kellogg, *Marathon Fighters and Men of Maple*.

61. See Ruzicka, *Trouble in the West*, 27.

62. Herodotus, *Hist.* 3.1.3; translation: Kuhrt, *Persian Empire*, 236; Ruzicka, *Trouble in the West*, 27; Wijnsma, "And in the Fourth Year," 34–35.

63. Cruz-Uribe, "On the Existence of Psammetichus IV," 35–39; Wijnsma, "And in the Fourth Year," 43.

64. See Salmon, "Relations entre la Perse et l'Egypte," 148–51; Vleeming, *Gooseherds of Hou*; Wijnsma, "And in the Fourth Year," 49–53.

65. For a proposal to pinpoint the exact dates, see Wijnsma, "And in the Fourth Year."

66. Herodotus, *Hist.* 7.77; translation: Kuhrt, *Persian Empire*, 248; Wijnsma, "And in the Fourth Year."

67. See Sternberg-el Hotabi, "Die persische Herrschaft in Ägypten," 125; Ruzicka, *Trouble in the West*, 28.

7.2.4. Inaros

In the period between 465 and 463 BCE, the Egyptians rebelled against Persian rule. In coalition with the Lybian chief Inaros, Amyrtes of Sais fought—in vain—against the Persians.[68] After Xerxes had defeated the rebellion by Psammetichus IV, he appointed his brother Achaemenes as satrap over Egypt. Herodotus notes, "While governing Egypt, this Achaemenes was at a later time slain by a Libyan, Inaros son of Psammetichus."[69] Achaemenes, also known as Haxāmaniš, the brother of Xerxes, was the satrap of Egypt from 484 until his death in 460 BCE.[70] In 480 BCE, he was commissioned to command the Persian fleet at the battle of Salamis.[71] According to Jeffrey Rop, the satrap's absence from Egypt led to the revolt by Inaros.[72] In my view, Rop is correct about the absence leading to rebellion, but wrong about the date.

In 465 BCE, Xerxes was killed by Artabanus, the commander of the royal bodyguard, with the helped by Aspamitres, a eunuch. Artabanus was one of the most powerful officials in the Persian court. The narrative of this assassination is present in three classical sources, albeit with some differences. Ctesias relates, "Artapanus and Aspamitres the eunuch, the confidential advisers of Xerxes, resolved to kill their master. Having done so, they persuaded Artaxerxes that his brother Dariaeus had murdered him. Dariaeus was taken to the palace of Artaxerxes, and, although he vehemently denied the accusation, he was put to death."[73] The reports by Diodorus Siculus[74] and Justin[75] only differ in details. Quite different is a remark in a Babylonian astronomical text. In connection to an eclipse on June 5–6, 465 BCE, it states: "Abu, 14 (+ x); Xerxes's son killed him."[76] Matthew Stolper has argued that since some other Babylonian and Persian texts mention events that are dated later than his assumed death, this reference might be a "ghost fact."[77] In view of the struggles that eventually

68. See Porten, *Archives*, 26; Kuhrt, *Ancient Near East*, 671; Sternberg-el Hotabi, "Die persische Herrschaft in Ägypten," 125–26; Ruzicka, *Trouble in the West*, 26–34; Rohrmoser, *Götter, Tempel und Kult*, 21–25.

69. Herodotus, *Hist.* 7.7; translation: Kuhrt, *Persian Empire*, 248; this claim is not corrorated by Diodorus Siculus who indicates that this same Achaemenes lead the Persian campaign against Egypt.

70. Achaemenes life ended during the battle of Papremis in the western Nile delta.

71. On this battle and its significance, see Strauss, *Battle of Salamis*.

72. See Rop, "Assassination of Tissaphernes," 58.

73. Ctesias, *Persica* =*FrGrH* 688 F1 3 (33); see Lenfant, *Ctésias de Cnide*, 127; Kuhrt, *Persian Empire*, 307.

74. Diodorus Siculus, *Bibliotheca historica* 11.69; translation by Kuhrt, *Persian Empire*, 307–8.

75. Justin, *Epitome* 3.1; translation by Kuhrt, *Persian Empire*, 309.

76. BM 32234, still unpublished; see Kuhrt, *Persian Empire*, 306; Stolper, "Some Ghost Facts," 196–98; Abu is the fifth month in the Babylonian calendar.

77. Stolper, "Some Ghost Facts."

lead to the enthronement of Artaxerxes, it might also be that scribes continued to date events after the deceased king, awaiting a final solution to the struggles. Nevertheless, this cuneiform text assumes that Xerxes was killed not by this high official but by an unnamed son. Diodorus Siculus offers a detailed report on the rebellion by Inaros:

> But when the inhabitants of Egypt learned of the death of Xerxes and of the general attempt upon the throne and the disorder in the Persian kingdom, they decided to strike for their liberty. At once, then, mustering an army, they revolted from the Persians, and after expelling the Persians whose duty it was to collect the tribute from Egypt, they set up as king a man named Inaros. He at first recruited soldiers from the native Egyptians, but afterward he gathered also mercenaries from the other nations and amassed a considerable army. He dispatched ambassadors also to the Athenians to effect an alliance, promising them that, if they should liberate the Egyptians, he would give them a share in the kingdom and grant them favors many times greater than the good service they had rendered. And the Athenians, having decided that it was to their advantage to humble the Persians as far as they could and to attach the Egyptians closely to themselves against the unpredictable shiftings of Fortune, voted to send three hundred triremes to the aid of the Egyptians. The Athenians, therefore, with great enthusiasm set about the preparation of the expedition. As for Artaxerxes, when he learned of the revolt of the Egyptians and their preparations for war, he concluded that he must surpass the Egyptians in the size of his armaments. So, he at once began to enrol soldiers from all the satrapies, build ships, and give his attention to every other kind of preparation.[78]

From this text, it becomes clear that the main reason for the revolt would have been the heavy burden of the Persian taxes on Egypt's economy. The Egyptians—under the leadership of Inaros—took advantage of the power vacuum after the death of Xerxes and the absence of the satrap Achaemenes.[79] They joined forces with the Athenians to become as strong as possible for the expected Persian reaction. The new Persian king, Artaxerxes I, took a set of measures leading to a major expansion of his military forces.

Later on, Artaxerxes appointed Achaemenes to lead the campaign against Egypt. His large army, however, was beaten by the allied forces of Egypt and

78. Diodorus Siculus, *Bibliotheca historica* II.71:3–6; translation by Kuhrt, *Persian Empire*, 319; see Sternberg-el Hotabi, "Die persische Herrschaft in Ägypten," 125.

79. As in the later case of Arshames whose absence was seized by Vidranga and the priests of Khnum to attack vital elements of the Persian power at Elephantine—above §6.3—the power-vacuum was a momentum for rebellion.

Athens.[80] After having tried in vain to bribe the Lacedaemonians to make war against Athens, Artaxerxes appointed Artabazus and Megabyzus, men of outstanding merit, to campaign against Egypt.[81] They marched through the Sinai to reach Memphis, where they overpowered the Greeks and the Egyptians. Egypt became a satrapy again and the Athenians were allowed to go home in view of their exceptional courage. The tragic fate of Inaros is mentioned by Ctesias:

> Having appointed Sarsamas satrap of Egypt, Megabyzus took Inaros and the Greeks to Artaxerxes, who was greatly enraged with Inaros because he had slain his brother Achaemenides. Megabyzus told him what had happened, how he had given his word to Inaros and the Greeks when he occupied Byblos, and earnestly entreated the king to spare their lives. The king consented, and the news that no harm would come to Inaros and the Greeks was immediately reported to the army.
>
> But Amestris, aggrieved at the idea that Inaros and the Greeks should escape punishment for the death of her son Achaemenides, asked the king [to give them up to her], but he refused; she then appealed to Megabyzus, who also dismissed her. At last, however, through her constant importunity she obtained her wish from her son, and after five years the king gave up Inaros and the Greeks to her. Inaros was impaled on three stakes; fifty of the Greeks, all that she could lay hands on, were decapitated.[82]

Inaros (II) was named after Inaros I, who rebelled against the Assyrians in the seventh century BCE. Later reflections on Inaros I in Demotic texts underscore the importance of this rebel. He was part of the Egyptian cultural memory.[83] Inaros II is mentioned in an Egyptian contract concerning water rights in the Kharga oasis.[84] Although his rebellion was ultimately in vain, his deeds kept the Egyptian dream of casting off the Persian yoke alive, as reflected in many Demotic tales and documents referring to this story.[85]

80. Diodorus Siculus, *Bibliotheca historica* 11.74:1–4; translation by Kuhrt, *Persian Empire*, 319; Thucydides, *Hist.* 1.104, 109–10; translation by Kuhrt, *Persian Empire*, 321–22; see Kahn, "Inaros' Rebellion against Artaxerxes I," 424–40.

81. Diodorus Siculus, *Bibliotheca historica* 11.74:5–6; translation by Kuhrt, *Persian Empire*, 319.

82. Ctesias, *Persica =FrGrH* 688 F13 (38–39); see Lenfant, *Ctésias de Cnide*, 129–31; Kuhrt, *Persian Empire*, 323–24.

83. See Ryholt, "Assyrian Invasion of Egypt," 384–511; Holm, "Sheikh Fadl Inscription," 193–224; Köhler, Driaux, Marchand, Holm and Capirci, "Preliminary Report."

84. See Chauveau, "Inaros, prince des rebelles," 39–46; Holm, "Sheikh Fadl Inscription," 208.

85. See Thissen, "Homerischer Einfluss," 369–87; Ryholt, "Assyrian Invasion of Egypt," 384–511; Rutherford, "Earliest Cross-Cultural Reception of Homer?," 83–105.

7.2.5. *Amyrtes/Psammetichus V*

The desire for independence did not die. In 411 BCE Amyrtes, most likely the grandson of Amyrtes who was a companion of Inaros II,[86] started a rebellion against Darius II, leading eventually to the throwing off of the Persian yoke. A late fifth-century letter from the satrap Arshames to Artavant concerning the Cilicians who were employed at the various estates of Arshames in Egypt[87] mentions an Egyptian uprising: "When the Egyptians rebelled and the garrison had to be mobilized, this Pariyama[88] and his coworkers were unable to get into the fortress."[89] Grelot connected this unspecified rebellion with the revolt by Amyrtes.[90] He might be correct, although a connection with the "evil act" of Vidranga and the priests of Khnum cannot be excluded.

In 404 BCE Amyrtes became the first and only pharaoh of the Twenty-Eighth Dynasty, ruling only over the delta region.[91] Not many details of his rebellion or his reign are known. Amyrtes took advantage of the struggle between Artaxerxes II and Cyrus the Younger, who both claimed the Persian throne after the death of Darius II. Their hostilities prevented the Persians from interfering in Egypt.[92] In the Demotic Chronicle, an ancient "prophetic" text based on the traditional proto-apocalyptic alternation of "good kings and bad kings," it is stated: "The first ruler who came after the foreigners who are the Medes (Persians) was Pharaoh Amenirdais (Amyrtaios)."[93] This report is corroborated by a remark in Manetho: "The Twenty-Eighth Dynasty. Amyrteos of Saïs, for 6 years."[94] Upper Egypt remained under Persian control up to 398 BCE, when Nepherites I succeeded in a rebellion, killed Amyrtes II, and was able to inaugurate the Twenty-Ninth Dynasty controlling all of Egypt.[95] This began a period of independence for Egypt that lasted until 343 BCE, when Artaxerxes III succeeded in bringing Egypt back under Persian control, albeit only for a few decades.

86. See Ruzicka, *Trouble in the West*, 37.
87. *TADAE* A6.7; see §3.2 above.
88. The leader and foreman of the Cilicians.
89. *TADAE* A6.7:6–8; see Sternberg-el Hotabi, "Die persische Herrschaft in Ägypten," 126–27.
90. Grelot, *Documents araméens d'Égypte*, 308.
91. See Ruzicka, *Trouble in the West*, 37 (with lit.); Rohrmoser, *Götter, Tempel und Kult*, 22.
92. See Ruzicka, *Trouble in the West*, 37–40; Waters, *Ancient Persia*, 189–90.
93. Demotic Chronicle, edited by Spiegelberg, *Die sogenannte demotische Chronik* 3.18–19; Johnson, "Demotic Chronicle as an Historical Source," 1–17; Kuhrt, *Persian Empire*, 393.
94. Manetho, *Hist. Egypt.* = *FrGrH* 609 F3; Kuhrt, *Persian Empire*, 390; Siljanen, *Judeans of Egypt*, 33.
95. See Ruzicka, *Trouble in the West*, 41; Waters, *Ancient Persia*, 190.

7.3. *Histoire Conjoncturelle*

When considering the Achaemenid period in the history of ancient Egypt, the historian feels like a psychiatrist analyzing an absent patient. The only evidence on hand is a set of reports created for some purpose other than diagnosis, and it is not possible to interview anyone with firsthand experience of the patient. Nevertheless, I dare to make a few remarks.

The struggle for independence was an ongoing undercurrent in Achaemenid Egypt. Next to ethnic or national pride, the fact that Persian taxes in kind and money throttled the local economy was very important.[96] To see the surplus of your agricultural endeavor skimmed off to a foreign country is a perennial reason for rebellion. This constant undercurrent also made the various ethnic groups who were working for the Persian administration and army vulnerable at moments of political weakness. To the Egyptians, all of them were accomplices of the Persians, who were coresponsible for the sometimes dire situation of the local Egyptians.

On several occasions, domestic pressures and uncertainties after the death of a Persian ruler affected the empire's outer territories, thus leading to changes and challenges. This pattern is discernible throughout the history of other larger states as well.[97]

Elephantine can be construed as a peripheral but complex and multiethnic community. As such, it was to a great degree dependent upon the core power in the center of the empire. The harmony in the peripheral communities could be disturbed by the influx of new ethnic groups (or the dramatic population increase of one of them) or by the core power favoring one of group over the others. I have argued that Papyrus Amherst 63 gives evidence of an inflow of Yehudites that took place in the years before 520 BCE. The so-called Passover Letter is evidence of the fact that the Yehudites were granted a religious privilege; whatever the details of this grant, it triggered hostility from the Egyptians. The Egyptian desire for independence began to undermine the local *pax persica*. The center was gradually losing its grip on the periphery, resulting in decreased security for any ethnicities other than Egyptians at Elephantine.

96. See Sternberg-el Hotabi, "'Die persische Herrschaft in Ägypten," 124–27.
97. See Binetti, "How Ancient States Rise and Fall," 30–45.

CHAPTER 8

Beyond the Final Curtain: The Aftermath of Elephantine

WHAT HAPPENED AFTER THE *PAX PERSICA* had perished? Is anything known about the fate of the various ethnic groups at Elephantine and Syene, or did they just disappear into the fog of the past? Not much is known about this period, therefore the following discussion will be limited.

8.1. Independent Under Nepherites

In 398 BCE, Nepherites I killed his rival Amyrtes II. Both had their power base in the delta region. The shift of power is subtly referred to in a fragmentary letter dated to 398 BCE: "When [this] le[tter] will reach you [. . .] they [will] bring to Memphis the king, Amyrt⸢es . . .⸣ King Nepherites ascended (the throne) [in] Epiphi [. . .]."[1] It is obvious that Shewa, the sender of this letter, tries to make clear to the unknown recipient that the former king—now incarcerated—has been replaced by Nepherites. Nepherites succeeded in liberating Upper Egypt from Persian rule: the whole land of the Nile was now independent again.[2] It is notable that the manner of dating documents in the texts from Elephantine changed at this time.[3] Up to 401 BCE, letters and documents were dated according to the regnal years of Artaxerxes. For instance, "On the 18th of Paophi, in the fourth year of Artaxerxes the king, in Yeb the fortress, said Malchiah, son of Joshibiah, Armaean, holding property in Yeb the fortress."[4] In the latest-dated Aramaic document from Elephantine, the shift to Amyrtes is visible. In this letter, Menaḥem, son of Shallum solemnly declares he will give the two sheqels that he had to give in fulfilment of the terms of a marriage contract to Sallua,

1. *TADAE* A3.9; see Kuhrt, *Persian Empire*, 392; Vittmann, "Arameans in Egypt," 249.
2. See Clarysse, "Nephorites, Founder of the 29th Dynasty and his Name," 215–17; Ruzicka, *Trouble in the West*, 41.
3. See Ruzicka, *Trouble in the West*, 39.
4. *TADAE* B7.2:1–3; for the identification of ארתחשסש with Artaxerxes II, see Porten, "Cowley 7 Reconsidered," 89–92.

daughter of Sa/ttuah, within a few months. The text is dated thus: "On the 21st (?) of Phamenoth, year 5 of Amyrtaeus (אמורטיס), the king, said Menaḥem, son of Shallum, an Armaean of Yeb the fortress, of the detachment of Nabukudurri, to Sallua, daughter of Sa/ttuah."[5] I do not interpret this dating as an indication that Upper Egypt was already under Egyptian control by 401 BCE; rather, I understand it as a sign that the Egyptians' desire for independence and Persia's slipping grip on Elephantine was felt by the Yehudite community.

No texts dated to the reign of Nepherites are found. He is, however, mentioned in later king lists. According to Manetho, Nepherites reigned for six years:

> The Twenty-Ninth Dynasty: four kings of Mendês.
> 1. Nepheritês, for six years.[6]

The Demotic Chronicle depicts him as a "bad king," in fitting with the alternation between good times and bad times characteristic of proto-apocalyptic texts: "The second ruler who came after the Medes, namely Pharaoh Nafiwert (Nepherites I), after he had done what he did conscientiously, his son was allowed to succeed him. He was only given a short time to himself because of the many transgressions that began in his time."[7] The character of these transgressions is not revealed. According to Diodorus Siculus, Nepherites helped Agesilaus, king of Sparta, in his war against Persia, probably in 396 BCE: "While these events were taking place, the Lacedaemonians dispatched ambassadors to Nephereus, the king of Egypt, to conclude an alliance; he, in place of the aid requested, made the Spartans a gift of equipment for one hundred triremes and five hundred thousand measures of grain."[8]

8.2. The Fate of the Yehudites and Other Minorities

The sources available give no clear evidence of the fate of the ethnic groups in and around Elephantine. It can be taken for granted that the local Egyptians enjoyed the regained freedom and the fact that the local resources now were to their own disposal. The Persians who had worked in the administration and the garrison were no longer of any use to the Egyptians.[9] There is no evidence of

5. *TADAE* B4.6:1–3

6. Manetho, *Hist. Egypt.* = *FrGrH* 609 F3; Kuhrt, *Persian Empire*, 390.

7. Demotic Chronicle, edited by Spiegelberg, *Die sogenannte demotische Chronik* 3.18–19; Johnson, "Demotic Chronicle as an Historical Source," 1–17; Kuhrt, *Persian Empire*, 393.

8. Diodorus Siculus, *Hist.* 14.79.4–5; Kuhrt, *Persian Empire*, 370.

9. Ruzicka, *Trouble in the West*, 40; Rohrmoser, *Götter, Tempel und Kult*, 81, assumes that the contracts of the mercenaries were simply discontinued.

what most likely happened: the Persians being killed or imprisoned by the new rulers.[10] But archaeological evidence indicates that the houses in the Yehudite/Aramean quarter of Elephantine came to be used as stables.[11]

There is one small piece of evidence hinting at the fate of the Yehudites of Elephantine. A letter in Demotic written to a lady in Elephantine contains the clearly Yehudite name *yhyḥy*, "May Yahô live."[12] Following Porten, Ruzicka assumes that the majority of them remained in Elephantine now serving new masters.[13] He might be correct, but there is nothing to prove the assumption. If he is correct, then a change in mentality must have occurred among the Egyptians, since they previously construed all these non-Egyptians as accomplices of the Persian oppressor. Redford's view of what befell the Yehudites is entirely different. In his view, the new Egyptian leadership wanted to restore Upper Egypt in all its glory, including the cult of Khnum. In that restored glory there would be no place for the Yehudites and other people from the border garrison who would then be killed, deported, or enslaved. Either way, the became invisible in the historical record.[14] To make a decision between these opposing views will require new evidence.

In the Egyptian city of Edfu, somewhat to the North of Elephantine, a Jewish minority community was present in Ptolemaic and Roman times, as is evidenced by tax receipts and a list of people propbably made up for the purposes of taxation.[15] They were integrated and assimilated into the local community, partly through intermarriage. According to some scholars, these "Jews" were the offspring of the Yehudites from Elephantine who, after the collapse of their community, migrated north.[16] Fitzpatrick-McKinley seems to toy with the idea that this Jewish community at Edfu consisted of descendants of Yehudite mercenaries installed there by the Persians.[17] Although this assumption is possible, the time-gap between fifth-century BCE Elephantine and Ptolemaic Edfu is too large to exclude other explanations for the existence of this Jewish community at Edfu.

In the first half of the fourth century BCE, Egypt played a new role on the international stage. In 343 BCE, Artaxerxes III conquered Egypt and turned it

10. Redford, "Some Observations on the Traditions," 279–364.

11. See Krekeler, "Stadtgrabung am Westkom von Elephantine," 107–15.

12. P.Berl. 23592, to be edited by Karl-Theodor Zauzich; see Vittmann, "Arameans in Egypt," 249–50.

13. B. Porten, *Archives*, 296–98 Ruzicka, *Trouble in the West*, 40.

14. See Redford, "Origin and Termination of the Foreign Colony," 154.

15. See *Corpus Papyrorum Judaicarum*, edited by V.A. Tcherikover, in collaboration with A. Fuks, 1:108; Kornfeld, "Zu den aramäischen Inschriften aus Edfu," 49–52.

16. See Honigman, "Jewish Communities of Hellenistic Egypt," 117–35; LaCoste, *Waters of the Exodus*, 30.

17. Fitzpatrick-McKinley, "Preserving the Cult of Yhwh," 428–31.

once again into a Pesian satrapy.[18] No traces of Yehudites, Judeans, or Jews from that period are known. This might be an indication that the Yehudites from Elephantine—as well as the other ethnic groups discussed above—were absorbed in the melting pot of Egypt in those days and lost their clear or traceable ethnic identity.

8.3. Some Speculations

Diodorus Siculus narrates that when the last Egyptian pharaoh, Nectanebo II, saw the army of Artaxerxes III entering into and conquering Egypt, he made a decision: "But King Nectanebôs, while still tarrying in Memphis and perceiving the trend of the cities toward betrayal, did not dare risk battles for his dominion. So, giving up hope of his kingship and taking with him the greater part of his possessions, he fled into Aethiopia."[19] On the fate of Nectanebo at the court in Nubia, not much is known. Burstein argues on the basis of an inscription of the Kushite king Nastasen that Nastasen had tried to reinstate Nectanebo II but was restrained from doing so since he had to bow before the Persian fleet under Artaxerxes II.[20] This remark has given rise to speculations on the fate of the Yehudites of Elephantine. David Kessler has suggested that they had followed the pharaonic example by taking refuge in Nubia.[21] The migration of some of the offspring of the Yehudites of Elephantine to Nubia, though unprovable, is far from impossible. Kessler, however, takes a further step by trying to connect these migrating Yehudites with the Falashas—or, more correctly, Beith Israel—in Ethiopia.[22] He admits the speculative nature of his proposal, though, and points out three problems with it. First, there is a time-gap of thirteen centuries between the assumed migration and the first written traces on the Falashas in Ethiopia. The diaries recording the travels of Eldad ha-Dani, in which he claims to be a Jew from an independent Jewish state "on the other side of the river Kush"—if not pure legendary—date from the ninth century CE.[23] Over this

18. As narrated in Diodorus Siculus, *Hist.* 16.46.4–7; 16.51; Kuhrt, *Persian Empire*, 413–14. See Kuhrt, *Ancient Near East*, 674–75; Briant, *Histoire de l'Empire Perse*, 713–833; Sternberg-el Hotabi, "Die persische Herrschaft in Ägypten," 127; Wiesehöfer, "Achaemenid Empire," 11–30.

19. Diodorus Siculus, *Hist.* 16.51.1; Kuhrt, *Persian Empire*, 413–14; Ladynin, "Nectanebo in Ethiopia," 527–34.

20. See Burstein, "Kush and the External World," 225–30; the Nastasen-stele (Berlin 2268) has been edited by Gauthier, *Livre des rois d'Égypte*, 62. Note that in the legendary *Alexander Romance* Nectanebo is said to have fled to Macedon where he would become the father of Alexander the Great.

21. Kessler, *Falashas*, 44–45.

22. Kessler, *Falashas*.

23. Kessler, *Falashas*, 77.

long period, greater demographic changes could have taken place. Second, the Jews from Ethiopia possessed a translation of the Hebrew Bible. In Elephantine no fragments of Tanak have been found.[24] Third, no traces of the veneration of deities like Eshem-Bethel or Anat-Yahô are found among the members of Beith Israel.[25] Kessler argues that the presence of Judeo-Aramaic words in the Geʿez language of Ethiopia—as signalled by Ullendorff[26]—hint at a background of the Falashas in ancient Elephantine,[27] but his view remains speculative.

Even more bewildering is the claim of British journalist Graham Hancock elaborating on the ideas of Kessler—on the ark of the covenant. This portable sanctuary was allegedly constructed during Israel's journey of forty years through the desert and later placed in the temple built by Solomon. This idea has roots in a fourteenth-century CE Ethiopian manuscript. The national epic of Ethiopia, the *Kebra Nagast*, "Glory of the Kings," narrates—among many other things how the Judeans had fallen out of grace as keepers of the ark of the covenant, and so a new Zion was founded in Ethiopia and the ark was transported to its new and better home in Africa:

> And Azâyâs rose up straightway, and woke up the three men his brethren, and they took the pieces of wood, and went into the house of God—now they found all the doors open, both those that were outside and those that were inside—to the actual place where Azâyâs found Zion, the Tabernacle of the Law of God; and it was taken away by them forthwith, in the twinkling of an eye, the Angel of the Lord being present and directing. And had it not been that God willed it Zion could not have been taken away forthwith. And the four of them carried Zion away, and they brought it into the house of Azâyâs, and they went back into the house of God, and they set the pieces of wood on the place where Zion had been, and they covered them over with the covering of Zion, and they shut the doors, and went back to their houses. And they took lamps and set them in the place where [Zion] was hidden, and they sacrificed the sheep thereto, and burned offerings of incense thereto, and they spread purple cloths over it and set it in a secret place for seven days and seven nights.[28]

From that day onward, the ark of the covenant would have resided in a sanctuary in Ethiopia. According to Hancock, the ark was transported to Elephantine

24. Kessler, *Falashas*, 24–57.
25. Kessler, *Falashas*, 24–57; see already Ullendorff, *Ethiopia and the Bible*.
26. Ullendorff, *Ethiopia and the Bible*, 124.
27. Kessler, *Falashas*, 44.
28. *Kebra Nagast* §48 = E.A. Wallis Budge, *Kebra Nagast*, 71–72; on this text, see now Shahîd, "Kebra Nagaśt," 253–98; Johnson, "Dating the Kebra Nagaśt, 299–311.

by Judeans who fled to Egypt during the reign of King Manasseh. Eventually, it was brought to the Church of St. Mary Zion in the small town of Axum, Ethiopia, where, according to him, it exists to this day.[29] The *Kebra Nagast*—if not pure legend—does not mention Elephantine as a halfway house for the ark. Hancock's book, while amusing and easy reading, is not based on confirmable facts and should be dismissed as an example of pseudoscience.[30]

8.4. Conclusions

How was the *pax persica* possible? With which instruments was it maintained? And why didn't it last? After analyzing the available documents and reading them against their historical and social background, I arrived at the following answers.

The *pax persica* in fifth-century BCE Egypt was made possible by the Persian military conquest of Egypt; the Persian Empire's military and economic control over its satrapy on the borders of the Nile; and the presence of many middlemen, including mercenaries and merchants from all over the empire, who served and supported the Persians.

The Persians, through institutions of scribal education, indoctrinated the *literati* by having the scribes read and write texts containing the Persian royal ideology of loyalty to the crown—the Sayings of Aḥiqar and the Bisitun inscription. The open society of respect for and acceptance between the various ethnic groups in Elephantine—and probably elsewhere—functioned as binding cement in the community. In addition, the Persian military, judicial, and administrative presence functioned as mechanisms of enforcement that discouraged disruptions and rebellions.

There are various reasons why the *pax persica* did not last. The most important of them is the internal weakening of the immense empire after the death of Darius II. As for Egypt, the ongoing struggle for independence eventually turned out to be stronger than the Persian enforcement.

29. Hancock, *Sign and the Seal.*

30. Porten, "Did the Ark Stop at Elephantine?," 54–77; Van Dyk and Enstrom, "What Happened to the Ark?," 50–60.

BIBLIOGRAPHY

Abe, T. "Dascylium: An Overview of the Achaemenid Satrapal City." *Acta Academiae Antiquitatis Kiotoensis* 12 (2012): 1–17.

Abou-Assaf, A., P. Bordreuil, and A. R. Millard. *La statue de Tell Fekherye et son inscription bilingue assyro-araméenne.* Études assyriologiques 10. Paris: Recherche sur les civilisations: 1982.

Adiego, I. J. *The Carian Language*. HdO 86. Leiden: Brill, 2007.

Africa, T. W. "Herodotus and Diodorus on Egypt." *JNES* 22 (1963): 254–58.

Aggoula, B. "Studia Aramaica, II." *Syria* 62 (1985): 61–76.

Ahlström, G. W. *The History of Ancient Palestine from the Palaeolithic Period to Alexander's Conquest.* JSOTSup 146. Sheffield: Sheffield Academic Press, 1993.

Alavoine, V. "Le *mrzḥ* est-il un banquet funéraire? Études des sources épigraphiques et bibliques (Am. 6, 7 et Ier. 16, 5)." *Le Muséon* 113 (2000): 1–23.

Albani, M. "Israels Feste im Herbst und das Problem des Kalenderwechsels in der Exilszeit." Pages 111–56 in *Festtraditionen in Israel und im Alten Orient.* Edited by E. Blum and R. Lux. VWGTh 28. Gütersloh: Gütersloher Verlagshaus, 2006.

Albertz, R. "The Controversy About Judean versus Israelite Identity and the Persian Government: A New Interpretation of the Bagoses Story (Antiquitates XI.297–301)." Pages 483–504 in Lipschits, Knoppers, and Oeming, *Judah and the Judeans in the Achaemenid Period.*

———. *Religionsgeschichte Israels in alttestamentlicher Zeit.* Grundrisse zum Alten Testament 8/1–2. Göttingen: Vandenhoeck & Ruprecht, 1992.

Albertz, R., and R. Schmitt. *Family and Household Religion in Ancient Israel and the Levant*. Winona Lake, IN: Eisenbrauns, 2012.

Albright, W. F. "The North Canaanite Epic of 'Al'êyan Ba'al and Môt." *Journal of the Palestine Oriental Society* 12 (1932): 185–208.

Alstola, T., *Judeans in Babylonia: A Study of Deportees in the Sixth and Fifth Centuries BCE.* CHANE 109. Leiden: Brill, 2019.

Amadasi Guzzo, M. G., and J. Á. Zamora. "The Phoenician *Marzeaḥ*—New Evidence from Cyprus in the 4th Century BC." *Studia Eblaitica* 4 (2018): 187–214.

Amin, M. A. "Ancient Trade and Trade Routes Between Egypt and the Sudan, 4000 to 700 BC." *Sudan Notes and Records* 51 (1970): 23–30.

Anneler, H. *Zur Geschichte der Juden von Elephantine*. Bern: Drechsel, 1912.

Arnold, W. R. "The Passover Papyrus from Elephantine." *JBL* 31 (1912): 1–33.

Athas, G. *The Tel Dan Inscription: A Reappraisal and a New Interpretation.* JSOTSup 360. Sheffield: Sheffield Academic, 2003.
Avishur, Y., and M. Heltzer. "Carians as Skilled Masons in Israel and Mercenaries in Judah in the Early I Millennium BCE." *Kadmos* 42 (2004): 87–90.
Ayad, B. A. "From the Archive of Ananiah Son of Azariah: A Jew from Elephantine." *JNES* 56 (1997): 37–50.
Ayali-Darshan, N. "The Sequence of Sir 4:26–27 in Light of Akkadian and Aramaic Texts from the Levant and Later Writings." *ZAW* 130 (2018): 436–49.
Azzoni, A. *The Private Lives of Women in Persian Egypt.* Winona Lake, IN: Eisenbrauns, 2013.
———. "'Where Will Yehoyišma' Go?' A Reconstruction of *TAD* B3.8." Pages 1–5 in *Puzzling Out the Past: Studies in Northwest Semitic Languages and Literatures in Honor of Bruce Zuckerman.* Edited by M. J. Lundberg, S. Fine, and W. T. Pitard. CHANE 55. Leiden: Brill, 2012.
Baines, J. "On the Composition and Inscriptions of the Vatican statue of Udjahorresnet." Pages 83–92 in *Studies in Honor of William Kelly Simpson.* Edited by P. Der Manuelian. Boston: Museum of Fine Arts, 1996.
Barkworth, P. R. "The Organization of Xerxes' Army." *IrAnt* 27 (1993): 149–67.
Bassir, H. "Neshor at Elephantine in Late Saite Egypt." *JEgH* 9 (2016): 66–95.
Bateman, J. A. *Multimodality and Genre: A Foundation for the Systematic Analysis of Multimodal Documents.* New York: Palgrave Macmillan, 2008.
Beaulieu, P.-A. *The Pantheon of Uruk During the Neo-Babylonian Period.* Cuneiform Monographs 23. Leiden: Brill, 2003.
———. *The Reign of Nabonidus King of Babylon, 556–539 B.C.* New Haven: Yale University Press, 1989.
Becking, B. "Burglars, Diplomats, or Victims? Remarks on the Interpretation of a Document from Elephantine." *Zeitschrift für altorientalische und biblische Rechtgeschichte* 23 (2017): 223–28.
———. "Centre, Periphery, and Interference: Notes on the 'Passover/Mazzot'-Letter from Elephantine." Pages 65–78 in *Centres and Peripheries in the Early Second Temple Period.* Edited by E. Ben Zvi and C. Levin. FAT 108. Tübingen: Mohr (Siebeck), 2016.
———. "Exchange, Replacement, or Acceptance? Two Examples of Lending Deities among Ethnic Groups in Elephantine." Pages 30–43 in *Jewish Cultural Encounters in the Ancient Mediterranean and Near Eastern World.* Edited by M. Popović, M. Schoonover, and M. Vandenberghe. JSJSup 178. Leiden: Brill, 2017.
———. "Die Gottheiten der Juden in Elephantine." Pages 203–26 in *Der eine Gott und die Götter: Polytheismus und Monotheismus im antiken Israel.* Edited by M. Oeming and K. Schmid. Abhandlungen zur Theologie des Alten und Neuen Testaments 82. Zürich: TVZ, 2003.
———. "Jeremiah 44: A Conflict on History and Religion." Pages 255–64 in *Religious Polemics in Context: Papers Presented to the Second Conference of the Leiden Institute for the Study of Religion (LISOR) held at Leiden, 27–28 April 2000.* Edited by T. L. Hettema and A. Van der Kooij. Studies in Theology and Religion 11. Assen: Van Gorcum, 2004.
———. "The Other Groups That Were . . . : Some Remarks on Different Minor Ethnicities in Persian Period Elephantine." *Journal for Semitics* 26 (2017): 820–48.
———. "Temple, *marzēaḥ*, and Power at Elephantine." *Transeu* 29 (2005): 37–47.

Becnel, K., and R. A. Moeller. "What, Why, and How They Read: Reading Preferences and Patterns of Rural Young Adults." *Journal of Adolescent and Adult Literacy* 59 (2015): 299–307.

Benz, F. L. *Personal Names in the Phoenician and Punic Inscriptions: A Catalogue, Grammatical Study and Glossary of Elements*. Studia Pohl 8. Roma: Pontificum Institutum Biblicum, 1972.

Berlejung, A., and K. Radner. "Aḫi-iaqar." Page 63 in *The Prosopography of the Neo-Assyrian Empire 1/1: A*. Edited by K. Radner. Helsinki: The Neo-Assyrian Text Corpus Project and the Finnish Foundation for Assyriological Research, 1998.

Bernand, A., and O. Masson. "Les inscriptions grecques d'Abou-Simbel." *Revue des Études Grecques* 70 (1957): 1–46.

Betlyon, J. W. *The Coinage and Mints of Phoenicia: The Pre-Alexandrine Period*. Harvard Semitic Monographs, 26. Atlanta: Scholars Press, 1982.

Bettles, E. A. *Phoenician Amphora Production and Distribution in the Southern Coastal Levant: A Multi-Disciplinary Investigation into Carinated-Shoulder Amphorae of the Persian Period (539–332 BC)*. British Archaeological Reports 1183. Oxford: BAR Publishing, 2003.

Binetti, C. "How Ancient States Rise and Fall: Pre-Democratic Regime Typology, Representation, and Domestic and International Balances of Power." *Geopolitics, History and International Relations* 10 (2018): 30–45.

Blau, P., and J. E. Schwartz. *Crosscutting Social Circles: Testing a Macrostructural Theory of Intergroup Relations*. New York: Routledge, 2018.

Bledsoe, S. A. "Conflicting Loyalties: King and Context in the Aramaic Book of Ahiqar." Pages 239–68 in Silverman and Waerzeggers, *Political Memory in and after the Persian Empire*.

Blenkinsopp, J. "The Mission of Udjahorresnet and those of Ezra and Nehemiah." *JBL* 106 (1987): 409–21.

Boiy, T. *Late Achaemenid and Hellenistic Babylon*. OLA 136. Leuven: Peeters, 2004.

Bolin, T. M. "The Temple of יהו at Elephantine and Persian Religious Policy." Pages 127–42 in *The Triumph of Elohim: From Yahwisms to Judaisms*. Edited by D. V. Edelman. CBET 13. Kampen: Kok Pharos, 1995.

Bonfiglio, R. P. "Visualizing Literacy: Images, Media, and Method." *Biblical Interpretation* 25 (2017): 293–319.

Borneman, J. *Death of the Father: An Anthropology of End in Political Authority*. New York: Berghahn Books, 2004.

Botta, A. F. *The Aramaic and Egyptian Legal Traditions at Elephantine: An Egyptological Approach*. LSTS 64. London: T&T Clark, 2009.

———. "Aspects of the Daily Life of the Jewish Colony of Elephantine." *Antiguo Oriente* 9 (2011): 63–84.

———. "Hated by the Gods and Your Spouse: Legal Use of שנא in Elephantine and its Ancient Near Eastern Context." Pages 105–29 in *Law and Religion in the Eastern Mediterranean: From Antiquity to Early Islam*. Edited by A.C. Hagedoorn and R.G. Kratz. Oxford: Oxford University Press, 2013.

Bresciani, E. "La satrapia d'Egitto." *Studi Classici e Orientali* 7 (1958): 132–88.

Bresciani, E., and M. Kamil. *Le lettere aramaiche di Hermopoli*. Accademia nazionale dei Lincei. Classe di scienze morali, storiche e filologiche 8/12, fasc. 5. Roma: Scienze e lettere editore commerciale, 1966.

Briant, P. *Histoire de l'Empire Perse: De Cyrus à Alexandre*. Paris: Fayard, 1996.

Briant, P., W. F. M. Henkelman, and M. Stolper. *L'archive des fortifications de Persépolis. État des questions et perspectives de recherches*. Persika 12. Paris: de Boccard, 2008.

Brodersen, K., *Polyainos: Strategika* Sammlung Tusculum, Berlin: de Gruyter, 2017.

Brosius, M. "Pax Persica: Königliche Ideologie und Kriegführung im Achämenidenreich." Pages 135–61 in *Krieg-Gesellschaft-Institutionen. Beiträge zu einer vergleichenden Kriegsgeschichte*. Edited by B. Meißner, O. Schmitt, and M. Sommer. Berlin: de Gruyter, 2005.

———. *The Persians*. New York: Routledge, 2006.

Brown, T. S. "Herodotus' Portrait of Cambyses." *Historia: Zeitschrift für Alte Geschichte* 31 (1982): 387–403.

Burstein, S. M. "Kush and the External World: A Comment." *Meroitica* 10 (1989): 225–30.

Callataÿ, F. de. "White Gold: An Enigmatic Start to Greek Coinage." *American Numismatic Society Magazine* 12, no. 2 (2013): 6–17.

Cameron, G. C. "Darius, Egypt, and the 'Lands Beyond the Sea.'" *JNES* 2 (1943): 307–13.

Candelora, D. "Defining the Hyksos: A Reevaluation of the Title *hk3 h3swt* and Its Implications for Hyksos Identity." *Journal of the American Research Center in Egypt* 53 (2018): 203–21.

Capps, D. "The Beatitudes and Erikson's Life Cycle Theory." *Pastoral Psychology* 33 (1985): 226–44.

Carp, B. L. *Defiance of the Patriots: The Boston Tea Party and the Making of America*. New Haven: Yale University Press, 2010.

Carter, A. *Marshal Tito: A Bibliography.* Westport, CT: Greenwood, 1989.

Cartledge, P. *Thermopylae: The Battle that Changed the World*. New York: Vintage Books, 2007.

Carty, A. *Polycrates, Tyrant of Samos: New Light on Archaic Greece*. Stuttgart: Franz Steiner Verlag, 2015.

Cawkwell, C. *The Greek Wars: The Failure of Persia*. Oxford: Oxford University Press, 2006.

Chauveau, M. "Inaros , prince des rebelles." Pages 39–46 in *Res Severa Verum Gaudium: Festschrift für Karl-Theodor Zauzich zum 65. Geburtstag.* Edited by F. Hoffmann and H. J. Thissen. StD 6. Leuven: Peeters, 2004 .

Clarysse, W. "Nephorites, Founder of the 29th Dynasty and His Name." *CdE* 69 (1994): 215–17.

Cohen, S. J. D. *The Beginnings of Jewishness: Boundaries, Varieties, Uncertainties,* Berkeley: University of California Press, 1999.

Colburn, H. P. "Connectivity and Communication in the Achaemenid Empire 1." *Journal of the Economic and Social History of the Orient* 56 (2013): 29–52.

Collins, J. J. *The Invention of Judaism: Torah and Jewish identity from Deuteronomy to Paul*. Taubman Lectures in Jewish Studies . Oakland: University of California Press, 2017.

Conklin, B. *Oath Formulas in Biblical Hebrew*. Linguistic Studies in Ancient West Semitic 5. Winona Lake, IN: Eisenbrauns, 2011.

Cornell, C. "Cult Statuary in the Judean Temple at Yeb." *JSJ* 47 (2016): 1–19.

———. "The Forgotten Female Figurines of Elephantine." *Journal of Ancient Near Eastern Religions* 18 (2018): 111–32.

Coulson, W. D. E., and A. Leonard. "A Preliminary Survey of the Naukratis Region in the Western Nile Delta." *Journal of Field Archaeology* 6 (2013): 151–68.
Cowley, A. E. *Aramaic Papyri of the Fifth Century BC*. Oxford: Clarendon, 1923.
Cross, F. M. "An Aramaic Inscription from Daskyleion." *BASOR* 184 (1966): 7–10.
Cruz-Uribe, E. "The Lake of Moeris: A Reprise." Pages 63–66 in *Life in a Multi-cultural Society: Egypt from Cambyses to Constantine and beyond* Edited by J. H. Johnson. Studies in Ancient Oriental Civilizations 51. Chicago: Oriental Institute, 1992.
———. "On the Existence of Psammetichus IV." *Serapis* 5 (1980): 35–39.
———. *Translations, Commentary, Discussions and Sign List*. Vol. 1 of *Hibis Temple Project*. San Antonio: Van Siclen, 1988.
Dandamaev, M. A. *Persien unter den ersten Achämeniden (6. Jh. v. Chr.)*. Beiträge zur Iranistik 8. Wiesbaden: Reichert, 1976.
Dandamaev, M. A., and V. G. Lukonin. *The Culture and Social Institutions of Ancient Iran*. Cambridge: Cambridge University Press, 2004.
Davis, A. "Moving Beyond the Single Mediated Arena Model: Media Uses and Influences Across Three Arena's." Pages 167–86 in *How Political Actors Use the Media: A Functional Analysis of the Media's Role in Politics*. Edited by P. Van Aelst and S. Walgrave. Cham: Palgrave Macmillan, 2017.
Depuydt, L. "Murder in Memphis: The Story of Cambyses's Mortal Wounding of the Apis Bull (ca. 523 BCE)." *JNES* 54 (1995): 119–26.
Deutsch, R., and M. Helzer. *New Epigraphic Evidence from the Biblical Period*. Tel Aviv: Archaeological Center Publications, 1995.
Donker van Heel, K., ed. *The Legal Manual of Hermopolis (P. Mattha): Text and Translation*. Leiden: Papyrologisch Instituut, 1990.
Doyle, D. "Ritual Male Circumcision." *Journal of the Royal College of Physicians Edinburgh* 35 (2005): 279–85.
Dubovský, P. *Hezekiah and the Assyrian Spies: Reconstruction of the Neo-Assyrian Intelligence Services and its Significance for 2 Kings 18–19*. Biblica et Orientalia 49. Roma: Pontifico Instituto Biblico, 2006.
Dupont-Sommer, A. '"Bêl et Nabû, Šamaš et Nergal" sur un ostracon araméen inédit d'Éléphantine." *Revue de l'Histoire des Religions* 128 (1944): 28–39.
———. "Une inscription araméenne inédite d'époque perse trouvée à Daskyléion (Turquie)." *Comptes rendus de l'Académie des inscriptions et belles-lettres* (1966): 44–57.
Dušek, J. *Les manuscripts araméens du Wadi Daliyeh et la Samarie vers 450–332 av. J.-C.* CHANE 30. Leiden: Brill, 2007.
Dušek, J., and J. Mynářová. "Phoenician and Aramaic Inscriptions from Abusir." Pages 53–69 in *In the Shadow of Bezalel. Aramaic, Biblical, and Ancient Near Eastern Studies in Honor of Bezalel Porten*. Edited by A. F. Botta. CHANE 60. Leiden: Brill, 2012.
Dvorjetski, E. "From Ugarit to Madaba: Philological and Historical Functions of the *marzēaḥ*." *JSS* 61 (2016): 17–39.
Dyk, P. J. van, and P. L. Enstrom, "What Happened to the Ark?" *Religion and Theology* 4 (1997): 50–60.
Eilberg-Schwartz, H. *The Savage in Judaism: An Anthropology of Israelite Religion and Ancient Judaism*. Bloomington: Indiana University Press, 1990.
Eilers, W. *Iranische Beamtennamen in der keilschriftlichen Überlieferung*. Abhandlungen für die Kunde des Morgenlandes 25/5. Leipzig: Brockhaus, 1940.

Elayi, J. *Histoire de la Phénicie*. Paris: Perrin, 2013.
Evans, J. A. S. "What Happened to Croesus?" *Classical Journal* 74 (1978): 34–40.
Fales, F. M. "Aramaic Letters and Neo-Assyrian Letters: Philological and Methodological Notes." *JAOS* 107 (1987): 451–69.
Fantalkin, A., and E. Lytle. "Alcaeus and Antimenidas: Reassessing the Evidence for Greek Mercenaries in the Neo-Babylonian Army." *Klio* 98 (2016): 90–117.
Ferrier, R. W. "Persepolis." *Asian Affairs* 3 (1972): 23–27.
Finkel, I. L., ed. *The Cyrus Cylinder: The King of Persia's Proclamation from Ancient Babylon*. London: I. B. Tauris, 2013.
Finn, J. "Gods, Kings, Men: Trilingual Inscriptions and Symbolic Visualizations in the Achaemenid Empire." *Ars Orientalis* 41 (2011): 219–75.
Fischer-Bovet, C. *Army and Society in Ptolemaic Egypt*. Cambridge: Cambridge University Press, 2014.
Fitzmeyer, J. A. "A Re-study of an Elephantine Aramaic Marriage Contract (AP 15)." Pages 137–68 in *Near Eastern Studies in Honor of William Foxwell Albright*. Edited by Hans Goedicke. Baltimore: Johns Hopkins Press, 1971.
Fitzpatrick-McKinley, A. *Empire, Power, and Indigenous Elites: A Case Study of the Nehemiah Memoir*. JSJSup 169. Leiden: Brill, 2015.
———. "Preserving the Cult of YHWH in Judean Garrisons: Continuity from Pharaonic to Ptolemaic Times." Pages 375–408 in *Sibyls, Scriptures, and Scrolls: John Collins at Seventy*. Edited by J. Baden, H. Najman, and E. J. C. Tigchelaar. JSJSup 175. Leiden: Brill, 2017.
Flowerdew, J. "Problems of Speech Act Theory From an Applied Perspective." *Language Learning* 40 (1990): 79–105.
Folmer, M. L. "De Achikar Traditie." Pages 73–83 in *Wijsheid*. Edited by J. Dubbink, N. A. Riemersma, K. Spronk, W. C .G. van Wieringen. Amsterdamse Cahiers voor Exegese van de Bijbel en Zijn Tradities 31. Bergambacht: 2VM, 2017.
———. *The Aramaic Language in the Achaemenid Period: A Study in Linguistic Variation*. OLA 68. Leuven: Peeters, 1995.
Franklin, N. "Masons' Marks from the Ninth Century BCE Northern Kingdom of Israel: Evidence of the Nascent Carian Alphabet?" *Kadmos* 40 (2001): 107–16.
Frey, J. "Temple and Rival Temple—The Cases of Elephantine, Mt. Gerizim and Leontopolis." Pages 173–80 in *Gemeinde ohne Tempel—Community without Temple*. Edited by B. Ego, A. Lange, P. Pilhofer. Wissenschaftliche Untersuchungen zum Neuen Testament 118. Tübingen: Mohr Siebeck, 1999.
Fried, L. S. "Cyrus the Messiah? The historical background to Isaiah 45:1." *Harvard Theological Review* 95 (2002): 373–93.
———. *Ezra: A Commentary*, Sheffield: Sheffield Phoenix, 2015.
———. *The Priest and the Great King: Temple-Palace Relations in the Persian Empire*. Biblical and Judaic Studies from the University of California, San Diego 10. Winona Lake, IN: Eisenbrauns, 2004.
Friedman, T. "The Sabbath in Israel: Law and Life." *Judaism* 31 (1982): 93–98.
Friedrich, J., and M. von Oppenheim. *Die Inschriften vom Tell Halaf: Keilschrifttexte und aramäische Urkunden aus einer assyrischen Provinzhauptstadt*. Archiv für Orientforschung Beiheft 6. Osnabruck: Biblio-Verlag, 1967.
Gale, N. H., and Z. A. Stos-Gale. "Ancient Egyptian Silver." *JEA* 67 (1981): 103–15.
Gardiner, A. H. *Ancient Egyptian Onomastica*. Oxford: Oxford University Press, 1947.

Garland, R. *Athens Burning: The Persian Invasion of Greece and the Evacuation of Attica*. Baltimore: Johns Hopkins University Press, 2016.
Gass, E. "Der Passa-Papyrus (Cowl 21I): Mythos oder Realität?" *Biblische Notizen* 99 (1999): 55–68.
Gates-Foster, J. "Achaemenids, Royal Power, and Persian Ethnicity." Pages 175–93 in *A Companion to Ethnicity in the Ancient Mediterranean*. Edited by J. McInerney. Blackwell Companions to the Ancient World 119. Malden, MA: Wiley-Blackwell, 2014.
Gauthier, H. *Le Livre des rois d'Égypte: Recueil de titres et protocoles royaux, noms propres de rois, reines, princes, princesses et parents de rois, 4: De la XXVe dynastie àla fin des Ptolémées*. Cairo: Institut français d'archéologie orientale, 1916.
Geertz, C. *The Interpretation of Cultures: Selected Essays*. New York: Harper Collins, 1973
Gensler, H. J. *Ethics and the Golden Rule*. New York: Routledge, 2013.
George, A. R. "The Gods Išum and Ḫendursanga: Night Watchmen and Street-Lighting in Babylonia." *JNES* 74 (2015): 1–8.
Ginzburg, C. *Clues, Myths and the Historical Method*. Baltimore: Johns Hopkins University Press, 1989 .
Glick, L. B. "Real Men: Foreskin Cutting and Male Identity in the Philippines." Pages 155–74 in *Circumcision and Human Rights*. Edited by G. C. Denniston, F. Hodges, and M. F. Milos. Dordrecht: Springer, 2009.
Goldstein, B. R., and A. Cooper. "The Festivals of Israel and Judah and the Literary History of the Pentateuch." *JAOS* 110 (1990): 19–31.
Gosline, S. L. "Carian Quarry Markings on Elephantine Island." *Kadmos* 31 (1992): 43–50.
Gottlieb, I. "Succession in Elephantine and Jewish Law: Brooklyn Museum Aramaic Papyrus 2." *JSS* 26 (1981): 193–203.
Grabbe, L. L. *A History of Jews and Judaism in the Second Temple Period* 1. LSTS 47. New York: Continuum, 2004.
———. "Israel's Reality After the Exile." Pages 9–32 in *The Crisis of Israelite Religion: Transformation of Religious Traditions in Exilic and Post-Exilic Times* Edited by B. Becking and M. C. A. Korpel. OTS 42. Leiden: Brill, 1999.
———. *Judaic Religion in the Second Temple Period: Belief and Practice from Exile to Yavneh*. New York: Routledge, 2000.
Granerød, G. "By the Favour of Ahuramazda I Am King: On the Promulgation of a Persian Propaganda Text among Babylonians and Judaeans." *JSJ* 44 (2013): 455–80.
———. "Canon and Archive: Yahwism in Elephantine and Āl-Yāḫūdu as a Challenge to the Canonical History of Judean Religion in the Persian Period." *JBL* 138 (2019): 345–64.
———. *Dimensions of Yahwism in the Persian Period: Studies in the Religion and Society of the Judaean Community at Elephantine*. BZAW 488. Berlin: de Gruyter, 2016.
Grassi, G. F. "Bemerkungen zu Ostrakon Clermont-Ganneau J8 (175+185) aus Elephantine." *ZAW* 129 (2017): 84–97.
Grätz, S. "The Question of 'Mixed Marriages' (Intermarriage): The Extra-Biblical Evidence." Pages 192–204 in *Mixed Marriages, Intermarriage and Group Identity in the Second Temple Period.* Edited by C. Frevel. The Library of Hebrew Bible/Old Testament Studies 547. New York: Bloomsbury, 2011.
Green, P. *The Greco-Persian Wars*. Berkeley: University of California Press, 1996.

Greenfield, J. C., and B. Porten, eds. *The Bisitun Inscription of Darius the Great: Aramaic Version; Text, Translation and Commentary*. London: Lund Humphries, 1982.

Grelot, P. *Documents araméens d'Égypte*. Littératures Anciennes du Proche-Orient 5. Paris: Cerf, 1972.

———. "Études sur le 'Papyrus Pascal' d'Éléphantine." *VT* 4 (1954): 361–62.

———. "Notes d'onomastique sur les textes araméens d'Égypte." *Semitica* 21 (1971): 95–117.

———. "Le papyrus pascal d'Éléphantine nouvel examen." *VT* 17 (1967): 114–17.

Gröndahl, F. *Die Personennamen der Texte aus Ugarit*. Studia Pohl 1. Rome: Biblical Institute Press, 1967.

Gropp, G. "The Development of Near Eastern Culture During the Persian Empire." Pages 17–24 in *Mehregan in Sydney: Proceedings of the Seminar in Persian Studies During the Mehregan Persian Cultural Festival, Sydney, Australia 28 October–6 November 1994*. Edited by G. Trompf and M. Honari. Sydney Studies in Religion. Sydney: University of Sidney, 1998 .

Grund, A. *Die Entstehung des Sabbats: Seine Bedeutung für Israels Zeitkonzept und Erinnerungskultur*. FAT 75. Tübingen: Mohr Siebeck, 2011.

Handy, L. K. *Among the Host of Heaven: The Syrian-Phoenician Pantheon as Bureaucracy*, Winona Lake, IN: Eisenbrauns, 1994.

Hanfmann, G. M. A. "The New Stelae from Daskylion." *BASOR* 184 (1966): 10–13.

Harrison, T. "Upside Down and Back to Front: Herodotus and the Greek Encounter with Egypt." Pages 161–72 in *Ancient Perspectives on Egypt*. Edited by R. Matthews and C. Roemer. Encounters with Ancient Egypt. New York: Routledge, 2016.

Hartenstein, F. "Der Sabbath als Zeichen und heilige Zeit. Zur Theologie des Ruhetages im Alten Testaments." Pages 103–31 in *Das Fest: Jenseits des Alltags*. Edited by I. Fischer and C. Markschies. Jahrbuch für Biblische Theologie 18. Neukirchen-Vluyn: Neukirchener Verlag, 2003.

Heckl, R. "Inside the Canon and Out: The Relationship Between Psalm 20 and Papyrus Amherst 63." *Semitica* 56 (2014): 359–79.

Heidorn, L. A. "The Saite and Persian Period Forts at Dorginarti." Pages 205–19 in *Egypt and Africa: Nubia from Prehistory to Islam*. Edited by W. V. Davies. London: British Museum Press, 1991.

Henkelman, W. F. M. *The Other Gods Who Are: Studies in Elamite-Iranian Acculturation based on the Persepolis Fortification Texts*. Achaemenid History 14. Leiden: Nederlands Instituut voor het Nabije Oosten, 2008.

Hensel, B. *Juda und Samaria. Zum Verhältnis zweier nach-exilischer Jahwismen*. FAT 1/110. Tübingen: Mohr Siebeck, 2016.

Herrenschmidt, C. "Designation de l'empire et concepts politiques de Darius Ier d'apres ses inscriptions en vieux-perse." *Studia Iranica* 5 (1976): 33–65.

Herrera, P. D. "P. 13497. 'Ofrecerán la oblación y el incienso.' Limitación del culto en Elefantina. Santuarios de Jerusalén y Khnum, los dos pilares de la decisión persa." *Estudios Bíblicos* 85 (2017): 421–49.

Herzfeld, E. *The Persian Empire: Studies in Geography and Ethnography of the Ancient Near East*. Wiesbaden: Harrasowitz, 1968.

Hintze, A. "Monotheism the Zoroastrian Way." *Journal of the Royal Asiatic Society* 24 (2014): 225–49.

Hobson, R. "Localized Scribal Systems at Elephantine and Qumran." *Journal of the Ancient Near Eastern Society* 33 (2018): 77–100.

Hoftijzer, J. "An Unpublished Aramaic Fragment from Elephantine." *Oudheidkundige Mededelingen uit het Rijksmuseum van Oudheden te Leiden* 68 (1988): 45–48.

Holladay, W. L. *Chapters 26–52*. Vol. 2 of *A Commentary on the Book of the Prophet Jeremiah. Chapters 26–52*. Hermeneia: A Critical and Historical Commentary on the Bible. Minneapolis: Fortress, 1989.

Holm, T. L. "Memories of Sennacherib in Aramaic Texts." Pages 295–323 in *Sennacherib at the Gates of Jerusalem: Story, History, and Historiography*. Edited by I. Kalimi and S. Richardson. CHANE 71. Leiden: Brill, 2014.

———. "Nanay and Her Lover: An Aramaic Sacred Marriage Text from Egypt." *JNES* 76 (2017): 1–37.

———. "The Sheikh Fadl Inscription in its Literary and Historical Context." *Aramaic Studies* 5 (2007): 193–224.

Honigman, S. "Jewish Communities of Hellenistic Egypt: Different Responses to Different Environments." Pages 117–35 in *Jewish Identities in Antiquity: Studies in Memory of Menahem Stern*. Edited by L. E. Levine and D. R. Schwartz. Texts and Studies in Ancient Judaism / Texte und Studien zum Antiken Judentum. Tübingen: Mohr Siebeck, 2009.

Honroth, W., O. Rubensohn, and F. Zucker. "Bericht über die Ausgrabungen auf Elephantine in den Jahren 1906–1908." *Zeitschrift für ägyptische Sprache und Altertumskunde* 46 (1910): 162–209.

Hoonacker, A. van. *Une communauté Judéo-Araméenne à Éléphantine, en Égypte, aux VIe et Ve siècles avant J.-C.* The Schweich Lectures, 1914. London: The British Academy, 1915.

Hoyland, R. G. *Arabia and the Arabs: From the Bronze Age to the Coming of Islam*. New York: Routledge, 2001.

Hudson, K. *Breaking the South Slav Dream: The Rise and Fall of Yugoslavia*. London: Pluto, 2003.

Hughes, G. R. "The So-Called Pherendates correspondence." Pages 75–86 in *Grammata Demotika: Festschrift für Erich Lüddeckens zum 15. Juni 1983*. Edited by H.-J. Thissen and K.-T. Zauzich. Würzburg: Zauzich, 1984.

Ilan, T. "Women's Archives from Elephantine and the Judean Desert: Law Codes and Archaelogial Founds." Pages 171–78 in *Structures of Power: La and Gender across the Ancient Near East and Beyond*. Edited by I. Peled. Oriental Institute Seminars 12. Chicago: Oriental Institute, 2018.

Janowski, B. "Die Tat kehrt zum Täter zurück: Offene Fragen im Umkreis des 'Tun-Ergehen-Zusammenhangs' Harmut Gese zum 65. Geburtstag." *Zeitschrift für Theologie und Kirche* 91 (1994): 247–71.

Jaussen, A., and R. Savignac. *Mission archéologique en Arabie*. Paris: Société des fouilles archéologiques, 1909–22.

Joffe, A. H. "Egypt and Syro-Mesopotamia in the 4th Millennium: Implications of the New Chronology." *Current Anthropology* 41 (2000): 113–23.

Johns, W. E. *Biggles Flies South*. Oxford: Oxford University Press, 1949.

Johnson, J. H. "The Demotic Chronicle as an historical source." *Enchoria* 4 (1974): 1–17.

———. "Ethnic Considerations in Persian Period Egypt." Pages 211–22 in *Gold of Praise: Studies on Ancient Egypt in Honor of Edward F. Wente*. Edited by E. Teeter and J. A. Larson. Studies in Ancient Oriental Civilization 58. Chicago: Oriental Institute, 1999.

———. "The Social, Economic and Legal Status of Women in Ancient Egypt." Pages 82–97 in *The Life of Meresamun: A Temple Singer in Ancient Egypt.* Edited by E. Teeter and J. H. Johnson. Oriental Institute Publications 59. Chicago: Oriental Institute, 2009.

Joisten-Pruschke, A. *Das religiöse Leben der Juden von Elephantine in der Achämenidenzeit.* Göttinger Orientforschungen 3: Iranica 2. Wiesbaden: Harrasowitz, 2008.

Jong, A. F. de, *Traditions of the Magi: Zoroastrianism in Greek and Latin Literature.* Religions in the Graeco-Roman World 133. Leiden: Brill, 1997.

Jonker, L. C. "Achaemenid Understanding of Law and Justice in Darius I's Tomb Inscriptions: Are There Any Connections with Hebrew Bible Pentateuchal Conceptions?" *Scandinavian Journal of the Old Testament* 33 (2019): 24–41.

Junod, H. A. *Social Life.* Vol. 1 of *The Life of a South African Tribe.* London: Macmillan, 1927.

Kaan, I. "A New Discovery in Dascylium: The Persian Destruction level." Pages 249–64 in *Proceedings of the 6th International Congress of the Archaeology of the Ancient Near East, 5 May–10 May 2009.* Edited by P. Matthiae, F. Pinnock, L. Nigro, and N. Marchetti. Wiesbaden: Harrasowitz, 2010.

Kahn, D. "The Assyrian Invasions of Egypt (673–663 BC) and the Final Expulsion of the Kushites." *Studien zur Altägyptischen Kultur* 34 (2006): 251–67.

———. "Inaros' Rebellion against Artaxerxes I and the Athenian Disaster in Egypt." *Classical Quarterly* 58 (2008): 424–40.

———. "Nebuchadnezzar and Egypt: An Update on the Egyptian Monuments." *Hebrew Bible and Ancient Israel* 7 (2018): 65–78.

———. "Note on the Time-Factor in Cambyses' Deeds in Egypt as Told by Herodotus." *Transeu* 34 (2007): 103–12.

Kalmijn, M. "Intermarriage and Homogamy: Causes, Patterns, Trends." *Annual Review of Sociology* 24 (1998): 395–421.

Kaper, O. E., ' "Petubastis IV in the Dakhla Oasis: New Evidence About an Early Rebellion against Persian Rule and Its Suppression in Political Memory." Pages 125–49 in Silverman and Waerzeggers, *Political Memory in and after the Persian Empire.*

Kaplan, B. J. *Calvinists and Libertines: Confession and Community in Utrecht, 1578–1620.* Oxford: Clarendon, 1995.

Kaplan, P. "Cross-Cultural Contacts Among Mercenary Communities in Saite and Persian Egypt." *MHR* 18 (2003): 1–31.

———. "Sojourner in the Land: The Resident Alien in Late Period Egypt." Pages 396–414 in *Walls of the Prince: Egyptian Interactions with Southwest Asia in Antiquity. Essays in Honor of John S. Holladay, Jr.* Edited by T. P. Harrison, E. B. Banning, S. Klassen (CHANE 77), Leiden: Brill, 2015.

Karrer, C. *Ringen um die Verfassung Judas: Eine Studie zu den theologische-politischen Vorstellungen im Esra-Nehemia-Buch.* BZAW 308. Berlin: de Gruyter, 2000.

Kaufman, S. A. *The Akkadian Influences on Aramaic.* Assyriological Studies 19. Chicago: University of Chicago Press, 1974.

Keel, O. *Goddesses and Trees, New Moon and Yahweh: Ancient Near Eastern art and the Hebrew Bible.* JSOTSup 261. Sheffield: Sheffield Academic, 1998.

Kellogg, D. L. *Marathon Fighters and Men of Maple.* Ancient Acharnai. Oxford: Oxford University Press, 2013.

Kessler, D. *The Falashas: A Short History of the Ethiopian Jews.* 3rd ed. London: Frank Cass, 1996.

Klinkott, H. *Der Satrap: Ein achaimenidischer Amtsträger und seine Handlungsspielräume.* Oikumene Studien zur Weltgeschichte 1. Frankfurt: Verlag Antike, 2005.

Klotz, D. "Darius I and the Sabaeans: Ancient Partners in Red Sea Navigation." *JNES* 74 (2015): 267–80.

Knauf, E. A. "Elephantine und das vor-biblische Judentum." Pages 179–88 in Kratz, *Religion und Religionskontakte.*

———. *Ismael: Untersuchungen zur Geschichte Palästinas und Nordarabiens im 1. Jahrtausend v. Chr.* Abhandlungen des Deutschen Palastina-Vereins. Wiesbaden: Harrassowitz, 1985.

———. "The Persian Administration in Arabia." *Transeu* 2 (1990): 201–17.

Koch, K. "Weltordnung und Reichsidee im alten Iran und ihre Auswirkungen auf die Provinz Jehud." Pages 133–325 in *Reichsidee und Reichsorganisation im Perserreich.* 2nd ed. Edited by P. Frei and K. Koch. OBO 55. Göttingen: Vandenhoeck & Ruprecht, 1996.

Kornfeld, W. *Onomastica aramaica aus Ägypten.* Sitzungsberichte der Österreichischen Akademie der Wissenschaften 333. Wien: Verlag der Osterreichischen Akademie der Wissenschaften, 1978.

———. "Zu den aramäischen Inschriften aus Edfu." *Wiener Zeitschrift für die Kunde des Morgenlandes* 71 (1979): 49–52.

Korpel, M. C. A. "Disillusion among Jews in the Postexilic Period." Pages 135–57 in *The Old Testament in Its World.* Edited by R. P. Gordon and J. C. de Moor. OTS 52. Leiden: Brill, 2005.

Kosmin, P. J. "A New Hypothesis: The Behistun Inscription as Imperial Calendar." *Iran: Journal of the British Institute of Persian Studies* 56 (2018): 1–10.

Kottsieper, I. "Anmerkungen zu Pap. Amherst 63.I.12, 11–19—Eine Aramäische Version von Psalm 20." *ZAW* 100 (1988): 217–44.

———. "El–ferner oder naher Gott? Zur Bedeutung einer semitischen Gottheit in verschiedenen sozialen Kontexten im 1. Jtsd. v. Chr." Pages 25–74 in *Religion und Gesellschaft.* Edited by R. Albertz. AOAT 248. Münster: Ugarit-Verlag, 1997.

———. "Die literarische Aufnahme assyrischer Begebenheiten in frühen aramäischen Texten." Pages 283–89 in *La circulation des biens, des personnes et des idées dans le Proche-Orient ancien. XXXVIIIe RAI.* Edited by D. Charpin and F. Joannès. Paris: Editions Recherche sur les Civilisations, 1992 .

———. "Die Religionspolitik der Achämeniden und die Juden von Elephantine." Pages 150–78 in Kratz, *Religion und Religionskontakte im Zeitalter der Achämeniden.*

———. *Die Sprache der Ahiqarsprüche.* BZAW 194. Berlin: de Gruyter, 1990.

Kraeling, E. G. H. *The Brooklyn Museum Aramaic Papyri.* New Haven: Yale University Press, 1953.

Kratz, R. G."Elephantine und Alexandria: Nicht-biblisches und biblisches Judentum in Ägypten." Pages 193–208 in *Alexandria.* Edited by T. Georges, F. Albrecht, and R. Feldmeier. Civitatum Orbis Mediterranei Studia 1. Tübingen: Mohr Siebeck, 2013.

———. *Historical and Biblical Israel: The History, Tradition, and Archives of Israel and Judah.* Translated by Paul Michael Kurtz. Oxford: Oxford University Press, 2015.

———. *Historisches und biblisches Israel: Drei Überblicke zum Alten Testament.* Tübingen: Mohr Siebeck, 2013.

———. "Judäische Gesandte im Achämenidenreich: Hananja, Esra und Nehemia." Pages 377–98 in *From Daena to Din: Religion, Kultur und Sprache der iranischen Welt* (Festschrift Philip Kreyenbroek zum 60. Geburtstag). Edited by C. Allison, A. Joisten-Pruschke, and A. Wendtland. Wiesbaden: Harrasowitz, 2009.

———. "Judean Ambassadors and the Making of Jewish Identity: The Case of Hananiah, Ezra, and Nehemiah." Pages 421–44 in Lipschits, Knoppers, and Oeming, *Judah and the Judeans in the Achaemenid Period.*

———. "*Mille Ahiqar:* 'The Words of Ahiqar' and the Literature of the Jewish Diaspora in Ancient Egypt." *Al-Abhath* 60–61 (2012–13): 39–58.

———. *Religion und Religionskontakte im Zeitalter der Achämeniden.* VGWTh 22. Gütersloh: Gütersloher Verlagshaus, 2001.

———. "The Second Temple of Jeb and of Jerusalem." Pages 247–64 in *Judah and the Judeans in the Persian Period.* Edited by O. Lipschits and M. Oeming. Winona Lake, IN: Eisenbrauns, 2006.

———. "Temple and Torah: Reflections on the Legal Status of the Pentateuch Between Elephantine and Qumran." Pages 77–103 in *The Pentateuch as Torah: New Models for Understanding Its Promulgation and Acceptance.* Edited by G. N. Knoppers and B. M. Levinson. Winona Lake, IN: Eisenbrauns, 2007.

———. "Zwischen Elephantine und Qumran: Das Alte Testament im Rahmen des Antiken Judentums." Pages 129–46 in *Congress Volume Ljubljana 2007.* Edited by A. Lemaire. Supplements to Vetus Testamentum 133. Leiden: Brill, 2010.

Krekeler, A. "Stadtgrabung am Westkom von Elephantine/Wohnbauten des 1. Jahrtausends v. Chr." Pages 107–15 in *Haus und Palast im Alten Ägypten.* Edited by M. Bietak. Untersuchungen der Zweigstelle Kairo des Österreichischen Archäologischen Instituts 14. Wien: Verlag der Osterreichischen Akademie der Wissenschaften, 1996.

Krul, J. *The Revival of the Anu Cult and the Nocturnal Fire Ceremony at Late Babylonian Uruk.* CHANE 95. Leiden: Brill, 2018.

Kuhrt, A. "The Achaemenid Concept of Kingship." *Iran: Journal of the British Institute of Persian Studies* 22 (1984): 156–60.

———. *The Ancient Near East, c. 3000–330 BC*, New York: Routledge, 1995.

———. *The Persian Empire: A Corpus of Sources from the Achaemenid Period*, New York: Routledge, 2007.

LaCoste, N. *Waters of the Exodus: Jewish Experiences with Water in Ptolemaic and Roman Egypt.* JSJSup 190. Leiden: Brill, 2018.

Ladynin, I. "Nectanebo in Ethiopia: A Commentary to Diod. XVI 51.1." Pages 527–34 in *Between the Cataracts: Proceedings of the 11th Conference of Nubian Studies.* Edited by W. Godlewski and A. Łajtar. PAM Supplement Series 2.2/1–2. Warsaw: Warsaw University Press, 2010.

Lankester Harding, G. *An Index and Concordance of Pre-Islamic Arabian Names and Inscriptions.* Near and Middle East Studies 8. Toronto: University of Toronto Press, 1971.

Lecoq, P. *Les inscriptions de la Perse achéménide*. Paris: Gallimard, 1997.

Lee, K.-J. *The Authority and Authorization of Torah in the Persian Period.* CBET 64. Leuven: Peeters, 2011.

Lemaire, A. "Everyday Life According to the Ostraca from Elephantine." Pages 365–73 in Lipschits, Knoppers, and Oeming, *Judah and the Judeans in the Achaemenid Period.*

Lemaire, A., and A. Yardeni. "New Hebrew Ostraca from the Shephelah." Pages 197–223 in *Biblical Hebrew in Its Northwest Semitic Setting: Typological and Historical Perspectives.* Edited by S. E. Fassberg and A. Hurvitz. Winona Lake, IN: Eisenbrauns, 2006.

Lenfant, D. *Ctésias de Cnide. La Perse. L'Inde. Autres fragments.* Paris: Les Belles Lettres, 2004.

Le Roux, M. *The Lemba—A Lost Tribe of Israel in Southern Africa?* Pretoria: University of South Africa, 2003.

Lichtheim, M. *The Late Period.* Vol. 3 of *Ancient Egyptian Literature.* Berkeley: University of California Press, 2006.

Lidzbarski, M. *Phönizische und aramäische Krugaufschriften aus Elephantine.* Abhandlungen der Königlich Preussischen Akademie der Wissenschaften. Berlin: Verlag der Königlich Akademie der Wissenschaften, 1912.

Lincoln, B. *Religion, Empire, and Torture: The Case of Achaemenian Persia, with a Postscript on Abu Ghraib.* Chicago: University of Chicago Press, 2010.

Lindenberger, J. M. *Ancient Aramaic and Hebrew Letters.* Writings from the Ancient World 14. Atlanta: SBL Press, 1994.

———. *The Aramaic Proverbs of Ahiqar.* Baltimore: Johns Hopkins University Press, 1983

———. "The Gods of Ahiqar." *Ugarit-Forschungen* 14 (1982): 105–17.

———. "What Ever Happened to Vidranga? A Jewish Liturgy of Cursing from Elephantine." Pages 134–57 in *Studies in Language and Literature in Honour of Paul-Eugène Dion.* Vol. 3 of *The World of the Arameans.* Edited by P. M. M. Daviau, J. W. Wevers, and M. Weigl. JSOTSup 326. Sheffield: Sheffield Academic, 2001.

Lipiński, E. *The Aramaeans: Their Ancient History, Culture, Religion.* OLA 100. Leuven: Peeters, 2000.

Lipschits, O., G. N. Knoppers, and M. Oeming, eds. *Judah and the Judeans in the Achaemenid Period: Negotiating Identities in an International Context.* Winona Lake, IN: Eisenbrauns, 2011.

Livschits, V. "Some Khwarezmian Names." Pages 317–24 in *Studies on Iran and the Caucasus In Honour of Garnik Asatrian.* Edited by U. Bläsing, V. Arakelova, and M. Weinreich. Leiden: Brill, 2015.

Lloyd, A. B. "The Egyptian Attitude to the Persians." Pages 185–98 in *A Good Scribe and an Exceedingly Wise Man: Studies in Honour of W. J. Tait.* Edited by A. Dodson, J. Johnston, and W. Monkhouse. London: Golden House, 2014.

———. "The Inscription of Udjaḥorresnet: A Collaborator's Testament." *JEA* 68 (1982): 166–80.

Lopez, F. *Democede di Crotone e Udjahorresnet di Sais: Medici primari alla corte achemenide di Dario il Grande.* Pisa: Pisa University Press, 2015.

Lorenz, C. *Konstruktion der Vergangenheit: Eine Einführung in die Geschichtstheorie.* Wien: Böhlau, 1997.

Lozachmeur, H. *La collection Clermont-Ganneau: Ostraca, épigraphes sur jarre, étiquettes de bois.* 2 vols. Paris: de Boccard, 2006.

Machinist, P. "Mesopotamian Imperialism and Israelite Religion: A Case Study from the Second Isaiah." Pages 237–64 in *Symbiosis, Symbolism and the Power of the*

Past: Canaan, Ancient Israel, and Their Neighbors from the Late Bronze Age through Roman Palestina. Edited by W. G. Dever and S. Gitin. Winona Lake, IN: Eisenbrauns, 2003.

MacKay, H. A. *Sabbath and Synagogue: The Question of Sabbath Worship in Ancient Judaism*. Religions in the Graeco-Roman World 122. Leiden: Brill, 2001.

MacLaurin, E. C. B. "Date of the Foundation of the Jewish Colony at Elephantine." *JNES* 27 (1968): 89–96.

Madreiter I. "Der Raum alltäglicher weiblicher Literalität im Achaimeniden-Reich." Pages 113–41 in *Literacy in Ancient Everyday Life*. Edited by A. Kolb. Berlin: de Gruyter, 2018.

Magen, Y., H. Misgav, and L. Tsfania. *The Aramaic, Hebrew and Samaritan Inscriptions*. Vol. 1 of *Mount Gerizim Excavations*. Judea and Samaria Publications 2. Jerusalem: Israel Antiquites Authority, 2004.

Masson, O. "Le nom des cariens dans quelques langues de l'Antiquité." Pages 406–14 in *Mélanges linguistiques offerts à Émile Benveniste*. Paris: Société de Linguistique de Paris, 1975.

May, N. N., "City Gates and their Functions in Mesopotamia and Ancient Israel." Pages 77–121 in *The Fabric of Cities: Aspects of Urbanism, Urban Topography and Society in Mesopotamia, Greece and Rome*. Edited by N. N. May and U. Steinert, Leiden: Brill, 2014.

Mazar, A. "Pottery Plaques Depicting Goddesses Standing in Temple Facades." *Michmanim* 2 (1985): 5–18.

McLaughlin, J. L. *The marzēah in the Prophetic Literature: References and Allusions in Light of the Extra-Biblical Evidence*. Supplements to Vetus Testamentum 86. Leiden: Brill, 2001.

Meinhold, A. "Scheidungsrecht bei Frauen im Kontext der jüdischen Militärkolonie von Elephantine im 5. Jh. v.Chr." Pages 247–59 in *"Sieben Augen auf einem Stein" (Sach 3,9): Studien zur Literatur des Zweiten Tempels*. Edited by F. Hartenstein and M. Pietsch. Neukirchen-Vluyn: Neukirchener Verlag, 2007.

———. "Vergleichbar-/Unvergleichbarkeit des Wiederaufbaus der Tempel von Jerusalem und Elephantine in persischer Zeit." *Orientwissenschaftliche Hefte* 6 (2003): 35–59.

Mettinger, T. N. D. *The Dethronement of Sabaoth: Studies in the Shem and Kabod Theologies*. Coniectanea Biblica, Old Testament Series 18. Lund: Gleerup, 1982.

———. *In Search of God: The Meaning and Message of the Everlasting Names*, Philadelphia: Fortress, 1988.

———. *No Graven Image? Israelite Aniconism in its Ancient Near Eastern Context.* Coniectanea Biblica, Old Testament Series 42. Stockholm: Almqvist & Wiksell, 1995.

Meyer, E. *Der Papyrusfund von Elephantine: Dokumente einer jüdischen Gemeinde aus der Perserzeit und das älteste erhaltene Buch der Weltliteratur*. Leipzig: Hinrichs, 1912.

Mitchell, C. "Achaemenid Persian Concepts Pertaining to Covenant and Haggai, Zechariah, and Malachi." Pages 291–306 in *Covenant in the Persian Period*. Edited by R. J. Bautch and G. N. Knoppers. Winona Lake, IN: Eisenbrauns, 2015.

———. "Berlin Papyrus P. 13447 and the Library of the Yehudite Colony at Elephantine." *JNES* 76 (2017): 139–47.

———. "The Testament of Darius (DNa/DNb) and Constructions of Kings and Kingship in 1–2 Chronicles." Pages 363–80 in Silverman and Waerzeggers, *Political Memory in and after the Persian Empire*.

Mondriaan, M. E. "Anat-Yahu and the Jews at Elephantine." *Journal for Semitics* 22 (2013): 537–52.
Monson, A. "Egyptian Fiscal History in a World of Warring States, 664–30 BCE." *JEgH* 8 (2015): 1–36.
Morgenstern, M. "Mandaic Magic Bowls in the Moussaieff Collection: A Preliminary Survey." Pages 157–70 in *New Inscriptions and Seals Relating to the Biblical World*. Edited by M. Lubetski and E. Lubetski. Atlanta: SBL Press, 2012.
Morrow, A. R. "I Hate My Spouse: The Performative Act of Divorce in Elephantine Aramaic." *Journal of Northwest Semitic Languages* 43 (2017): 7–25.
Muffs, Y. *Studies in the Aramaic Legal Papyri from Elephantine*. HdO 66. Leiden: Brill, 2003.
Müller, M. "Among the Priests of Elephantine Island Seen from Egyptian Sources." *Die Welt des Orients* 46 (2016): 213–43.
Muraoka, T., and B. Porten. *A Grammar of Egyptian Aramaic*. 2nd ed. HdO 32. Leiden: Brill, 2003.
Na'aman, N. "Four Notes on the Ancient Near Eastern Marzeah." Pages 215–22 in *Open-Mindedness in the Bible and Beyond: A Volume of Studies in Honour of Bob Becking*. Edited by M. C. A. Korpel and L. L. Grabbe. The Library of Hebrew Bible/Old Testament Studies 616. London: T&T Clark, 2015.
Naveh, J., and S. Shaked. *Aramaic Documents from Ancient Bactria from the Khalili Collections*. London: Khalili Family Trust, 2012.
Neuffer, J. "The Accession of Artaxerxes I." *Andrews University Seminary Studies* 6 (1968): 60–87.
Neugebauer, O. "The Origin of the Egyptian Calendar." *JNES* 1 (1942): 396–403.
Neusner, J., and B. D. Chilton, eds. *The Golden Rule: The Ethics of Reciprocity in World Religions*. New York: Bloomsbury, 2008.
Newby, G. D. *A History of the Jews of Arabia: From Ancient Times to Their Eclipse Under Islam*. Columbia: University of South Carolina Press, 1988.
Niehr, H. *Aramäischer Aḥiqar*. Jüdische Schriften aus hellenistisch-römischer Zeit: Neue Folge 2. Gütersloh: Gütersloher Verlagshaus, 2007.
———. *Der höchste Gott: Alttestamentlicher JHWH-Glaube im Kontext syrisch-kanaänischer Religion des 1. Jahrtausends v. Chr.* BZAW 190. Berlin: de Gruyter, 1990.
———. "JHWH in der Rolle des Baalšamem." Pages 307–26 in *Ein Gott Allein? JHWH-Verehrung und biblischer Monotheismus im Kontext der israelitischen und altorientalischen Religionsgeschichte* Edited by M. Klopfenstein and W. Dietrich. OBO 139. Göttingen: Vandenhoeck & Ruprecht, 1994.
———. *Religionen in Israels Umwelt: Einführung in die nordwestsemitischen Religionen Syrien-Palästinas*. Die Neue Echter Bibel: Alten Testament 5. Würzburg: Echter Verlag, 1998.
Nihan, C. *From Priestly Torah to Pentateuch: A Study in the Composition of the Book of Leviticus*. FAT 2/25. Tübingen: Mohr Siebeck, 2007.
Nims, C. F. "The Term Hp, 'Law, Right,' in Demotic." *JNES* 7 (1948): 243–60.
Nims, C. F., and R. C. Steiner. "A Paganized Version of Psalm 20:2-6 from the Aramaic Text in Demotic Script." *JAOS* 103 (1983): 261–74.
Nodet, E. *A Search for the Origin of Judaism: From Joshua to the Mishnah*. JSOTSup 248. Sheffield: Sheffield Academic, 2004.
Nutkowicz, H. "Concerning the Verb *śn'* in the Judaeo-Aramaic Contracts from Elephantine." *JSS* 52 (2007): 211–25.

———. *Destins de femmes à Eléphantine au Vè siècle avant notre ère*. Paris: Harmattan, 2015.

———. "Note sur une institution juridique à Éléphantine, *'dh*, la «cour»." *Transeu* 27 (2004): 181–85.

Olyan, S. M. *Biblical Mourning: Ritual and Social Dimensions*. Oxford: Oxford University Press, 2004.

Oppenheim, A. L. "Akk. *arad ekalli* = Builder." *Archív Orientální* 17 (1949): 227–35.

Oshima, T. M. "How 'Mesopotamian' Was Ahiqar the Wise? A Search for Ahiqar in Cuneiform Texts." Pages 141–67 in *Wandering Arameans: Arameans Outside Syria: Textual and Archaeological Perspectives*. Edited by A. Berlejung, A. M. Maeir, and A. Schüle. Leipziger Altorientalistische Studien 5. Wiesbaden: Harrasowitz, 2017.

Papatheophanes, M. "Heraclitus of Ephesus, the Magi, and the Achaemenids." *IrAnt* 20 (1985): 101–61.

Pardee, D. *Ritual and Cult at Ugarit*. Writings from the Ancient World 10. Atlanta: Society of Biblical Literature, 2002.

Parpola, S. "Il retroterra assiro di Ahiqar.' Pages 91–112 in *Il saggio Ahiqar. Fortuna e transformazioni di uno scritto sapienziale. Il testo più antico e le sue versioni*. Edited by R. Contini and C. Grottanelli. Brescia: Paideia 2005.

Pearce, L. E., and C. Wunsch. *Documents of Judean Exiles and West Semites in Babylonia in the Collection of David Sofer*. Cornell University Studies in Assyriology and Sumerology 28. Bethesda: CDL, 2014.

Peden, A. J. *The Graffiti of Pharaonic Egypt: Scope and Roles of Informal Writings (c 3100–332 BC)*. Probleme der Ägyptologie 17. Leiden: Brill, 2001.

Pérez Gondar, D. "Culto, autoridad y tradición: La comunidad judía de Elefantina y la religiosidad vinculada a su templo." *Scripta Theologica* 50 (2018): 23–52.

Perrot, J., ed. *The Palace of Darius at Susa: The Great Royal Residence of Achaemenid Persia*. London: I. B. Tauris, 2013.

Petry, S. *Die Entgrenzung JHWHs: Monolatrie, Bilderverbot und Monotheismus im Deuteronomium, in Deuterojesaja und im Ezechielbuch*. FAT 2/27. Tübingen: Mohr Siebeck, 2007.

Pham, X. H. T. *Mourning in the Ancient Near East and the Hebrew Bible*. JSOTSup 302. Sheffield: Sheffield Academic, 2000.

Pilgrim, C. von. "Textzeugnis und archäologischen Befund: Zur Topographie Elephantines in der 27. Dynastie." Pages 485–97 in *Stationen: Beiträge zur Kulturgeschichte Ägyptens Rainer Stadelman gewidmet*. Edited by H. Guksch and D. Polz. Mainz: von Zabern, 1998.

Pons Mellado, E. "Trade of Metals Between Egypt and Other Countries from the Old Until the New Kingdom." *CdE* 81 (2006): 7–16.

Porten, B. "The Address Formulae in Aramaic Letters: A New Collation of Cowley 17." *RB* 90 (1983): 396–415.

———. "The Aramaic Boat Papyrus (P. Ber. 23000): New Collation." *Or* 57 (1988): 76–81.

———. "An Aramaic Oath Contract: A New Interpretation." *RB* 90 (1983): 563–75.

———. "Aramaic Papyrus Fragments in the Egyptian Museum of West Berlin." *Or* 57 (1988): 14–54.

———. *Archives from Elephantine: The Life of an Ancient Jewish Colony*. Berkeley: University of California Press, 1968.

———. "The Calendar of Aramaic Texts from Achaemenid and Ptolemaic Egypt." Pages 13–32 in *Irano-Judaica II: Studies relating to Jewish Contacts with Persian Culture throughout the Ages*. Edited by S. Shaked and A. Netzer. Jerusalem: Ben-Zvi Institute for the Study of Jewish Communities in the East, 1990.

———. "A Comprehensive Table of Bethel Names in Ancient Inscriptions." *Maarav* 21 (2014): 223–44.

———. "Cowley 7 Reconsidered." *Or* 56 (1987): 89–92.

———. "Did the Ark stop at Elephantine?" *Biblical Archaeology Review* 21 (1995): 54–77.

———. "Egyptian Names in Aramaic Texts." Pages 283–328 in *Acts of the Seventh Conference of Demotic Studies, Copenhagen 23–17 August 1999*. Edited by K. Ryholt. Carsten Niebuhr Institute Publications 27. Copenhagen: Museum Tusculanum Press, 2002.

———. *The Elephantine Papyri in English: Three Millennia of Cross-Cultural Continuity and Change*. 2nd ed. Documenta et Monumenta Orientis Antiqui 220. Atlanta: SBL Press, 2011.

———. "Fragmentary Aramaic Deeds of Obligation and Conveyance: New Collations and Restorations." *JNES* 48 (1989): 161–83.

———. "The Jews in Egypt." Pages 372–400 in *The Cambridge History of Judaism* 1. Edited by W. D. Davies and L. Finkelstein. Cambridge: Cambridge University Press, 1984.

———. "Persian Names in Aramaic Documents from Ancient Egypt." Pages 165–86 in *Irano-Judaica V: Studies relating to Jewish Contacts with Persian Culture throughout the Ages*. Edited by S. Shaked and A. Netzer. Jerusalem: Yad Ben-Zvi Press, 2003.

———. "The Prophecy of Hor bar Punesh and the Demise of Righteousness: An Aramaic Papyrus in the British Library." Pages 427–66 in *Res Severa Verum Gaudium: Festschrift für Karl-Theodor Zauzich zum 65. Geburtstag am 8. Juni 2004*. Edited by F. Hoffmann and H. Thissen. StD 6. Leuven: Peeters, 2004.

———. "The Religion of the Jews of Elephantine in Light of the Hermopolis Papyri." *JNES* 28 (1969): 116–21.

———. "Settlement of the Jews at Elephantine and the Arameans at Syene." Pages 451–70 in *Judah and the Judeans in the Neo-Babylonian Period*. Edited by O. Lipschits and J. Blenkinsopp. Winona Lake, IN: Eisenbrauns, 2003.

Porten, B., and H. Z. Szubin. "'Abandoned Property' in Elephantine: A New Interpretation of Kraeling 3." *JNES* 41 (1982): 123–31.

———. "The Status of the Handmaiden Tamet: A New Interpretation of Kraeling 2 (TAD B3.3)." *Israel Law Review* 29 (1995): 43–64.

Porten, B., R. Zadok, and L. Pearce. "Akkadian Names in Aramaic Documents from Ancient Egypt." *BASOR* 375 (2016): 1–12.

Posener, G. *La première domination perse en Egypte: Recueil d'inscriptions hiéroglyphiques*. Bibliothèque des études 11. Cairo: l'Institut français d'archéologie orientale, 1936.

Prag, K. "Byblos and Egypt in the Fourth Millennium BC." *Levant* 18 (1986): 59–74.

Quack, J. F. "The Interaction of Egyptian and Aramaic Literature." Pages 375–401 in Lipschits, Knoppers, and Oeming, *Judah and the Judeans in the Achaemenid Period.*

———. "Zum Datum der persischen Eroberung Ägyptens unter Kambyses." *JEgH* 4 (2011): 228–46.

Quinn, J. C. *In Search of the Phoenicians*. Princeton: Princeton University Press, 2018.

Radner, K. "How to Reach the Upper Tigris: The Route Through the Ṭūr ʿAbdīn." *State Archives of Assyria Bulletin* 15 (2006): 273–305.

Ramet, S. P. *Balkan Babel: The Disintegration of Yugoslavia from the Death of Tito to the Fall of Milosevic*. New York: Routledge, 2018.

Ray, J. D. "The Carian Inscriptions from Egypt." *JEA* 68 (1982): 181–98.

———. "Soldiers to Pharaoh: The Carians of Southwest Anatolia." Pages 1185–94 in *Civilizations of the Ancient Near East* 2. Edited by J. M. Sasson. New York: Hendrickson, 1995.

Redford, D. B. *Egypt, Canaan and Israel in Ancient Times*. Princeton: Princeton University Press, 1992.

———. "The Hyksos Invasion in History and Tradition." *Or* 39 (1970): 1–52.

———. "The Origin and Termination of the Foreign Colony-Garrison at Elephantine." Pages 149–57 in *Cultural Contact and Appropriation in the Axial-Age Mediterranean World: A Periplos*. Edited by B. Halpern and K. Sacks. CHANE 86. Leiden: Brill, 2016.

———. "Some Observations on the Traditions Surrounding 'Israel in Egypt.'" Pages 279–364 in Lipschits, Knoppers, and Oeming, *Judah and the Judeans in the Achaemenid Period.*

Redmount, C. A. "The Wadi Tumilat and the 'Canal of the Pharaohs.'" *JNES* 54 (1995): 127–35.

Reisner, G. A. *Sumerisch-babylonische Hymnen nach Thontafeln griechischer Zeit*. Berlin: W. Spemann, 1896.

Retso, J. *The Arabs in Antiquity: Their History from the Assyrians to the Umayyads*. London: Routledge, 2003.

Robinson, G. *The Origin and Development of the Old Testament Sabbath*. Beiträge zur biblischen Exegese und Theologie 21. Frankfurt am Main: Lang, 1988.

Roche, M.-J. "Introduction aux religions préislamiques d'Arabie du Nord. Recherches sur les divinités du paganisme arabe, à travers l'épigraphie et l'iconographie. Conférences des années 2008–2009, 2009–2010 et 2011–2012." *Annuaire de l'École pratique des hautes études (EPHE), Section des sciences religieuses. Résumé des conférences et travaux* 121 (2014): 119–28.

Rohrmoser, A. *Götter, Tempel und Kult der Judäo-Aramäer von Elephantine: Archäologische und schriftliche Zeugnisse aus dem perserzeitlichen Ägypten*. AOAT 396. Münster: Ugarit-Verlag, 2014.

Rollinger, R. "Altorientalisches bei Herodot: Das wiehernde Pferd des Dareios I." Pages 13–42 in *Zwischen Assur und Athen: Altorientalisches in den Historien Herodots.* Edited by H. Klinkott and N. Kramer. Spielräume der Antike 4. Stuttgart: Steiner, 2017.

Rop, J. "The Assassination of Tissaphernes: Royal Responses." Pages 51–73 in *Brill's Companion to Military Defeat in Ancient Mediterranean Society.* Edited by J. H. Clark and B. Turner. Brill's Companions to Classical Studies 2. Leiden: Brill, 2017.

Rosen, L. von. *Lapis Lazuli in Geological Contexts and in Ancient Written Sources*. Partille: Paul Åströms Förlag, 1988.

Rosenberg, S. G. "The Jewish Temple at Elephantine." *Near Eastern Archaeology* 67 (2004): 4–13.

Rössler-Köhler, U. "Zur Textkomposition der naophoren Statue des Udjahorresnet/ Vatikan Inv. Nr. 196." *Göttinger Miszellen* 85 (1985): 43–54.

Rottpeter, M. "Initiatoren und Träger der 'Aufstände' im persischen Ägypten." Pages 9–49 in *Ägypten unter fremden Herrschern zwischen persischer Satrapie und römischer Provinz*. Edited by S. Pfeiffer. Frankfurt am Main: Antike, 2007.

Roy, J. *The Politics of Trade: Egypt and Lower Nubia in the 4th Millennium BC*. CHANE 47. Leiden: Brill, 2011.

Rubinstein, A. Z. *Yugoslavia and the Nonaligned World*. Princeton: Princeton University Press, 2015.

Rutherford, I, "The Earliest Cross-Cultural Reception of Homer? The Inaros Narratives of Greco-Roman Egypt." Pages 83–105 in *Greco-Egyptian Interactions: Literature, Translation and Culture, 500BC-AD 300*. Edited by I. Rutherford. Oxford: Oxford University Press, 2016.

Ruzicka, S. *Trouble in the West: Egypt and the Persian Empire, 525–332 BC*. Oxford: Oxford University Press, 2012.

Ryholt, K. S. B. "The Assyrian Invasion of Egypt in Egyptian Literary Tradition." Pages 384–511 in *Assyria and Beyond: Studies Presented to Mogens Trolle Larsen*. Edited by J. G. Dercksen. Leiden, Nederlands Instituut voor het Nabije Oosten, 2004.

———. *The Political Situation in Egypt During the Second Intermediate Period*. Carsten Niebuhr Institute Publications 20. Copenhagen: Museum Tusculanum Press, 1997.

Sachau, E. *Aramäische Papyrus und Ostraka aus einer jüdischen Militär-Kolonie zu Elephantine: Altorientalische Sprachdenkmäler des 5. Jahrhunderts vor Chr*. Leipzig: Hinrichs, 1911.

———. *Drei aramäische Papyrus-Urkunden aus Elephantine*. Philosophische und historische Abhandlungen der Königlich preussischen Akademie der Wissenschaften. Berlin: Verlag der Königlichen Akademie der Wissenschaften, 1907.

Salmon, P. "Les Relations entre la Perse et l'Egypte du VIe au IVe siècle av J.-C." Pages 147–68 in*The Land of Israel: Cross-roads of Civilizations*. Edited by E. Lipiński. OLA 19. Leuven: Peeters, 1985.

Schäfer, P. *Judeophobia: Attitudes Towards the Jews in the Ancient World*. Cambridge: Harvard University Press, 1977.

Schama, S. *The Story of the Jews: Finding the Words (1000 BCE–1492 CE)*. London: Vintage Books, 2014.

Schaudig, H. "Bel Bows, Nabu Stoops! The Prophecy of Isaiah xlvi 1-2 as a Reflection of Babylonian Processional Omens." *VT* 58 (2008): 557–72.

Schipper, B. U. *Die Erzählung des Wenamun: Ein Literaturwerk im Spannungsfeld von Politik, Geschichte und Religion*. OBO 209. Göttingen: Vandenhoeck & Ruprecht, 2005.

———. "Joseph, Ahiqar, and Elephantine: The Joseph Story as Diaspora Novella." *Journal of Ancient Egyptian Interconnections* 18 (2018): 71–84.

Schmitz, P. C. "The Phoenician Contingent in the Campaign of Psammetichus II against Kush." *JEgH* 3 (2010): 321–37.

———. *The Phoenician Diaspora: Epigraphic and Historical Studies*. Winona Lake, IN: Eisenbrauns, 2012.

Schulz, R. "Zwischen Eroberungskrieg und Präventivschlag? Neue Perspektiven zu den Perserkriegen und ihren Voraussetzungen." *Historische Zeitschrift* 306 (2018): 647–84.

Schwiderski, D. *Die alt-und reichsaramäischen Inschriften: Texte und Bibliographie* 2. Berlin: de Gruyter, 2004.

———. *Handbuch des nordwestsemitischen Briefformulars. Ein Beitrag zur Echtheitsfrage der aramäischen Briefe des Esrabuches*. BZAW 295. Berlin: de Gruyter, 2000.

Sear, D. R. *Asia and Africa*. Vol. 2 of *Greek Coins and Their Values*. London: Spink, 1994.

Segal, J. B. *Aramaic Texts from North Saqqâra with some Fragments in Phoenician*. London: Egypt Exploration Society, 1983.

Seidl, U. "Ein Monument Darius' I. aus Babylon." *Zeitschrift für Assyriologie* 89 (1999): 101–14.

Serrano Delgado, J. M. "Cambyses in Sais: Political and Religious Context in Achaemenid Egypt." *CdE* 79 (2004): 31–52.

Shaked, S. *Le satrape de Bactriane et son gouverneur: Documents araméens du IVᵉ s. avant notre ère provenant de Bactriane*. Persika 4. Paris: de Boccard, 2003.

Shayegan, M. R. "Bardiya and Gaumāta: An Achaemenid Enigma Reconsidered." *Bulletin of the Asia Institute* 20 (2006): 65–76.

Shortland, A. J. "Evaporations of the Wadi Natrun: Seasonal and Annual Variation and its Implication for Ancient Exploitation." *Archaeometry* 46 (2004): 497–516.

Siljanen, E. *Judeans of Egypt in the Persian Period (539–332 BCE) in Light of the Aramaic Documents*. Helsinki: Unigrafia, 2017.

Silverman, J. M., and C. Waerzeggers, eds. *Political Memory in and after the Persian Empire*. Ancient Near East Monographs/Monografías sobre el Antiquo Cercano Oriente 13. Atlanta: SBL Press, 2015.

Silverman, M. H. *Religious Values in the Jewish Proper Names at Elephantine*. AOAT 217. Neukirchen-Vluyn: Neukirchener Verlag, 1985.

Simonson, B. "A Demotic Parallel to the Aramaic *hnṣl* of Elephantine." *Aramaic Studies* 14 (2016): 242–64.

Sims-Williams, N. *Biblical and Other Christian Sogdian Texts from the Turfan Collection.* Berliner Turfan Texte 32. Turnhout: Brepols, 2014.

———. "The Final Paragraph of the Tomb-Inscription of Darius I (DNb, 50–60): The Old Persian Text in the Light of an Aramaic Version." *Bulletin of the School of Oriental and African Studies* 44 (1981): 1–7.

Skjaervo, P. O. "Ahura Mazdā and Ārmaiti, Heaven and Earth, in the Old Avesta." *Journal of the American Oriental Society* 122 (2002): 399–410.

———. "Farnah-: Mot Mède en Vieux-Perse?" *Bulletin de la Société de Linguistique de Paris* 78 (1983): 241–59.

Smith-Christopher, D. L. *The Religion of the Landless: The Social Context of the Babylonian Exile*. Eugene, OR: Wipf & Stock, 2015.

Soden, W. von. "Die Unterweltsvision eines assyrischen Kronprinzen. Nebst einige Beobachtungen zur Vorgeschichte des Aḥiqar-Romans." *Zeitschrift für Assyriologie* 43 (1936): 1–31.

Spalinger, A. "Esarhaddon and Egypt: An Analysis of the First Invasion of Egypt." *Or* 43 (1974): 295–326.

Spiegelberg, W. *Drei demotische Schreiben aus der Korrespondenz des Pherendates, des Satrapen Darius' I., mit den Chnumpriestern von Elephantine*. Berlin: Akademie der Wissenschaften, 1928.

———. *Die sogenannte demotische Chronik des pap. 215 der Bibliothèque nationale zu Paris: Nebst den auf der Rückseite des Papyrus stehenden Texten*. Leipzig: Hinrichs, 1914.

Steiner, R. C. "The Aramaic Text in Demotic Script: The Liturgy of a New Year's Festival Imported from Bethel to Syene by Exiles from Rash." *JAOS* 111 (1991): 362–63.

———. *Early Northwest Semitic Serpent Spells in the Pyramid Texts*. Harvard Semitic Studies 61. Winona Lake, IN: Eisenbrauns, 2011.

———. "Papyrus Amherst 63: A New Source for the Language, Literature, Religion, and History of the Aramaeans." Pages 199–207 in *Studia Aramaica: New Sources and New Approaches. Papers Delivered at the London Conference of the Institute of Jewish Studies University College-London, 26th–28th June.* Edited by M. J. Geller, J. C. Greenfield, and M. P. Weitzman. Journal of Semitic Studies Supplement 4. Oxford: Oxford University Press, 1991.

Steiner, R. C., and C. F. Nims. "The Aramaic Text in Demotic Script: Text, Translation, and Notes." Yeshiva Academic Institutional Repository. https://hdl.handle.net/20.500.12202/51.

———. "Ashurbanipal and Shamash-shum-ukin: *A Tale of Two Brothers* from the Aramaic Text in Demotic Script." *RB* 92 (1985): 60–81.

Stern, S. "The Babylonian Calendar at Elephantine." *Zeitschrift für Papyrologie und Epigraphik* 130 (2000): 159–71.

———. *Calendars in Antiquity: Empires, States, and Societies*. Oxford: Oxford University Press, 2012.

Sternberg-el Hotabi, H. "Die persische Herrschaft in Ägypten." Pages 111–49 in Kratz, *Religion und Religionskontakte im Zeitalter der Achämeniden.*

Stieglitz, R. R. "Hebrew Seafaring in the Biblical Period." *MHR* 15 (2004): 5–15.

Strauss, B. *The Battle of Salamis: The Naval Encounter That Saved Greece—And Western Civilization.* New York: Simon & Schuster, 2005.

Streck, M. *Assurbanipal und die letzten assyrischen Könige bis zum Untergange Niniveh's.* Vorderasiatische Bibliothek 7. Leipzig: Hinrichs, 1916.

Szubin, H. Z., and B. Porten. "'Ancestral Estates' in Aramaic Contracts: The Legal Significance of the Term *mhḥsn*." *Journal of the Royal Asiatic Society of Great Britain and Ireland (New Series)* 114 (1982): 3–9.

———. "An Aramaic Joint Venture Agreement: A New Interpretation of the Bauer-Meissner Papyrus." *BASOR* 288 (1992): 67–84.

———. "A Life Estate of Usufruct: A New Interpretation of Kraeling 6." *BASOR* 269 (1988): 29–45.

———. "The Status of a Repudiated Spouse: A New Interpretation of Kraeling 7 (TAD B3. 8)." *Israel Law Review* 35 (2001): 46–78.

———. "Testamentary Succession at Elephantine." *BASOR* 252 (1983): 35–46.

Tairan, S. A. *Die Personennamen in den altsabäischen Inschriften: Ein Beitrag zur altsüdarabischen Namengebung*. Texte und Studien zur Orientalistik 8. Hildesheim: Olms, 1992.

Tal, O. "On the Identification of the Ships of *kzd/ry* in the Erased Customs Account from Elephantine." *JNES* 68 (2009): 1–8.

Talay, S. "Die Geschichte und die Sprüche des Aḥiqar im neuaramäischen Dialekt von Mlaḥsō." Pages 695–712 in *Sprich doch mit deinen Knechten aramäisch, wir verstehen es! Festschrift for Otto Jastrow*. Edited by W. Arnold and H. Bobzin. Wiesbaden: Harrassowitz, 2002.

Tamber-Rosenau, C. "Female Diplomats in Jewish Elephantine? A New Look at a Papyrus from the Yedaniah Archive." *JSOT* 40 (2016): 491–510.

Tammuz, O. "Mare clausum? Sailing Seasons in the Mediterranean in Early Antiquity." *MHR* 20 (2005): 145–62.
Tavernier, J. "An Achaemenid Royal Inscription: The Text of Paragraph 13 of the Aramaic Version of the Bisitun Inscription." *JNES* 60 (2001): 161–76.
———. *Iranica in the Achaemenid Period (ca. 550–330 B.C.): Lexicon of Old Iranian Proper Names and Loanwords, Attested in Non-Iranian Texts*. OLA 158. Leuven: Peeters, 2007.
Taylor, J. H. *Death and the Afterlife in Ancient Egypt*. Chicago: University of Chicago, 2001.
Teixidor, J. *The Pagan God: Popular Religion in the Greco-Roman Near East*. Princeton: Princeton University Press, 1977.
Thissen, H. J. "Homerischer Einfluss im Inaros-Petubastis-Zyklus?" *Studien zur Altägyptischen Kultur* 27 (1999): 369–87.
Thompson, T. L. "The Intellectual Matrix of Early Biblical Narrative." Pages 107–26 in *The Triumph of Elohim: From Yahwisms to Judaisms*. Edited by D. V. Edelman. CBET 13. Kampen: Kok Pharos, 1995.
Toorn, K. van der. "Anat-Yahu, Some Other Deities, and the Jews of Elephantine." *Numen* 39 (1992): 80–101.
———. *Becoming Diaspora Jews: Behind the Story of Elephantine*. Anchor Yale Bible Reference Library. New Haven: Yale University Press, 2019.
———. "Celebrating the New Year with the Israelites: Three Extrabiblical Psalms from Papyrus Amherst 63." *JBL* 136 (2017): 633–49.
———. "Eshem-Bethel and Herem-Bethel: New Evidence from Amherst Papyrus 63." *ZAW* 128 (2016): 668–80.
———. "Ethnicity at Elephantine: Jews, Arameans, Caspians." *Tel Aviv* 43 (2016): 147–64.
———. "Ezra in Egypt? The Significance of Hananyah's Mission." *VT* 67 (2017): 602–10.
———. "Herem-Bethel and Elephantine Oath Procedure." *ZAW* 98 (1986): 282–85.
———. *Papyrus Amherst 63*. AOAT 448. Münster: Ugarit-Verlag, 2018.
———. "Previously, at Elephantine." *JAOS* 138 (2018): 255–70.
———. "Psalm 20 and Amherst Papyrus 63, XII, 11–19: A Case Study of a Text in Transit." Pages 244–61 in *Le-ma'an Ziony: Essays in Honor of Ziony Zevit*. Edited by F. E. Greenspahn and G. A. Rendsburg. Eugene, OR: Cascade, 2017.
———. *Scribal Culture and the Making of the Hebrew Bible*. Cambridge: Harvard University Press, 2007.
Tuland, C. G. "*'Uššayyā'* and *'Uššarnâ*: A Clarification of Terms, Date, and Text." *JNES* 17 (1958): 269–75.
Tuplin, C. "Mercenaries and Warlords in the Achaemenid Empire." Pages 17–35 in *War, Warlords, and Interstate Relations in the Ancient Mediterranean*. Edited by T. Ñaco del Hoyo and F. López Sánchez. Impact of Empire 28. Leiden: Brill, 2018.
Turri, J. "Epistemic Invariantism and Speech Act Contextualism." *Philosophical Review* 119 (2010): 77–95.
Uehlinger, C. "Leviathan und die Schiffe in Ps 104, 25–26." *Biblica* 71 (1990): 499–526.
Van Seters, J. *The Hyksos: A New Investigation*. Eugene, OR: Wipf & Stock, 2010.
Veijola, T. *Moses Erben: Studien zum Dekalog, zum Deuteronomismus und zum Schriftgelehrtentum*. Beiträge zur Wissenschaft vom Alten und Neuen Testament 149. Stuttgart: Kohlhammer, 2000.

Vittmann, G. *Ägypten und die Fremden im ersten vorchristlichen Jahrtausend*. Mainz: Harrasowitz, 2000.
———. "Arameans in Egypt." Pages 229–79 in *Wandering Arameans: Arameans Outside Syria: Textual and Archaeological Perspectives*. Edited by A. Berlejung, A. M. Maeir, and A. Schüle. Leipziger Altorientalistische Studien 5. Wiesbaden: Harrasowitz, 2017.
———. "Kursivhieratische und frühdemotische Miszellen." *Enchoria* 25 (1999): 111–27.
Vleeming, S. P. *The Gooseherds of Hou: (Pap. Hou); A Dossier Relating to Various Agricultural Affairs from Provincial Egypt of the Early Fifth Century BC*. StD 3. Louvain: Peeters, 1991.
Vleeming, S. P., and J. W. Wesselius. "An Aramaic Hymn from the Fourth Century B.C." *Bibliotheca Orientalis* 39 (1982): 501–9.
———. "Betel the Saviour." *Jaarbericht van het Vooraziatisch-Egyptisch Gezelschap (Genootschap) Ex oriente lux* 28 (1983): 110–40.
———. *Studies in Papyrus Amherst 63: Essays on the Aramaic Texts in Aramaic/Demotic Papyrus Amherst 63*. Vol. 2. Amsterdam: Juda Palache Instituur, 1990.
Vogelsang, W. "Early Historical Arachosia in South-East Afghanistan. Meeting-Place Between East and West." *IrAnt* 20 (1985): 55–99.
Waerzeggers, C. "The Carians of Borsippa." *Iraq* 68 (2006): 1–22.
Wagenaar, J. A. *Origin and Transformation of the Ancient Israelite Festival Calendar*. Beihefte zur Zeitschrift fur Altorientalische und Biblische Rechtsgeschichte 6. Wiesbaden: Harrasowitz, 2005.
Wainwright, G. A. "The Meshwesh." *JEA* 48 (1962): 89–99.
Wallis Budge, E. A. *Kebra Nagast: The Queen of Sheba and Her Only Son Menelik*. Oxford: Oxford University Press, 1932.
Wasmuth, M. "Political Memory in the Achaemenid Empire: The Integration of Egyptian Kingship into Persian Royal Display." Pages 203–37 in Silverman and Waerzeggers, *Political Memory in and after the Persian Empire* .
Waters, M. *Ancient Persia: A Concise History of the Achaemenid Empire, 550–330 BCE*. Cambridge: Cambridge University Press, 2014.
Weigl, M. *Die aramäischen Achikar-Sprüche aus Elephantine und die alttestamentliche Weisheitsliteratur*. BZAW 399. Berlin: de Gruyter, 2010.
Weiher, E. von. "Marduk-apla-uṣur und Nabû-šum-iškun in einem spätbabylonischen Fragment aus Uruk." *Baghdader Mitteilungen*15 (1984): 197–224.
Weippert, M. "Synkretismus and Monotheismus: Religionsinterne Konfliktbewältigung im alten Israel." Pages 143–79 in *Kultur und Konflikt* Edited by J. Assmann and D. Harth. Edition Suhrkamp NS 612. Frankfurt am Main: Suhrkamp, 1990.
Wesselmann K. "Se non è vero: On the Use of Untrue Stories in Herodotus." Pages 130–54 in *Truth and History in the Ancient World*. Edited by I. Ruffel and T. Hau. New York: Routledge, 2016.
Westbrook, R. "The Phrase 'His Heart Is Satisfied' in Ancient Near Eastern Legal Sources." *JAOS* 111 (1991): 219–24.
Whitehead, J. D. *Early Aramaic Epistolography: The Arsames Correspondence*. Chicago: Department of Near Eastern Studies, 1974.
Whitters, M. F. "Some New Observations About Jewish Festal Letters." *JSJ* 32 (2001): 272–88.
Wiesehöfer, J. "The Achaemenid Empire in the Fourth Century BCE: A Period of Decline?" Pages 11–30 in *Judah and the Judeans in the Fourth Century BCE*.

Edited by O. Lipschits, G. Knoppers, and R. Albertz. Winona Lake, IN: Eisenbrauns, 2007.

———. *Der Aufstand Gaumātas und die Anfänge Dareios' I.* Reihe Alte Geschichte 13. Bonn: Habelt, 1978.

———. *Das antike Persien von 550 v. Chr. bis 650 n. Chr.* Zürich: Artemis, 1994.

Wigand, A.-K. "Politische Loyalität und religiöse Legitimierung: Überlegungen zur Textpragmatik der aramäischen Achiqarkomposition." *Die Welt des Orients* 48 (2018): 128–50.

Wijnsma, U. Z. "'And in the Fourth Year Egypt Rebelled . . .': The Chronology of and Sources for Egypt's Second Revolt (ca. 487–484 BC)." *Journal of Ancient History* 7 (2019): 32–61.

———. "The Worst Revolt of the Bisitun Crisis: A Chronological Reconstruction of the Egyptian Revolt under Petubastis IV." *JNES* 77 (2018): 157–73.

Wilson, J. A. "The Oath in Ancient Egypt." *JNES* 7 (1948): 129–56.

Winlock, H. E. *The Temple of Hibis in el Khargeh Oasis.* Publications of the Metropolitan Museum of Art, Egyptian Expedition 13. New York: Metropolitan Museum of Art, 1941.

Winter, U. *Frau und Göttin: Exegetische und ikonographische Studien zum weiblichen Gottesbild im Alten Israel und in dessen Umwelt.* OBO 53. Göttingen: Vandenhoeck & Ruprecht, 1983.

Wright, B. G., III, *The Letter of Aristeas: "Aristeas to Philocrates" or "On the Translation of the Law of the Jews."* Commentaries on Early Jewish Literature 8. Berlin: de Gruyter, 2015.

Wu, X. "Land of the Unrule-ables: Bactria in the Achaemenid Period." Pages 258–88 in *Fitful Histories and Unruly Publics: Rethinking Temporality and Community in Eurasian Archaeology.* Edited by K. O. Weber, E. Hite, L. Khatchadourian, and A. T. Smith. Leiden: Brill, 2016.

Yamauchi, E. M. "Cambyses in Egypt." Pages 371–91 in *Go to the Land I Will Show You: Studies in Honor of Dwight W. Young.* Edited by J. Coleson and V. Matthews. Winona Lake, IN: Eisenbrauns, 1996.

———. "Mordecai, the Persepolis Tablets, and the Susa Excavations." *VT* 42 (1992): 272–75.

Yardeni, A. "Maritime Trade and Royal Accountancy in an Erased Customs Account from 475 B.C.E. on the Aḥiqar Scroll from Elephantine." *BASOR* 293 (1994): 67–78.

Yaron, R. "Aramaic Marriage Contracts from Elephantine." *JSS* 3 (1958): 1–39.

———. *Introduction to the Law of the Aramaic Papyri.* Oxford: Clarendon, 1961.

Zaia, S. "My Brother's Keeper: Assurbanipal versus Šamaš-šuma-ukīn." *Journal of Ancient Near Eastern History* 6 (2019): 19–52.

Zaibert, L. *Punishment and Retribution.* Law, Justice, and Power. London: Routledge, 2016.

Zarghamee, R. *Discovering Cyrus: The Persian Conqueror astride the Ancient World.* Iran's Age of Empire 1. Washington, DC: Mage, 2013.

Zauzich, K.-Th. "Demotische Fragmente zum Ahikar-Roman." Pages 180–85 in *Folia Rara Wolfgang Voigt LXV. diem natalem celebranti ab amicis et catalogorum codicum orientalium conscribendorum collegis dedicata.* Edited by H. Franke. Wiesbaden: Franz Steiner Verlag, 1976.

———. "Neue literarische Texte in demotischer Schrift." *Enchoria* 8 (1976): 33–38.

Zawadzki, S. "The Circumstances of Darius II's Accession." *Jaarbericht Ex Oriente Lux* 34 (1995–96): 45–49.
Zerubavel, E. "Easter and Passover: On Calendars and Group Identity." *American Sociological Review* 47 (1982): 284–89.

INDEX OF AUTHORS

Abe, T., 92
Abou-Assaf, A., 34
Abush, T., 88
Adiego, J. J., 62
Africa, T. W., 64
Aggoula, B., 140
Ahlström, G. W., 21
Alavoine, V., 152–53
Albani, M., 24
Albertz, R., 38, 40, 44, 139
Albright, W. F., 47
Alstola, T., 22, 87, 100
Amadasi Guzzo, M. G., 33, 153
Amin, M. A., 14
Anneler, H., 23, 26, 34, 96, 102, 130
Arnold, W. R., 25, 28
Avishur, Y., 61–62
Ayad, B. A., 34, 80
Ayali-Darshan, N., 105
Azzoni, A., 32, 82–83, 125–26

Badawi, A. M., 130
Baines, J., 4
Barkworth, P. R., 57
Bassir, H., 21
Bateman, J. A., 109
Beaulieu, P.-A., 92, 149
Becking, B., 21–22, 24, 33–35, 54, 57, 87, 120, 147
Becnel, K., 114
Benz, F. L., 66, 72, 88
Berlejung, A., 100
Bernand, A., 61–62
Betlyon, J. W., 70
Bettles, E. A., 66
Binetti, C., 162
Blau, P., 78
Bledsoe, S. A., 17, 19, 101, 103, 108, 146
Blenkinsopp, J., 4
Boiy, T., 92
Bolin, T. M., 37
Bonfiglio, R. P., 109
Borneman, J., 118
Botta, A. F., 15, 19, 25, 32–33, 57, 80–81, 85, 93–96, 112, 115–16, 121, 125
Bordreuil, P., 34
Bourdieu, P., 99
Bresciani, E., 12, 15, 46
Briant, P., 4, 6–8, 11–12, 14–16, 55, 63, 65, 67, 129–30, 166
Brodersen, K., 10
Brosius, M., 98
Brown, T. S., 4
Burstein, S. M., 166

Cameron, G. C., 10
Candelora, D., 1
Capirci, A., 2, 160
Capps, D., 31
Carter, A., 117
Carty, A., 4
Cawkwell, C., 73
Chauveau, M., 160
Chilton, B. D., 103

Clagett, M., 15, 25
Clarysse, W., 163
Cohen, S. J. D., 19
Colburn, H. P., 63
Collins, J. J., 19, 27, 52
Conklin, B., 43, 95–96
Contini, R., 100
Cooper, A., 152
Cornell, C., x, 87, 95, 97, 137–38
Coulson, W. D. E., 74
Cowley, A. E., 62, 70, 129, 137
Cross, F. M., 91
Cruz-Uribe, E., 11, 15, 157

Dandamaev, M. A., 9, 15
Davis, A., 114
Day, P. L., 45
De Callatay, F., 74
Depuydt, L., 4
Deutsch, R., 91
Donker van Heel, K., 130
Doyle, D., 31
Driaux, D., 2, 160
Dubovský, P., 125
Dupont-Sommer, A., 87–89, 91
Dušek, J., 65, 140
Dvorjetski, E., 33

Eilberg-Schwartz, H., 31
Eilers, W., 123
Elayi, J., 64
Enstrom, P. L., 168
Evans, J. A. S., 4

Fales, F. M., 138, 139
Fantalkin, A., 74
Farver, J. M., 114
Ferrier, R. W., 57
Finkel, I. L., 90
Finn, J., 108–9
Fischer-Bovet, C., 62, 64
Fitzmeyer, J. A., 32
Fitzpatrick-McKinley, A., 4, 15–16, 22, 61, 75, 130, 165
Flowerdew, J., 95
Folmer, M., x, 24, 52, 91, 102, 104, 127
Franklin, N., 61–62
Frey, J., 37, 39, 44, 48, 142
Fried, L., 4, 11–13, 116, 122–24, 132, 134, 137, 141
Friedman, Th., 29
Friedrich, J., 89

Gale, N. H., 14
Gardiner, A. H., 66
Garland, R., 73
Gass, E., 26
Gates-Foster, J., 99
Gauthier, H., 166
Geertz, C., 36, 121, 130–31
Gensler, H. J., 103
George, A. R., 48
Ginsberg, H. L., 87
Ginzburg, C., 14, 131
Glick, L. B., 31
Goldstein, B. R., 152
Gosline, S. L., 62
Gottlieb, I., 33
Grabbe, L. L., 4, 13, 19, 22, 26, 29–30, 137, 140, 143
Grätz, S., 80
Granerød, G., 7, 13, 23, 26–29, 32, 34, 36, 38, 43–44, 51, 62, 76, 80–81, 83, 86, 89, 93, 100, 102–6, 109, 114, 127, 129, 132–34, 137–43, 146, 153
Grassi, G. F., x, 36, 66
Green, P., 157
Greenfield, J. C., 109–10
Grelot, P., 19, 25, 58, 87, 100, 123, 128, 137, 161
Gröndahl, F., 88
Gropp, G., 58
Grottanelli, C., 100
Grund, A., 28

Hancock, G., 167–68
Handy, L. K., 49
Hanfmann, G. M. A., 91
Harrison, T., 154
Hartenstein, F., 28
Heckl, R., 148
Heidorn, L. A., 16, 65
Heltzer, M., 61–62, 91
Hensel, B., 141
Henkelman, W. F. M., 55–56, 63
Herrenschmidt, C., 114

Herrera, P. D., 142
Herzfeld, E., 58
Hintze, A., 37
Hinz, W., 58, 62–63
Hobson, R., 100
Hoedt, S., x
Hoftijzer, J., 60, 94
Holladay, W. L., 46
Holm, T., x, 2, 99–101, 148–49, 160
Honigman, S., x, 165
Honroth, W., 66 , 97
Hoyland, R. G., 75
Hoonacker, A. van, 19, 130
Hudson, K., 117
Hughes, G. R., 12

Ilan, T., 32, 81, 83
Israel, J., 154

Janowski, B., 103
Jaussen, A., 77
Joffe, A. H., 64
Johnson, J. H., 67, 98, 125, 161, 164, 168
Joisten-Pruschke, A., 26, 122–23
Jong, A. F. de, 55
Jonker, L. C., 27, 110–11
Junod, H. A., 31

Kaan, I., 92
Kahn, D., 1, 6, 7, 160
Kalmijn, M., 78
Kamil, M., 46
Kaper, O., 7, 8, 156
Kaplan, B. J., 153–54
Kaplan, P., 62–63, 72, 121, 130
Karrer, C., 42
Kaufman, S. A., 84, 127
Keel, O., 152
Kellogg, D. L., 157
Kessler, D., 166–67
Klinkott, H., 11, 138
Klotz, D., 11
Knauf, E. A., 41–42, 75
Knight, G. A. F., 99
Koch, K., 37, 142
Köhler, E. C., 2, 160
Kosmin, P. J., 111
Kornfeld, W., 66, 123, 165
Korpel, M. C. A., 18
Kottsieper, I., x, 27–28, 46–47, 92, 100, 102, 104, 122, 139, 142–43, 147–49
Kraeling, E. G. H., 38, 143
Kratz, R. G., x, 23, 25–27, 30, 34, 100–104, 107, 122, 129–30, 137, 145
Krekeler, A., 165
Krul, J., 48
Kuhrt, A., 2, 4, 6–12, 15, 17, 37, 56–57, 60, 62, 66–68, 89–90, 102, 108, 110, 113, 115, 142, 154, 157–61, 163–64, 166

LaCoste, N., 165
Ladynin, I., 166
Lankester Harding, G., 76–77
Lee, K.-J., 4, 7, 25, 115
Lemaire, A., 87
Lenfant, D., 158, 160
Leonard, A., 74
Lepper, V., x, 102
Leung, A. N. M., 114
Lichtheim, M., 61–62
Lidzbarski, M., 65–66, 76–77
Lincoln, B., xii, 28, 108
Lindenberger, J. M., 92, 100, 104–6, 124, 126–27, 132–33, 137, 139, 145
Lipiński, E., 88, 92, 135
Livingstone, A., 88
Livschits, V., 57
Lloyd, A. B., 4, 7, 15–16, 154
Lopez, F., 4
Lorenz, C., 144
Lozachmeur, H., 30, 36, 72, 87, 96
Lukonin, V. G., 15
Lytle, E., 74

Maclaurin, E. C. B., 20
Machinist, P., 89
MacKay, H. A., 29
Madreiter I., 100
Magen, Y., 141
Marchand, S., 2, 160
Masson, O., 61–62
Mazar, A., 97
May, N. N., 125, 127
McLaughlin, J. L., 33, 35, 43, 46, 153
Meinhold, A., 81, 129

Mertens, Th., 114
Mettinger, T. N. D., 34, 36, 47
Meyer, E., 140
Millard, A. R., 34 , 88
Misgav, H., 141
Mitchell, C., 102, 109–11, 114
Moeller, R. A., 114
Mondriaan, M. E., 43, 96
Monson, A., 11, 15
Moore, J. D., x, 102
Morgenstern, M., 92
Morrow, A. R., 81
Müller, M., 1, 12, 16
Muffs, Y., 96, 116
Muraoka, T., 24–25, 127
Mynářová, J., 65

Na'aman, N., 33, 153
Naveh, J., 60
Neuffer, J., 60
Neugebauer, O., 15, 24
Neusner, J., 103
Newby, G. D., 149
Niehr, H., 22, 38–39, 44–45, 47, 49, 86, 92, 100–102, 105
Nihan, C., 27
Nims, C. F., 46–48, 91, 115, 148–49, 151
Nodet, E., 30
Nutkowicz, H., 32, 43, 79–82, 85, 96, 121, 127

Olyan, S. M., 35, 139
Oppenheim, A. L., 84
Oshima, T. M., 100, 102
Otto, E., 130

Papatheophanes, M., 55
Pardee, D., 152
Parker, C. H., 154
Parpola, S., 102
Patton, M. H., 154
Pearce, L. E., 22, 54, 58, 72, 88–89, 100–101
Peden, A. J., 61
Perrot J., 13
Petry, S., 89
Pham, X. H. T., 139
Pons Mellado, E., 64
Porten, B., x, 7, 11–12, 18–21, 24–29, 31–35, 38–43, 50, 52, 54, 58, 60, 62–63, 66, 71–74, 79–89, 93–94, 99, 101–102, 104, 109–11, 121–24, 126–27, 129–30, 132–35, 137, 140, 142–44, 146, 158, 163, 165, 168
Posener, G., 4, 11
Prag, K., 64

Quack, J. F., x, 1, 9, 100
Quinn, J. C., 63

Radner, K., 100, 113
Ramet, S. P., 118
Ray, J. D., 61–62
Redford, D. B., 1, 21–22, 154, 165
Redmount, C. A., 11
Reisner, G. A., 92
Retso, J., 6, 75
Robinson, G., 29
Roche, M.-J., 86
Röllig, W., 45
Rössler-Köhler, U., 4
Roller, D. W., 6, 7
Rohrmoser, A., 4, 21, 23, 25–26, 28–30, 34, 36, 38–39, 43, 45, 55, 64, 70, 87, 96–97, 115, 117, 123, 130, 132–33, 135, 137–39, 142–43, 146, 158, 161, 164
Rollinger, R., 8
Rop, J., 158
Rosenberg, S. G., 18, 34
Rottpeter, M., 154
Roux, M. le, 31
Roy, J., 14
Rubensohn, O., 66, 97
Rubinstein, A. Z., 117
Rutherford, I. C., 160
Ruzicka, S., 2, 5, 6, 7, 8, 10, 12–13, 157–58, 161, 163, 164
Ryholt, K., x, 1, 2, 160

Sachau, E., 26, 44, 65–66, 100, 102, 140
Salmon, P., 157
Savignac, R., 77
Schäfer, P., 20, 97, 129, 132, 134, 137, 139, 142, 146
Schama, S., ix, 18, 22–23, 25, 30–31, 80, 83, 124, 145

Schaudig, H., 89
Schwartz, J. E., 78
Schipper, B. U., x, 64, 101
Schmitt, R., 38
Schmitz, P. C., 64
Schulz, R., 5, 6, 8, 11, 16
Schwiderski, D., 26, 37, 39
Sear, D. R., 74
Segal, J. B., 65, 75
Seidl, U., 90, 108
Serrano Delgado, J. M., 4, 155
Shaked, S., 59–60
Shayegan, M. R., 9
Shortland, A. J., 70
Siljanen, E., 5, 9, 20, 22–23, 28, 38, 43, 95, 137, 146
Silverman, M. H., 38, 44, 48
Simonson, B., 116
Sims-Williams, N., 110
Skjaervo, P. O., 37, 55
Smith-Christopher, D. L., 28
Smoláriková, K., 4
Spalinger, A., 2
Spiegelberg, W., 12, 75, 115, 161, 164
Steiner, R. C., 22–23, 46–48, 64, 91, 148–52
Stern, S., 111–12
Sternberg-el Hotabi, H., 6, 11, 13, 154, 157–59, 161–62, 166
Stieglitz, R. R., 62
Stolper, M. W., 55, 158
Stone, R. G., 105
Stos-Gale, Z., 14
Strauss, B., 73, 158
Streck, M., 2
Szubin, H. Z., 33, 50, 58, 73, 80–82, 121, 143

Tairan, S. A., 66
Tal, O., 68
Talay, Sh., 100
Tamber-Rosenau, C., 125–27
Tammuz, O., 67, 70
Tavernier, J., 55–57, 95, 110, 133
Taylor, J. H., 33
Teixidor, J., 51
Thissen, H. J., 160
Thompson, T. L., 38
Toorn, K. van der, x, 19–20, 22–23, 27–28, 42–48, 55, 58–59, 91, 95–96, 100, 115–16, 119–24, 126–27, 147–53
Tsfania, L., 141
Tuland, C. G., 136
Tuplin, C., 54
Turri, J., 95

Uehlinger, C., 69–70
Ullendorff, E., 167

Van de Mierop, M., 130
Van Dyk, P. J., 168
Van Seters, J., 1
Veijola, T., 29
Vittmann, G., 1, 19, 21, 61, 64–65, 75, 85, 129, 151, 163, 165
Vleeming, S. P., 46–47, 148, 157
Vogelsang, W., 13
Vogelstein, M., 140
Von Lieven, A., x
Von Oppenheim, M., 89
Von Pilgrim, C., 34, 71, 129
Von Rosen, L., 57
Von Soden, H., 101
Von Weiher, E., 101
Vriezen, Th.C., ix

Waerzeggers, C., 22
Wagenaar, J. A., 24–26, 28
Wallis Budge, E. A., 167
Wainwright, G. A., 75
Wasmuth, M., 11, 12, 15
Waters, M., 161
Weigl, M., 92, 100–102, 104–7
Weippert, M., 22
Wesselius, J. W., 46–47, 148, 151
Wesselmann K., 4, 5
Westbrook, R., 43, 96
Whitehead, J. D., 63
Whitters, M. F., 25
Wiesehöfer, J., 9, 55, 67, 110, 166
Wigand, A. C., x, 1, 101–2, 104, 107–11, 114
Wijnsma, U., 11, 156–57
Wilson, J. A., 96
Winlock, H. E., 15
Winter, U., 40, 42–44, 48
Wong, N., 114

Wright, B. G., 21
Wu, X., 60
Wunsch, C., 22, 100

Yamauchi, E. M., 5, 63
Yardeni, A., 24–25, 66–67, 74, 87, 100, 104
Yaron, R., 32, 116

Zadok, R., 54, 72, 88–90, 101
Zaibert, L., 103
Zaia, S., 148
Zamora, J. Á., 33, 153
Zarghamee, R., 3
Zauzich, K.-Th., 100, 165
Zawadzki, S., 135
Zerubavel, E., 24
Zucker, F., 66, 97

INDEX OF ANCIENT SOURCES

Biblical and Deuterocanonical Texts

Genesis
10:26 88
24:7 38
25:13 75
31:13 46

Leviticus
7:23 144
17:3 144
22:27 144
23:6–8 26
23:15–21 40

Numbers
18:17 144
28:17 26

Deuteronomy
7 78
34:3 149

Judges
1:16 149
3:13 149
9:8–15 102

2 Samuel
8:18 61
15:18 61
20:23 61

2 Kings
4:23 30
11:4 61
11:19 61
14:9b 102
25:27–30 154

Isaiah
46:1 89
60:7 75

Jeremiah
32:12 95
36:22–23 136
43:5–7 21
46:25 125
48:13 46
51:59 95

Ezekiel
27 121
30:14–16 125
45:18–25 40

Amos
4:2 68
8:5 30

Jonah
3:5 35

Nahum
3:8 125

Haggai
1–2 87

Psalms
20 151
81:3 30
81:4 152
104 69
131:1 105
136:16 38
141:3 106

Daniel
3:8, 12 18

Ruth
4 127

Esther 63

Proverbs
13:21 106

Ezra
1:2 38
4:12, 13 18
4:13 67
5:1 18, 87
5:3 136
5:5 18
5:9 136
5:12 38
6:2 140
6:7–8 18
6:9–10 38
6:14 18, 87
9–10 78

Nehemiah
1:4–5 38
2:4 38
2:20 38, 140
5:4 67
9:36–37 114

1 Chronicles
1:26 88
1:29 75

2 Chronicles
7:12 141
28:15 149
36:23 38

1 Maccabees
2:41 30

Sirach
11:29–30 122
21:14 104
22:27 106

Matthew
23:16 44

Other Jewish Texts
Corpus Papyrorum Judaicarum
1:108 165

Josephus, *Antiquitates*
11.297–301 139

Josephus, *Contra Apionem*
1.73 64

Letter of Aristeas
13 21

Qumran Scrolls
11QT 55.11 44
3QTr 9.6 44
3QTr 11.7 44

Targum Job
36:19 25

Targum Psalms
16:3 25
22:31 25
71:18 25
80:3 25

Targum Ruth
3:15 25

Mishnah Pesachim
3 25

Aramaic Documents

Aḥiqar (*TADAE* C1.1) 100–108, 153
II 17 127
II 23 127
II 24 103
IV 51–52 103
VI 6 (84) 104
VI 15 (92) 104
VI 16 (93) 104
VII 27 (107–8) 105
IX 51 (137) 104
IX 130 138
X 58–59 (142–44) 105
X 62 (147) 105
XI 81 (168–71) 107
XI 82 (171–72) 106
XIII 99 (191) 106

Collection Clermont-Ganneau (Lozachmeur)
#147:1 87
#205 30
#265 96
#266:4 87
#277 87
J8 36

Daskyleion Inscription 91

Louvre Stele Si Gabbor
KAI 226:2 140

Papyrus Amherst 63 19–20, 22–23, 148–54, 162
I–V 148
V–XI 148
V 1–17 152
VI 22 46
VIII:1–7 91
VIII 13 46
IX 7 153
IX 9.13 46
X 9 46
X 14 150
XI 17–18 46
XII–XIII 148
XII 1–11 148
XII 11–19 151
XIII 1–10 151
XIII 2 153
XIII 6 152
XIII 7 152
XIII 10 153
XIII 11–17 151
XVI 1 42, 47–48
XVI 13–17 47
XVI 14.15 42, 47
XVII 2 148
XVII 3–4 148
XVII 15 46
XX 4 149

Sefire Treaties
KAI 222 B:39 135
KAI 224:28 123

TADAE
A2.1 46
A3.3:1 34
A3.6 115
A3.6:1 37
A3.6:2 120
A3.7 39, 86
A3.8 115, 123
A3.8:3–4 37
A3.9 163
A3.10:1 86
A4.1 24–27, 122, 147, 151
A4.2 39, 86, 115, 122
A4.2:2–5 123
A4.2:6 125
A4.2:8 123
A4.2:14–15 123
A4.3 116, 119–22, 147, 151
A4.3:1 52
A4.3:1–2 37
A4.3:4 120
A4.4 124, 126
A4.4:3–4 126
A4.4:5–6 126
A4.4:5 79
A4.5 129, 131–37
A4.5:7 137
A4.5:12 137
A4.5:13 137
A4.7–9 36

TADAE (*cont'd*)
A4.7 27, 34, 36–37, 64, 121, 129, 136–37
A4.7:6–7 138
A4.7:9 42, 138
A4.7:9–10 136
A4.7:11 136
A4.7:11–13 136
A4.7:13–14 6, 23, 141
A4.7:14 20, 136
A4.7:15–17 139
A4.7:16–17 138
A4.7:17–19 139
A4.7:20 35
A4.7:20–22 139
A4.7:23 139
A4.7:23–24 139
A4.7:25–26 142
A4.8 27, 34, 36–37, 64, 121, 129, 136–37
A4.8:6 138
A.4.8:8 42, 138
A4.8:8–9 136
A4.8:11 136
A4.8:11–12 136
A4.8:12–13 6, 23, 141
A4.8:13 20
A4.8:13–16 139
A4.8:14 136
A4.8:16 138
A4.8:16–18 139
A4.8:18–20 139
A4.8:19 35
A4.8:22 139
A4.8:23 139
A4.8:24–25 142
A4.9 129, 137, 140–43
A4.9:1 140
A4.9:3 141
A4.9:9–11 142
A4.10 129, 137, 139, 143–44
A4.10:1 128
A4.10:6 143
A4.10:7–14 144
A4.10:13–14 144
A5.3 86
A6.1 39
A6.2 62
A6.2:5 136
A6.3 116–17
A6.7 62, 161
A6.7:6–8 161
A6.9 63
A6.11:1 52
A6.12:1 52
A6.13 67
A6.13:1 52
A6.15 63
B1.1 73
B2.1–11 83
B2.1:2–3 54
B2.2 57, 95, 115
B2.2:3–4 54, 58
B2.2:4 95
B2.3:5–6 95
B2.2:8 95
B2.2:11 95
B2.2:11–12 57, 95
B2.2:13 115
B2.2:19 101
B2.3 57, 84
B2.3:5–6 57
B2.3:24 115
B2.4 84
B2.4:3–4 84
B2.4:5–6 84
B.2.6 32–33, 79, 85
B2.6:2 84–85
B2.6:4 32
B2.7 59
B2.7:13–14 34
B2.7:18–19 59
B2.7:18 56
B2.8 32, 43, 76, 84–86, 96
B2.8:2 84
B2.8:13 76
B2.9 84
B2.10:3 85
B2.10:11.14 81
B3.1:9 89
B3.1:13.19 115
B3.2:6 115
B3.3 32, 79–80, 121
B3.3:4–7 80
B3.4 58, 81, 93
B3.4:4 93

B3.4:7–10 59
B3.4:9–10 81
B3.4:23–24 59
B3.5 56, 59, 81
B3.5:2–3 81
B3.5:4 81
B3.5:12 81
B3.5:16–22 82
B3.5:18 82
B3.5:23–24 56
B3.6 82
B3.6:4–5.6.7–8 82
B3.6:16–17 55
B3.7 82
B3.7:3 83
B3.8 32, 79, 83
B3.8:41 81
B3.9:12 44
B3.10 146
B3.10:5.12.17 81
B3.11:9 81
B3.12 59, 83, 146
B3.12:4–5.12 59
B3.12:5–6.14 74
B3.12:28 115
B3.13 94
B4.6:1–3 164
B4.6:2 54
B4.6:4 74
B4.6:14 115
B4.7:1 54
B4.4:6–10 50
B5.1:12 115
B5.2:10 81
B5.4:7 81
B5.5:2 81
B6.1 79
B6.1:3–4 32
B6.2 79
B6.3 79
B6.4 79
B7.1:6 96
B7.2 43, 50
B7.2:1–3 163
B7.2:2 44
B7.3 43, 50–51, 96
B8.1 75
B8.3 74, 121
B8.4:2 115
B8.9:3–4 96
B8.10:2 115
C1.1 *see* Aḥiqar
C1.2 99
C2.1 108–14
C2.1:54 111
C2.1 I 25–28 113
C2.1 IV 1–7 113
C2.1 IV 6 113
C2.1 V 13 112–13
C2.1 V 16 112
C2.1 V 17 113
C2.1 V 19–21 113
C2.1 V 22 112
C2.1 V 23 113
C2.1 VII 30 112
C2.1 VII 33 112
C2.1 VII 36 113
C2.1 VII 43 112
C2.1 VII 46 112
C2.1 VII 56 112
C2.1 XI 64–73 110
C2.1:74–75 56
C3.4 94
C3.4:4 71
C3.6 94
C3.7 66–70
C3.7 FR 1:6 67
C3.7 FV 3:25 67
C3.7 GR 2:7 67
C3.7 KR 2:23–24 67, 74
C3.8 69
C3.12 ii:7 71
C3.12 ii:8 71
C3.12 ii:9 71
C3.12 ii:15 71
C3.12 ii:22 71
C3.12 ii:27 71
C3.12 ii:28 71
C3.12 ii:32 71
C3.15 39, 87, 125, 152
C3.15:1 39
C3.15 VII:126–28 34, 40
D1.13 86
D1.22 88
D1.33 frg. d:2 89
D.2.4. 152

TADAE (*cont'd*)
D2.12 94
D2.12:2–4 60
D3.39 71
D3.39b:3 58, 71
D3.39b:4–5 72
D3.40:1 72
D6.7 63, 153
D7.6:9 28
D7.10 29
D7.12:9 30
D7.16:1–9 29
D7.18 34
D7.21 39, 85
D7.24 28
D7.28 30
D7.29 33, 35, 87, 152
D7.30 87
D7.30:2–3 39, 87
D7.35 30
D7.48:4–5 30
D9.10 94
D11.4 76
D11.10:1 38
D18:1 89

Mount Gerizim Inscriptions
Text 199 141

Tayma Stele
KAI 228 A:15 140

Assyrian and Babylonian Texts
Assurbanipal
Annals
1:74 2

Rassam Cylinder
Col II:37–39 2

Babylonian Bisitun Inscription
Bab. 41446 108
BE 3627 108

Borsippa Texts
BM 27797 90

Cyrus Cylinder
20–22 90
33–35 90

El Amarna Letters
244:16 127

Esarhaddon
Victory Stele from Sinjirli
rev. 36–44 2

Neo-Assyrian Letters
SAA XVII 68 125
SAA XVII 73 125

Neo-Assyrian Treaties and Loyalty Oaths
SAA II 5 iv:6–7 45
SAA II 6:467 45

Persepolis Fortification Texts
81 63
412 63
489 63 1858
758 56
1858 63

Sumerisch-Babylonische Hymnen
No. 8 92
No. 56 92

Tell Halaph Documents
Text 117:3–4 89

Unpublished
BM 32234 158

Demotic Texts
Aḥiqar Cairo Papyrus 100

Codex Hermopolis West 130

Demotic Aḥiqar Fragments (Papyrus Berlin)
23729 (Aḥiqar) 100
15658 (Aḥiqar) 100

Demotic Chronicle (Papyrus BN 215)
Recto C:1–16 115
Recto C:7–8 9
Verso D:1–17 13, 154
Verso D:3 161, 164
Verso D:18–19 161, 164

Pherendates Correspondence (Papyrus Berlin)
13540 12
23592 165

Papyrus Loeb
1 75

Egyptian Texts
Autobiography of Udjaḥoresnet
11–12 4
14 7
33–34 7, 156
40–41 7, 156

Dakhla Oasis Inscriptions 156

Darius I
Heliopolis Stela (DSab) 15

Horus Myth C from Edfu
VI, 111,4 37

Nastasen Stele (Berlin 2268) 166

Stela of Psammetichus II 61, 64

Ethiopic Texts
Ethiopic Version of Ahiqar 100

Kebra Nagast
§48 168

Greek Texts
Abou-Simbel Inscription 61, 64

Aeschylus, *Persians*
765–79 9

Alexander Romance 166

Aristotle, *History of Animals*
3.19 155

Arrian, *Anabasis of Alexander*
4.15.4 57

Ctesias, *Persica*
3:688 Fr. F 3 158
3:688 Fr F 13 (38–39) 160
3:688 Fr. F 9 57, 60
3:688 Fr. F 13 (10) 6
3:688 Fr. F 13 (11–15) 9
3: 688 Fr. F 14 (35) 60

Diodorus Siculus, *Bibliotheca historica*
11.69 158
11.71:3–6 159
11.74:1–4 160
11.74:5–6 160
14.79.4–5 164
16.46.4–7 166
16.51 166

Heraclitus of Ephesus (apud Clement of Alexandria, *Protrepticus*)
2.13 55

Herodotus, *Histories*
1.79–81.84 4
1.101 55
1.131 37
2.112 64
2.152, 154 61
2.178–79 74
2.182 5
3.1 5
3.1.3 157
3.6 66
3.7–9 6
3.10–11 6
3.11 61
3.14–15 6, 7, 154
3.14.10–11 154
3.15.4 154
3.17–21 6

Herodotus, *Histories* (*cont'd*)
3.19, 44 5
3.25 7
3.26–27 6, 7–8
3.30 8
3.61–68 9
3.65–68 9
3.70–73 10
3.76–79 10
3.84–89 8
3.88 75
3.89–97 11
3.90 62
3.91 11, 14–15
3.92 58
3.93 57–58
3.120–25 4
4 142
4.165–67 11
4.191 75
4.200 11
6.112–16 157
7.7 13, 158
7.66 57
7.77 157
8.113 60

Homer, *Iliad*
2.867 61

Justin, *Epitome of the Philippic History*
1.9.4–13 9
3.1 158

Manetho, *Aegyptiaca*
FrGrH 609 F3 161, 164

Plutarch, *Themistocles*
31 154

Polyaenus, *Strategemata*
7.11.7 10

Pseudo-Skylax, *Periplus*
3.35 67

Quintus Curtius Rufus, *History of Alexander*
VII 4:30 60

Strabo, *Geography*
17.1.5 6

Thucydides, *Histories*
1.104 160
1.109–10 160

Xenophon, *Cyropaedia*
8.2.10–12 17

Xenophon, *Hellenica*
2.4.33 74

Persian Inscriptions
Artaxerxes II
Persepolis Tomb Inscription (A2Pa) 58

Darius I
Bisitun Inscription (DB)
§ 1 108
§ 1–5 108
§6 56, 60
§ 6–58 108
§10 8–9, 154
§11 111
§13 10
§16–75 10
§18–20 114
§21 10, 114, 156
§25 113
§27 112–13
§28 112–13
§29 113
§30 112–13
§31 113
§37 112
§38 112
§40 112
§41 112
§42 112
§45 112
§50 114

§59–75 108

Chalouf Stela (DZc)
§3 11

Empire List from Susa (DSe)
31 133

Naqsh-e Rustam Burial Inscription b (DNb) 110
§2b 110
§9:50–60 110

Naqsh-e Rustam Inscription e (DNe) 58

Susa Trilingual Inscription (DSf) 13
§10 56
§11 13

Xerxes
Burial Inscription (XPl) 110

Daiva Inscription (XPh)
§3 57, 60

§42 133

Other Inscriptions

Abusir Inscriptions 65

Arad
17:3 91

CIS I
112 61, 64

Elephantine Inscriptions on Jar Fragments
Text 2 65
Text 10 65
Text 23 65

Mesha Inscription
KAI 181.17 44

Sabaean Rock Inscriptions
Text 1066 76

www.ingramcontent.com/pod-product-compliance
Lightning Source LLC
Chambersburg PA
CBHW020526080526
44583CB00013B/759
* 9 7 8 1 6 4 6 0 2 2 4 4 1 *